# Hard Time & Nursery Rhymes

# Hard Time
# &
# Nursery Rhymes

## A Mother's Tales of Law and Disorder

*Claudia Trupp*

RODALE

Mention of specific companies, organizations, or authorities in this book does not imply endorsement by the author or publisher, nor does mention of specific companies, organizations, or authorities imply that they endorse this book, its author, or the publisher.
Internet addresses and telephone numbers given in this book were accurate at the time it went to press.

Rodale books may be purchased for business or promotional use or for special sales. For information, please write to:
Special Markets Department, Rodale Inc., 733 Third Avenue, New York, NY 10017

Printed in the United States of America
Rodale Inc. makes every effort to use acid-free ∞, recycled paper ♻.

Book design by Anthony Serge

**Library of Congress Cataloging-in-Publication Data**

Trupp, Claudia.
    Hard time & nursery rhymes : explaining my work to my daughters / Claudia Trupp.
        p.     cm.
    Includes index.
    ISBN-13 978-1-59486-824-5 hardcover
    ISBN-10 1-59486-824-7 hardcover
    1. Trupp, Claudia   2. Women lawyers—New York (State)—New York—Biography.   3. Lawyers—New York (State)—New York—Biography.   4. Defense (Criminal procedure)—New York (State)—New York—Biography.   5. Criminals—New York (State)—New York—Anecdotes.   6. Working mothers—United States—Biography.   7. Mothers—United States—Biography.   8. Motherhood—United States—Anecdotes.   9. New York (N.Y.)—Biography.   I. Title.   II. Title: Hard time and nursery rhymes.
    CT275.T92A3 2009
    974.7'044092—dc22
    [B]
                                             2008025349

Distributed to the trade by Macmillan

2  4  6  8  10  9  7  5  3  1  hardcover

RODALE
LIVE YOUR WHOLE LIFE™

We inspire and enable people to improve their lives and the world around them
For more of our products visit **rodalestore.com** or call 800-848-4735

For Charlie, who always knew that

I didn't wear hats.

And for our daughters, who have taught me to wear many.

# Contents

# Preface

Green Haven Correctional Facility,
Stormville, New York, July 31, 2006

I never seem to be dressed right for Green Haven. Maximum security prisons are a lot like the fraternity houses scattered across most American college campuses. From their uniform, solid, slightly intimidating facades, it is difficult to tell one from the other. But once inside, there are subtle differences of institutional culture. Green Haven reminds me of Beta Delta Xi, the fraternity from my college days whose members were almost always football players. Not a good place for a woman to spend too much time alone.

On my first trip several years ago to visit a client convicted of murder, my entry was delayed for hours because the prison authorities deemed my knee-length brown crepe dress too short and enticing. I had to wait for a female corrections officer to come with a ruler and measure the distance from my hem to the top of my knee. She then explained the problem: The dress's bottom button was a full inch above my knee, and that violated some prison regulation somewhere. Like a seamstress taking up a hem, she knelt down and further secured my dress by pinning it closed with several safety pins. Only once these makeshift alterations were completed was I allowed inside.

For my next visit to Green Haven, I made sure to wear long pants—and this time it was my pockets that proved problematic. While clearing security, I pulled out a board book of *Peter Rabbit and Friends*, which I had earlier been reading to my daughter and had inadvertently taken with me as I flew out the door. The smirking guards informed me that children's books were not considered proper legal materials for an attorney to bring into the prison.

I walked back to store the book in the gray metal locker in which I had placed the other vestiges of my freedom—car keys, credit cards, cell phone, gum. But I could not bring myself to abandon it there. Some part of me feared that molecules of misery might settle on the glossy pictures of Jemima Puddle-Duck and Samuel Whiskers, diminishing the delight they brought their rightful owner and somehow contaminating my home. I closed the locker and left the reception center to walk the book out to my car.

On my third trip to Green Haven, I was determined to clear the gate without a hitch. Wearing pocketless pants so long they bagged over my ankles, I walked into the visitors' reception center and weaved my way through the wooden gates meant to corral the weekend crowds. But on this early weekday morning, there was only me, and my third time proved a charm.

I had come to visit a client serving a fifty-year sentence following his conviction for raping a teenage girl who was walking to her job at McDonald's—the nightmare of every mother. I pushed from my mind images of my own daughters, ages nine, six, and two, as I read over the police reports I had brought to review with my client.

There were things about the case that had troubled me from the start, among them the seeming incompetence of the defense trial attorneys and my client's vehement assertions of innocence in his letters to me. I was at the prison to hear him out. But before I could do that, I had to wait for the prison authorities to find him.

The corrections officer responsible for updating me on my client's precise location within the massive prison seemed embarrassed. He apologized several times and offered me water and snacks, as if he were the host of a dinner party responsible for my comfort and well-being. But it was not his hospitality I was after as I sat in the heavy, humid air, sweating beneath my black pantsuit, growing crankier by the minute.

Finally the corrections officer returned smiling, and I saw a man standing behind him in a prison uniform. The prisoner was tall, young, clean cut. *He doesn't look like a rapist,* I thought to myself as I stood to shake my client's hand and sat down again to listen to his story.

........................................

What kind of woman leaves three young daughters at home to spend her time representing convicted murderers and rapists? That would be me. For close to fifteen years, I have been a criminal defense attorney specializing in appellate litigation. For nine of those years, I have also been a mother of young children. First one, then two, and then, somewhat surprisingly, three.

The demands of small children can seem endless and far from rational: marshmallows for breakfast; refusing to wear anything but pajamas or to eat lunch in the school cafeteria because "it smells." All must be negotiated with skill and care.

After such delicate negotiations, I crave the morning commute, when I can sit on the train with a cup of coffee and read the paper uninterrupted. Because oddly, as intense as it is, my job provides me with a realm of calm, order, and rationality. Appellate litigation is a world consisting of demarcated rules, deadlines, and mandatory page limits for briefs. The office is a place with set routines and defined demands.

At dinner parties, people sometimes ask me how I can leave my kids to defend "those people." The truth is, I love my job not only for the intellectual challenge it poses but also because I get to represent "those people"—the ones who have been accused, and then convicted, of some of the most heinous acts you can imagine (and some you couldn't even if you tried).

Almost always my clients are respectful and courteous toward me. Unlike my children, they do not throw tantrums or accuse me of not understanding their problems. When someone is depending on you to bring him hope and to make sense of a system that is often arbitrary and always confusing, it's hard not to feel connected to that person.

But I didn't write this book to satisfy the curiosity of casual acquaintances. I wrote it to explain to my daughters why I choose to walk out the door each morning, despite their frequent pleas that I stay home. Sometimes I wish I could just tell them that we need the money. It would not take much effort to explain the necessity of paying the bills. A quick review of my credit card statements, the interest and late charges compounding by the second, could drive home that grim reality.

But the lessons I have learned and wanted to pass on are more complex. I held out little hope that I would be finished with this project any time soon and envisioned presenting these pages to my girls decades from now—around the time my first grandchild arrived. But shortly after I began, I was sitting at my computer, staring at a mostly blank screen, writing and deleting sentences in equal measure, when I received a call from my doctor's office. There had been some questionable findings on my most recent mammogram.

A few days later, sitting in the doctor's office, my husband, Charlie, at my side, I heard the radiologist finish reviewing a new batch of films and announce that I would definitely need a biopsy. Immediately Charlie was asking the right questions about surgeons and procedures in his steadiest voice, all business. I was crying too hard to hear the answers.

As Charlie drove me home from the doctor's office, he insisted that I was not sick, that everything was going to turn out fine. Ordinarily, simply being near my husband is enough to calm my nerves. This time there was no quelling my rising panic.

That evening I found myself sobbing silently on the pink and white tiled floor of my daughters' bathroom. After they had all finished brushing their teeth, I left the tap on and closed the door. As I cried, I could hear Charlie reading aloud.

A few minutes after the story ended, I got up, wiped my eyes, and walked down the hall to my oldest daughter, Jessica's, room. She was sitting in the overstuffed chair she had recently selected as a birthday present, so focused on her book that she did not notice me standing in the doorway. The ends of her long, light brown hair swept the opened pages on her lap. She looked up after a moment, her multicolored eyes, their irises speckled blue, green, and gold, registering my presence.

"Are you okay, Mommy?" Jessie asked, keenly attuned to my mood as always.

"I'm fine," I said with a forced smile.

"You look sad."

"No, just tired."

"I'll babysit the other two tomorrow if you want, so you can rest," my nine-year-old offered.

I could feel the tears rising again. Jessie was already too old for her years, a kid I had to encourage to break free of the rigid routines she set for herself, to eat dessert every once in a while before she finished her homework. Pushing from my mind the thought that I might not be around to remind her to do such things, I kissed the top of her head, thanked her for her generous offer, and left her to her book.

Next door, six-year-old Lila was already sleeping noisily, her straight dark hair fanned across the pillow, her smooth skin illuminated slightly by the solar system mobile hanging from her ceiling. The planets glowed green in the darkness, along with the myriad stars Lila had carefully positioned throughout the room. I pulled the covers she had managed to kick off during two minutes of sleep back over her shoulders. The lean muscles of her arms, without the benefit of any extra flesh, felt cold beneath my fingers as I bent to kiss her cheek. Various inventions and art projects in different stages of development were strewn over her bedroom floor, requiring me to choreograph my exit carefully.

Crossing the hall, I steeled myself for the greatest challenge of the evening. I knew that Maya would be awake, the only two-year-old who could rise before the sun, travel at warp speed throughout her day without a single nap, and keep going and going—long after I was ready to collapse. Sure enough, she was sitting straight up on her bed, her blonde hair shining in the bedroom's dimmed light, waiting for me, while Charlie dozed next to her, a copy of *Goodnight Moon* on his chest.

"Mama here!" Maya shouted, informing her father that he was dismissed.

"She's all yours," Charlie said, maneuvering his six-foot-two-inch, 235-pound frame off the tiny bed.

For the next half hour, I read the four books Maya had originally assigned me, followed by a fifth—to stave off an angry crying jag (hers, not mine). Then I dimmed the light further, told her the story of "The Three Little Pigs," and sang several lullabies while she splayed her body across mine, like a wrestler pinning an opponent, so as to thwart any effort to depart. Ordinarily this tactic worked; I would pass out long before Maya and awaken hours later still in her bed, my contact lenses plastered to the insides of my eyelids.

But I could not hope to sleep with the doctor's words swimming in my head, his descriptions of the various biopsy methods I needed to research, the surgeons I needed to meet. *I do not have time for this,* I thought, as I considered my schedule for the upcoming days. I had promised to make cupcakes for a party at Jessie's school, was due to appear in court, had set up a meeting with a client's mother to discuss his case, and had scheduled a well-baby visit for Maya—all on top of the regular doses of brief writing and train dashing. It was a typical week, suddenly grown atypical by the discovery of specks and shadows.

In fact, many weeks of screenings, consultations, and biopsies followed. During that uncertain time, I could not stop writing. On the train, walking to court, waiting to see yet another doctor, I would compose the pages in my head and then stay up typing deep into the night. I needed to record for my daughters the joy I had found in being their mother, the value of my work, the importance of finding what you are meant to do in this life. The doctors eventually assured me that no further tests were needed. By that time, I was more or less done writing, too.

I selected each of these clients' stories because they taught me something invaluable: the importance of perspective, of faith, of accepting limitations—hard-won wisdom for which I am grateful. Names have been changed to protect the guilty. We're all guilty of something.

# part 1

# Weeping on the Job

I was eager to get to my office in Lower Manhattan that chilly Monday morning in December 2001. The weekend had been a long and tense one at my house. It should have been celebratory, since I had just won the biggest case of my career, and the decision was going to make the front page of the *New York Law Journal.* But by Friday afternoon, we had begun receiving a series of telephone calls during which the caller would simply breathe and hang up. Because of the nature of my work, I have an unlisted phone number. Therefore, the caller had to be some pervert who just happened to dial the number at random, someone I actually knew, or someone with the ability to access my unlisted number.

I had tried to convince my husband, Charlie, that the calls were just the acts of some random pervert, but he was pretty sure they had to do with the DeLuca decision. By the second night of harassing calls, Charlie was understandably upset. Finally, I unplugged the phone without telling him.

Arriving at my office on Monday morning, I saw my telephone message light. Expecting to hear the voices of my public defender colleagues from around the city calling to congratulate me, I happily picked up the phone and retrieved my messages.

"Fuck you," a gruff voice snarled.

Then I heard bagpipes. It took me a second to reconcile the angry cursing with the beautifully mournful music. We had all heard that music a lot recently. It was played at every law enforcement officer's funeral, and it had been played too many times in the months following the September 11 attacks. My entire body began to tremble as it became clear to me that my weekend harassment had not been an unfortunate coincidence but rather a calculated attempt to frighten me by someone who knew of my part in DeLuca's victory.

The phone on my desk was ringing again, and this time it sounded loud and threatening, like in those slasher films where the babysitter sits helplessly awaiting her fate. I snatched up the receiver before I lost my nerve.

"Who is this?!" I demanded with all the bravado I could muster.

"Hey, it's me. What's wrong?"

It was Charlie. Not wanting to alarm him, I evened my voice. "Nothing. What's up?"

"Did you fill out Jessie's forms?" he asked. The forms for my four-year-old daughter's kindergarten registration were due that day.

"I can't deal with that right now," I told him. "I'm in the middle of something here. I'll call you back later."

I hung up the phone. In my excitement over the DeLuca victory, I had entirely forgotten about Jessie's school forms. In addition to being reviled by countless strangers, I was also a terrible mother. Still trembling, I put my head on my desk and sobbed.

....................................

The world can be easily divided into two groups of people. The divide is not between rich and poor, men and women, prosecutors and defense attorneys. It is not between those who have children and the childless. The world is divided into those who cry easily, the "weepers," and those who do not, the "others." I always knew which camp I belonged in.

I remember in kindergarten the other kids complained during nap time because I was crying too loudly and keeping them up. It was not that I was a sullen or depressed kid. On the contrary, my parents have always described me as upbeat— and I would probably agree with that assessment. But throughout my life, whenever I would get stressed out or nervous or frustrated, I would crumple into sobs.

In law school, I remember crying for hours over getting a B in my Evidence course. The grade, received in the last semester of my third and final year of law school after already having secured a position at a white-shoe law firm, could not have impacted my future in any way. But I'd liked the class and respected my professor, and superstitiously I felt the grade somehow did not bode well for my prospects of becoming a real lawyer. My husband—whom I have seen cry exactly once in the seventeen years that I have known him—was horrified. To appear less insane, I told him I had failed the course. We were only engaged at the time, and I was afraid he would call off the wedding if he knew the truth.

My weeping jags continued well into my legal career. I cried when I lost cases I thought I should have won; when judges or supervisors criticized my arguments; when I made stupid mistakes, a sin I deemed unforgivable. If Stephen DeLuca's case had not come my way, I might still be crying over such things. I'll never know. But when you have suffered horrible morning sickness, total public humiliation, and your first trip to the pediatric emergency room—all in a single day—the discovery of a typographical error in a brief no longer seems a legitimate cause for hysterics.

## BABIES CRY

Some cases haunt you before they ever land on your desk. You hear about the crime and shudder. You follow the coverage in the media. Then, a year or two later you walk into the office on Monday morning, and there's the case record on your chair. Invariably, it's a monster, the trial transcript in multiple volumes, their pages numbering into the thousands. You crack the file, and it all comes back to you.

November 10, 1997, was my first day of work at the Office of the Appellate Advocate, the place where I have practiced ever since. It was also my first day as a working mother. I remember the date because my oldest daughter, Jessica, was exactly five months old. By any standards, Jessica was a difficult baby. Beautiful beyond my wildest expectations, with enormous blue eyes and perfectly formed light brown ringlets surrounding her china-doll face, Jessie did not smile for the first six months of her life. She slept little and ate with less regularity than she cried.

I would call my own mother to complain that Jessie's hour-long crying jags could not possibly be normal. My mother was unconcerned.

"Babies cry," she would tell me over and over again. "It's what they do. If she's still doing it when she's eighteen, then you can worry."

My mother would address all my concerns about Jessie in this way. According to my mother, Jessie could share our bed, wear diapers, and tantrum until she walked out the door to go to college and I would have no cause for concern. Of course, my mother knew what I only later learned, that just when you think you can't stand a child's tantrums or refusal to sleep alone, just as you feel your sanity starting to break, the clouds will part and you will wake up one morning next to your husband in your bed, alone, with your child sleeping peacefully in her own bed down the hall.

But in the weeks leading up to my return to work, I had not yet learned that lesson, and I tried mightily to force Jessie to take a bottle. Even as an infant, Jessie had an iron will. She remained exclusively breast fed, refusing any of my efforts to convince her to do otherwise. Needless to say, neither one of us was in particularly good spirits that day. I had not slept more than four hours the night before, worrying about whether she would starve herself and dehydrate to punish me for my abandonment.

Leaving your tiny, vulnerable infant with a person you barely know is inevitably part of a working mother's plight. That person might be a nanny, a day-care worker, or a husband/new father who has mutated overnight into a stranger of questionable competence. Unable to negotiate the complexities of day care, the mere thought of dressing a baby in time to catch the 8:05 train being more than I could fathom, I hired a nanny, Marie, who has cared for our family pretty much ever since.

My first day of work was Marie's as well. For the next few weeks, I would return to inspect the baby for bruises and question Marie about any slight discolorations I found. In retrospect, my daily inspections were comic, since every injury my children have suffered—a dislocated elbow, a broken arm, and worse—has been on my watch. Now I feel compelled on Monday mornings to account to Marie for my children's weekend-acquired bumps and bruises.

But in the absence of financial need, if a working mother has any hope of getting out the door, mixed in with the anxiety of leaving must be some measure of relief. At least, that was my experience. For five months, I had lived in the world of round-the-clock feedings, laundry, and errands. There were days when Charlie would leave for work and I felt envy. He was going to a land I knew well, the workplace, populated with people who thought about things other than diaper changing and who aspired to greater achievements than showering. I was left behind in the isolated and strange new world of mothering.

It was not a world to which I acclimated easily. One day Charlie arrived home while I was sitting in the nursery glider (traditional rocking chairs had apparently become too jarring for today's infants), nursing the baby for what seemed like the thirtieth time that afternoon. When he asked me what I had done that day, I burst into tears.

"This! This is what I've done today," I cried. "It's the exact same thing I did yesterday and the day before that." Charlie never posed that question again during any of my maternity leaves.

Every mother will tell you that children grow up too quickly. What few admit is that there are hours during the afternoon, as you wait for your husband to arrive home for dinner, when the laws of relativity are suspended and time actually stands still. You'll be cooking with a baby on your hip for an hour, but when you look up at the clock, only five minutes will have passed.

So that day in November 1997 when I started my new job in Lower Manhattan, I might have already been exhausted, but I was also guiltily gleeful about returning to the land of thinking adults. My new boss, Richard Smith, greeted me and showed me to my desk.

Back then it must have been clean, since the office had only opened four months earlier. Its existence was the result of the Legal Aid Society's disastrous strike in the early 1990s. The strike resulted from the constant clashing of the union and management following years of minuscule pay raises and escalating health insurance costs. Following the strike, the city had created alternative legal services providers for its indigent criminal defendants. In fact, I had participated in that strike and had even walked the picket line for two days until the Giuliani administration threatened me that I would lose my job. I went back to work, having lost two days of pay and gained nothing but blisters on my feet.

By the time the Office of the Appellate Advocate was finally formed in July 1997, I was working at a large private law firm. I had become used to working long hours and making more money than I had time to spend. Ordering dinner from a diner at midnight had become a bit too routine. Monday mornings found me just as exhausted as Friday afternoons, the weekend having done little to revive me.

On a rainy day when I was feeling particularly ground down, I received a call from Rich, whom I had known from my Legal Aid days, offering me a job at his newly formed office. Years earlier, one of the first cases I had worked on coincidentally involved the same arcane issue of statutory interpretation that Rich was also working on at the time. Despite the cases' similarities, I won my case and he lost his. My victory earned me Rich's respect.

When Rich learned that I was pregnant, he calculated that I might be willing to trade a larger paycheck for some evenings at home with my new family. He agreed to let me work as many or as few days as I wanted, with flexible hours. The salary was roughly half what I had been earning.

Charlie and I sat down at our kitchen table to discuss my options. We had a mortgage, two car payments, a new baby to support, and thousands of dollars remaining on Charlie's law school loans. Consideration of our debt burden would have turned any professional financial planner to stone. Add to this that Charlie had recently joined two friends who had started their own firm, leaving behind his big firm salary. The logical choice was clear.

Over the years, Charlie and I had mulled over many, many job offers and alternate career paths. We had met in August 1989 during law school orientation, before classes had started. At the welcoming reception for new students, I was standing alone next to a cheese platter, dressed for a garden party, in a long floral print dress and a straw hat. The hat was an unfortunate last-minute addition, donned in an attempt to appear more confident than I felt around my new classmates. Even on the crispest winter day, when the humidity is nil, I have wild hair that cannot be tamed by any product. In the New York August humidity, my hair was enormous; the straw hat had little hope of staying on my head. The first thing Charlie ever said to me was, "You don't usually wear hats, do you?" His tone was so genuinely curious, I had to laugh and admit the truth.

That first meeting pretty much sums up our relationship. I have never been a mystery to my husband. He had me pegged from the moment we met. And he has always been able to make me laugh. In the unlikely event that my daughters ever ask me for advice about whom to marry, I would depart from my own mother's advice that it is just as easy to love a rich man as a poor man. My advice would be to marry somebody who gets you, who understands what will make you happy, and who will encourage you to pursue that happiness even when doing so is not entirely logical.

It was my husband who encouraged me to take Rich's offer. The decision was obviously not wise financially—it seems even less so now that we have two more children than we did then. Still, I have never regretted it.

But on my first day back in 1997, I found myself staring out from my new office window, looking down at the Trinity Church graveyard, and wondering exactly how I was going to make this new life work. My musings were interrupted by the arrival of a pushcart filled with a huge trial record, which looked to be at least 3,000 pages long. I read the file jacket. Client name: Stephen DeLuca. Judgment date: January 5, 1995. Crime: Murder in the First Degree. Sentence: Fifty-Five Years to Life Imprisonment.

Just what I needed to ease myself back from the world of Peter Rabbit and friends—a first-degree murder case with a client serving a life term. To add to my joy, the client was already pissed off. I could tell from the thick pile of correspondence attached to the file's left interior jacket.

I soon discovered that my new client had every right to feel unsettled. He had been sentenced almost three years earlier and had filed a notice of appeal within a month of his sentencing date. It had taken the appellate court two years to assign him his first attorney. His case had then been sent to the Legal Aid Society, which accumulated the mountains of transcripts and file papers before advising the court that the society would not mind transferring the case to another office, an option because the new alternative providers needed to stock up. That transfer had been accomplished months earlier, and still DeLuca did not know the name of the person who would be handling his case. That was until I arrived to offer myself up as the object of his wrath. I dashed off a letter introducing myself to him, took a deep breath, and reminded myself that I would read this transcript like any other, one page at a time.

········································

Ordinarily, when I am not sleep deprived and worrying that my infant daughter might be starving, I love the experience of starting a new case. Every case is a story. Each has its own cast of characters through which to view the human condition: love, hate, stupidity, lust, rage, greed, envy. All of the seven deadly sins are there. I crack open trial transcripts the way others dive into new novels, letting the story wash over me. It always amazes me that in all the years I've practiced, I've never encountered two cases that are the same. Even though I sort of know how the story will end, with the jury announcing a guilty verdict, I still find the experience exciting.

It is said (mostly by prosecutors and judges) that a trial is a search for the truth. During that search, witnesses are called to the stand, place their hands on the Bible, and swear to tell the truth, the whole truth, and nothing but the truth. Questions are asked, answers are given, objections registered, arguments advanced. Inevitably mistakes are made. Every word uttered in open court is taken down dutifully by an official court reporter. If the jury reaches a guilty verdict and the defendant decides to appeal his conviction, the record will be typed up.

There is no constitutional right to appeal. Unlike the right to trial by jury, the right to appeal is not specifically listed in the Bill of Rights. Nonetheless, all fifty states have some mechanism through which a convicted person can challenge the justness of his conviction. The Supreme Court of the United States has held that if a state creates avenues of appellate review for convicted defendants, access to those avenues cannot be closed simply because a person cannot afford an attorney. That's where I come in.

Every person convicted of a crime who is too poor to pay for his own attorney is assigned one to represent him during one complete round of the appellate process. This first round is often referred to as the direct appeal. For example, in New York State, the jurisdiction in which I practice, felonies tried in the Supreme Court are appealed to the Appellate Divisions—the intermediate appellate courts to which every defendant can appeal "as of right." In other words, these courts have to consider the case whether they like it or not.

In contrast, a defendant does not have a right to have the highest court, the court of appeals, consider his case. That court reviews petitions and agrees to hear only those cases implicating legal issues of statewide importance. Once the court of appeals has denied a request to review a defendant's case, his direct appeal is concluded.

In theory, at that point, my job is done. But I tend to be slow to close out my files, especially when I think a client has suffered a real injustice. For a creative advocate (and I am nothing if not creative), the direct appeal is just the beginning of the process. In the right case, there are additional challenges that can be lodged in the federal courts and back in the trial parts. But such creative endeavors are considered "collateral" attacks, and an indigent defendant is not entitled to the representation of counsel to launch them. When I undertake such challenges on behalf of a client, my office receives no additional funds. We are essentially working for free. So the majority of our time is spent working on direct appeals.

An appeal is not a do-over. It is not a chance for the convicted defendant to ask the appellate court to revisit every issue already addressed by the trial court and jury. It is a common misperception that convicted criminals "get off" on appeal due to legal "technicalities." In fact, appellate judges are generally a conservative bunch when it comes to convicted felons, and they do not relish the thought of putting the state through the time, expense, and risk of a new trial, even when serious errors have occurred.

As an appellate lawyer, my job is to identify specific legal issues that warrant serious consideration and to argue that those issues merit awarding my client some relief—a new trial, a reduction in the grade of the offense, or a lesser sentence. To do that job, there are two separate stories that need to be told. There is the story of the crime: basically how, according to the prosecution's witnesses, my client did something ghastly, like sell a vial of crack to an undercover officer.

Then there is the story of the trial itself and the various proceedings that occurred in the lower courts. For example, in that case where my client allegedly sold crack, there might have been a pretrial hearing to determine whether the police unreasonably searched his knapsack for additional drugs in violation of the Fourth Amendment. Following any pretrial hearings, a jury will have to be selected and sworn according to established rules. The jurors will then have to consider evidence and arguments before being instructed on the law and returning a verdict. Each stage of the proceedings must be mined for appellate issues.

The story of Stephen DeLuca's crime started in January 1993, when the New York City Police Department began investigating some unsavory activities at a screen-printing shop located on the Lower East Side of Manhattan, near the legendary Katz's Deli. The shop was a place people would go to get logos sprayed on their T-shirts. Even the local police precinct had gone there to get their softball uniforms done up. But there were other, less wholesome items for sale, including guns and large quantities of marijuana.

In order to gain the trust of the people selling the guns and pot, detective Ronnie Ruiz had gone undercover, posing as a badass Colombian drug dealer in need of guns and a wholesale source of weed. Showing a surprising lack of creativity, Ruiz actually introduced himself as Colombia to those from whom he was trying to purchase.

Throughout January and February of 1993, Ruiz and his undercover partners had engaged in the accepted police practice of "buying up." They had placed small orders for pot and guns over a period of several months to gain the trust of their suspects, hoping that by so doing they would be led to the main source of the goods. By March 1993, they had ordered a total of ten pounds of marijuana from the owner of the screen-printing shop, Howard Green.

On March 10, 1993, Ruiz met with his supervisor, Sergeant David Matt, to plan the culmination of the investigation and the arrest of all its subjects. At that time, the police drew up a plan detailing how the arrests would go down. That "tactical" plan called for Ruiz to return to the store, check out the marijuana that he had ordered, and signal its arrival to the field team.

The police would need to gain access to the shop through a locked glass door, which presented a host of problems. Anybody inside the shop would be able to see the backup team coming. The team could not bash the door in without its shattering. Therefore, to ease the team's entry, the tactical plan required Ruiz to check out the pot and then pretend that he had to get the money to pay for it. Once the people inside the store let him back in to pay, Ruiz was to then hold open the glass door for the other team members, but he was not to re-enter the store to make the arrests himself. In other words, ideally, the subjects were never to realize they had been selling to a cop at all.

Several detectives were assigned to back up Ruiz during the transaction. Ruiz would have two "ghosts," officers whose primary responsibilities were to make sure he stayed safe. There was also a lieutenant, Michael Neff, who would supervise the entire operation. None of these officers would wear uniforms, not even those slickers often worn on television cop shows marked DEA or FBI or NYPD. These cops would wear street clothes, with shields around their necks.

This plan might have sounded good when it was being hatched back at the precinct, but it quickly went awry once it began to play out in the street. As planned, Ruiz met with Green and another man, Bob Vently, who was also inside the store. The two men told Ruiz that the goods had not yet been delivered. A short time later, Stephen DeLuca walked in, carrying a large shopping bag containing four pounds of marijuana, six less than Ruiz had ordered. Ruiz returned to his Jeep and transmitted to his field team, telling them that some of the pot had arrived. He then headed back to the store, carrying a bag of what was supposed to look like money.

As Ruiz crossed the street, the police backup team lined up along the outside of the building to avoid being seen through the store's glass door. A female officer, Beth Luz, positioned herself directly behind Ruiz. As anticipated, one of the men inside the store, Vently, let Ruiz back in.

That's when things started going wrong in a major way. Vently immediately saw the female officer coming toward him and began struggling to keep her out of the store. The struggle created a bottleneck in the entryway, around which the remainder of the team could not pass. While the officers claimed that they were yelling "Police!" Vently apparently could not wrap his mind around the idea of a female officer and responded, "You're no police!" as he continued to struggle with Luz.

With the struggle between Luz and Vently continuing at the front door, Ronnie Ruiz abandoned his undercover role, assumed a combat stance, and advanced toward the store's interior second room. Ruiz, who until that moment was known as Colombia the drug dealer to those inside, began screaming "Police!" and "Get on the fucking floor!" and "Let me see your hands!"—all the while pointing his gun directly at Harold Green, the store owner.

It was a dramatic departure from the tactical plan. A veteran officer, Franklin Nevins, who had participated in over 200 narcotics operations, would later testify at DeLuca's trial that he had never seen an officer abandon his undercover role during an operation. Even without twenty-twenty hindsight, the dangers of doing so seem obvious.

Suddenly, shots from my client's gun rang out from the store's back room. Immediately, Lieutenant Neff, supervising the operation from outside the store, radioed a "Ten-thirteen" message—the most dire call for assistance that an officer can make. Sergeant Matt, who had arrived at the store's threshold, began screaming "Shots fired!" and pushing his team members away from the store. Officer Nevins, who was described at trial as six-foot-eight and 280 pounds, somehow managed to push his way inside. He squeezed himself behind a filing cabinet in the store's front room. Luz finally made it past Vently in time to see Ruiz collapse.

Meanwhile, my client, Stephen DeLuca, extended his arm around the door frame of the store's back room and continued to fire a silver gun. The police returned fire. In the midst of the chaos, Ronnie Ruiz was carried outside.

Lieutenant Neff entered the store and positioned himself against the wall of the first room. From the back of the store, Neff heard my client screaming, "You're not the real police!" even as the police were ordering him to drop the gun. When their orders were not followed, Lieutenant Neff returned fire with his nine-millimeter Glock.

Amid this activity, my client begged the intruders to prove their identities as police officers by showing him a vest or some other official identification. Minutes later, when the marked backup police cars finally arrived at the scene, their lights flashing, my client surrendered. After screaming, "Okay, I know you're the police!" DeLuca threw down his weapon and walked unarmed toward the front of the store.

According to the police testimony, even after throwing down his weapon and being shot through the hip, my client continued to resist arrest. After seeing DeLuca gun down one of their brother officers, the police team was furious. My client would later testify that his "resistance" resulted in the officers beating the shit out of him, literally. I never really thought about the meaning of that expression until the DeLuca case. Apparently, if beaten severely enough, a human being will lose control of his bowels.

While my client was being beaten into unconsciousness, the undercover officer, Ruiz, died at the hospital from a single bullet wound. The gunshot had entered six inches below his left shoulder and passed through his torso, perforating his lungs and heart before exiting his back below his right shoulder. The trajectory suggested that Ruiz had been shot from the side, with his left arm outstretched, exposed to his assailant. The bullet made a clean path through the upper arm into his vital organs. Ruiz's bulletproof vest was useless.

# WHO'S CRYING NOW?

Every mother knows there are two sides to every story. At a recent dinner gathering—five adults, nine children—the grown-ups had reached that cherished stage of the evening when the children have been fed dinner, given dessert, and ordered to go play and the first bottle of red wine has been poured. But before we could hoist our glasses, the dreaded sound of crying could be heard echoing from upstairs. We all froze, trying to identify its source.

"It's Noah," my hostess stated with the certainty of a mother penguin attuned to her chick's unique call.

Sure enough, within moments Noah was in the dining room, face red, tears streaming down his cheeks.

"Lila hit me in the head!" Noah declared indignantly, identifying my six-year-old daughter as his assailant. I could feel my face flush as I was dispatched by the grown-ups to dispense swift justice. I set my wine glass on the table, its contents sloshing dangerously above the white tablecloth.

Following Noah up the stairs to the scene of the crime, I was ready to mete out punishment. There is no presumption of innocence when an older child strikes a younger one. I barged into the bedroom without knocking and demanded to know why Lila had hit Noah. Lila and her two oldest friends, Emma and Grace, were dancing joyfully to the upbeat tones of the *High School Musical* soundtrack, which had been playing the entire afternoon. Lila looked up at me, surprised and struck temporarily speechless by my angry entrance. Fortunately for her, Emma and Grace came to her immediate defense.

"We were making up a dance to this song and Noah walked into Lila's hand," Emma explained without hesitation, assuming the role of lead counsel.

"It was an accident!" Grace chimed in, as second chair.

Watching Lila's sideways glances at her two oldest friends, I knew that their version of events was not entirely true. I quickly determined that the girls had been dancing, Noah had been bugging them, and Lila didn't bother altering her dance moves to avoid his head. Still, the quick maneuverings of Lila's Dream Team raised enough doubt in my mind that she got off with just a strong warning. If I received any additional reports of hitting, the party would come to an immediate end, I promised. All was quiet for the rest of the evening, and I was able to drink my wine in peace, although I remained a glass behind the others.

The criminal justice system does not work with the same speed and efficiency as mommy justice. Because so much more is at stake than interrupting the choreography of a new dance number, a criminal defendant is accorded more procedural protections to guard against the arbitrary and capricious determination of his fate. The accused has no burden of proving his innocence. Instead, the prosecution must prove his guilt beyond a reasonable doubt to overcome the presumption of innocence. Many criminal defendants never take the stand to explain their version of events, preferring to keep the jury's focus on holding the prosecution to its burden of proof. While the strategy makes perfect sense from a legal standpoint, to satisfy my personal curiosity I prefer cases in which my client testifies in his own defense.

Stephen DeLuca's defense was the best type—the kind that's never changed. My client's version of the shooting was not so much different than the police account. Immediately after the incident and at trial, DeLuca explained that he had moved from New Jersey into Manhattan in 1992 and had been introduced to Howard Green through a mutual friend. In March 1993, Green contacted him and asked if he could score ten pounds of marijuana for a guy named Colombia, who ran a large drug operation. Green described Colombia as a tough guy.

At that time, DeLuca was selling pot to a select clientele, an unfortunate choice of profession that carried very real risks. DeLuca had friends who had been shot during drug rip-offs. Frightened by their experiences, he began carrying a nine-millimeter semiautomatic for protection. He also bought two guns for Green.

On the day of the shooting, DeLuca carried to the store a little less than four pounds of the pot Green had ordered for Colombia. Afraid of being robbed, he carried the nine-millimeter in his jacket pocket and had left the additional six pounds of pot with a friend. Once inside the store, DeLuca met with Colombia and showed him the marijuana. Colombia said he would go get the money, and DeLuca, undoubtedly nervous, went to the bathroom in the back of the shop.

Upon leaving the bathroom, DeLuca heard Vently being attacked and screaming in pain. When DeLuca walked toward the front of the store, he saw a huge African American, Nevins, with a gun, behind a filing cabinet, and Colombia, also with a gun in his hand. Colombia pointed the gun at DeLuca and then at Green, ordering Green to "give him the shit." As Colombia swung around to point the gun at Green, DeLuca reached for his gun. He testified that he had been shot before he himself fired. He then fired two or three more shots and hid behind the wall.

Only then did DeLuca hear people yelling "Police!" He became confused and asked to see a badge. Neff threw him a small gold detective's badge, not the big silver type worn by regular patrol officers. DeLuca was not convinced by the badge, but when marked police cars with flashing lights arrived and the intruders did not flee, DeLuca realized that they were the real thing.

He must have also realized at that point that he was completely fucked. The last thing he remembered was being tackled and beaten until he lost consciousness. He came to at the precinct. The statement he gave before receiving any medical attention reflected essentially the same story he would testify to months later.

The trial prosecutor sought to discredit DeLuca's account by questioning him about every unsavory detail from his past, including his bad treatment of ex-girlfriends (DeLuca had apparently dated more than one woman at a time and lied about it) and his ownership of pit bulls. As a pit bull owner myself, I found this latter line of questioning particularly offensive. But DeLuca's account of Ruiz's shooting remained pretty much unshaken.

After reading the story of the shooting, I remembered it well. In March 1993, I was a recent graduate from New York University School of Law. When we were in law school, Charlie used to take me to Katz's every once in a while so that we could get some real corned beef, the fatty kind, or some hot dogs, the salty kind. When I heard of the incident, which the media depicted simply as a cop killing during a shootout with a gang of drug dealers, I remember thinking that months earlier we could have been in the neighborhood.

One of my first cases at the Legal Aid Society involved a client accused of selling crack whose trial began the day after Ruiz was killed. The testifying undercover officers during that client's trial had been allowed to wear black stripes on their clothing as a sign of mourning. The defense attorney objected that such a display sought to appeal to the jurors' emotions and would prejudice his client by reminding the jurors just how dangerous undercover narcotics operations could be. That argument was rejected by the trial judge. Despite my best efforts, the appellate court did not embrace it either. No court was going to get in the way of the NYPD's right to mourn a slain officer in the manner it saw fit.

A case involving the killing of a police officer is like no other. Inevitably, the event is followed by a predictable outrage, calls for the death penalty, and televised coverage of the funeral, with bagpipes playing and hundreds of uniformed officers in attendance.

I don't have anything against police officers. I teach my children to respect them, that they are the good guys, and to look for the blue uniforms if they ever get lost. The New York City police department is larger than the population of a lot of small towns. Unavoidably in a group of people that size, there are good ones and not-so-good ones.

Unlike a lot of defense attorneys, I have represented a number of police officers, although none from the NYPD. One client was accused of offering to look the other way on a traffic violation when an attractive female motorist, a former Playboy Bunny (or was it a *Hustler* centerfold?), offered to go down on him for his consideration. Really, I could not muster too much moral outrage. I imagine the thought of striking that deal would have entered the minds of most men.

Another client was accused of unjustifiably shooting at a group of young men who, he believed, were looking to steal a car in a mall's crowded parking lot during the Christmas shopping season. The grand jury convened to investigate that case ultimately deemed it a justified shooting. My client walked away, his job and freedom intact.

While I fretted over the fate of my police clients, as I do with all my clients, I admit that I do not understand, on a gut level, why the killing of a police officer is treated so differently than the killing of a civilian. If Stephen DeLuca had intentionally shot and killed a newborn baby, his crime would have repulsed me to a far greater degree and he could not have been charged with first-degree murder. It is noble that police officers willingly face the dangers of protecting society from criminals. But they are adults who make that choice and assume that risk.

I also understand on an intellectual level that an attack on a police officer must be viewed as an attack on society itself. But I have to admit, the outrage it creates—the orchestrated response of the department, the PBA blowhards basking in the limelight—leaves me cold. My representation of Stephen DeLuca never made me feel morally conflicted. I dove right in.

· · · · · · · · · · · · · · · · · · · · · · · · · · ·

The second story of the DeLuca trial, the story of the legal proceedings, was equally dramatic. Just as every crime has its cast of characters—the suspect, the victim, the investigators—so too does every trial. The players in the crime story are usually a lot more interesting than these second-story players, namely the lawyers and the judges. Most of the time, the personalities of the lawyers don't fly off the page. The judges also usually act, at least on the record, judicious.

A lot of sniping takes place off the record, but as a general rule, what happens off the record stays off the record. When I was an intern at the Federal Defender's Office, I saw a knock-down, drag-out fight between the lawyer I was shadowing and the federal prosecutor she was up against that culminated in the defense lawyer's muttering, "Fuck off, you uptight bitch." The comments never made it onto the record. On that transcript, everything seemed perfectly cordial between the parties.

Not so in the DeLuca trial. DeLuca's parents had mortgaged the family home to be able to pay a private attorney to defend him. Unfortunately, they chose Herman Gross, a somewhat high-profile defense attorney, well known in New York's criminal justice system for being heavy on promises and salesmanship, light on legal research and factual investigation. A successful defense in the DeLuca trial would have required a good deal of both factual investigation and legal maneuvering, and while Gross is far from the worst criminal defense attorney in New York State, he is far from the best.

He is also one of those people whose face is so unlined, through either a meticulous skin care regimen or Botox injections, that it's hard to tell whether he's truly happy or sad, despite his attempts to seem sincere at all times. Gross loves the media and is ready to laugh or cry on cue for the cameras, depending on which demonstration of emotion is more likely to make the nightly news.

He's got some great lines that he uses in every criminal trial. He refers to criminal defense as "laboring in the vineyards of the criminal justice system." On particularly bad days, I sometimes think of that image, reflect upon the real vineyard laborers in *The Grapes of Wrath*, and remember to be grateful for my cushy desk job.

He also tells a story about stealing sugar out of his mother's sugar bowl when he was a child and how he and his brothers, after sticking their fingers into the bowl, would smooth over the sugar to leave no trace of their fingerprints. But their mother would always know they had been to the kitchen to steal the sugar, because the next morning, with her bare feet, she could feel the grains that had fallen on the floor. Gross always used the story to ask the jurors to feel for the grains of truth in the case that the prosecution had not been able to smooth over.

Harold Green, the print-shop owner, was tried along with DeLuca. His attorney was Jake Ortiz. Ortiz kept a lower profile than Gross. Green was not accused of murdering Ruiz or attempting to murder any of the field team members. His biggest problem was that he was sitting next to DeLuca. Ortiz's strategy was to try to emphasize at every opportunity that his client's case had to be considered separately from DeLuca's.

The prosecutor, Anthony Burns, was a careerist who must have been pretty high up to be assigned the DeLuca case. From the cold record, Burns seemed to be zealous but professional, though this initial assessment of him was destined to change.

The first piece of truly bad luck for DeLuca came when his case was assigned to Justice John Lake. Justice Lake was a legend in appellate circles because he simply did not care what any appellate court thought of his actions. He would disdainfully refer to recent court of appeals decisions, accusing the judges on New York State's highest court of lunacy. He actually referred to them on the record as the seven dwarfs.

There were stories that when the administrative law judge tried to transfer Lake to the civil side so that he could preside only over matters involving money, not people's freedom, Lake barricaded himself in his chambers and refused to move. The administrative judge ultimately relented, and Lake remained responsible for overseeing criminal trials.

By the time of the DeLuca trial, Justice Lake was old and sick and more crotchety than ever. As an appellate lawyer, I love that kind of judge. In any case tried before him, I can be sure that I will not have to slog through thousands of pages to find a good issue for appeal.

When it comes to appellate issues, usually the error has to hit you hard on the first read for there to be any hope of reversing a felony conviction, particularly a violent felony conviction. In a case involving the first-degree murder of a police officer, because of the institutional power of the police force and the severity of the crime, the error would have to be serious enough to knock the wind out of you for there to be any hope of achieving appellate relief.

But Justice Lake did not disappoint. Page 35 of the three-thousand-page record presented the issue that would come to dominate my professional life for the next seven years.

*Voir dire*, a French term meaning to speak the truth, is the portion of the trial when prospective jurors are questioned about their respective abilities to consider the case without bias or prejudice. In a case such as DeLuca's, finding unbiased jurors presented obvious problems for the defense. First, the case involved the murder of a police officer, the type of crime about which most people have strong feelings. Second, the case had an overlay of drug dealing, another unsympathetic fact.

Adding to the mix, DeLuca was a white boy from a suburban background selling marijuana for profit, who had killed a highly decorated, beloved minority officer. While conventional wisdom holds that minority jurors are more likely to be hostile to the police, it seemed unlikely that poor, minority jurors would have much sympathy for DeLuca. There was just no obvious demographic from which the defense could easily draw.

During every jury selection, the parties make snap judgments based on limited information. Because so little is known about the prospective jurors' attitudes and feelings, the law allows each side a certain number of peremptory challenges— challenges for which no reason needs to be stated. For example, if a juror says he hates black people because he has been robbed by them in the past and the defendant is African American and accused of robbery, a defense attorney would move to strike the juror for cause, meaning that the juror should be excused because his admitted bias means he cannot be fair. But if that same juror never admitted to being a racist and simply glared at the defendant with obvious hostility, the defense attorney would most likely be forced to expend a peremptory challenge. Peremptory challenges are treasured by defense attorneys everywhere. They are the only things that prevent you from having to suffer through weeks of that juror's hostile stares.

Jury selection began in DeLuca's trial at the beginning of November 1994. When the first twelve prospective jurors were questioned, neither side asked for their responses to be recorded by the court reporter. Following the questioning, the defense moved to excuse four jurors for cause. Juror number two, George Holmes, the first juror challenged, was a retired investment banker who had previously served as the foreman of a narcotics grand jury; Gross insisted that Holmes had stated he could not be fair and could not apply the law.

Justice Lake responded, "That is not so."

Because the individual jurors' responses had not been recorded, I could not tell who was correctly recalling those responses, the defense attorney or the judge. Same story when Gross next challenged prospective juror number five, Karl Capp, and set forth that Capp had friends who were police officers, including a close friend who worked in the narcotics division.

"He couldn't be fair," Gross argued. "That is what he actually said."

"That is denied," the judge responded.

Nor could Gross persuade Justice Lake that two additional jurors should be excused for cause: number eight, John Perlowitz, and number eleven, Michael Bon. Both jurors, Gross insisted, had said they had strong negative feelings about guns. Bon had stated that he had several friends who were police officers. Justice Lake contested that Perlowitz had said that he could not be fair, but concerning Bon, the judge merely stated, "That is denied."

Undeterred, Gross asked Justice Lake to question the four challenged jurors for himself.

The judge responded, "I am not going to do anything of the kind. Go ahead and take the peremptories."

Gross subsequently asked to approach the bench to urge the court to reconsider its ruling.

"What is your problem?" the judge snarled.

Gross repeated that he had spoken with Ortiz, Green's counsel, and certain jurors definitely said they could not be fair. If a prospective juror had said that he could not be fair, the trial court had to excuse him, unless the juror subsequently promised to set aside any bias. But Justice Lake apparently did not feel bound by this particular rule of criminal procedure.

"That is not enough," Justice Lake responded.

"Could you just question them?" Gross begged.

Again the judge refused. "I am not going to question any of them. Use your peremptories."

When Gross stated that he was being forced to use an inordinate amount of peremptory challenges during the round, Justice Lake quipped, "You got reversible error. Go ahead, use them."

From a legal standpoint, Justice Lake's comments were the equivalent of Clint Eastwood's Dirty Harry daring a thug to go for his gun. The judge could have just as easily asked Gross, "Do you feel lucky? Well, do ya, punk?"

The judge's ruling denying the challenges meant that Gross could either expend four valuable peremptories in the first round, a risky strategy given that he did not know who would be called to replace the challenged jurors, or he could accept some or all of them. Gross pulled the trigger and ate up four of the defense's twenty peremptory challenges.

But he did not prove lucky. By the final round of voir dire, Gross had no more peremptory challenges left. He was forced to accept a juror who had initially stated he could not be fair. After some prosecutorial questioning, however, the juror reversed himself and promised he *could* be fair, thereby securing himself a spot as the twelfth juror to decide Stephen DeLuca's fate.

Even back in the first round, Gross, sensing the seriousness of Lake's error, begged to make a record.

"Can we just do that?" he pleaded, without any success.

When a lawyer requests to just "make a record," he is invoking the higher power of the appellate court. The request signals that the lawyer accepts that the judge is not going to change his ruling but that the lawyer believes the error is sufficiently grave that it will warrant relief on appeal.

A trial court's refusal to allow a party to make a complete record is universally frowned upon by appellate courts. It justifiably creates suspicion that the trial judge is trying to hide his mistakes. But more important, the less clear the record, the harder the appellate judges' jobs become. Nobody appreciates more work.

Until the DeLuca trial, I had never seen a case in which a judge had actively thwarted the creation of the record. Reading Justice Lake's comments, his repeated rebuffing of the defense pleas to make a record, his adamant refusals to recall the jurors, took my breath away. *You got reversible error. Go ahead, use them.* He had *admitted* committing reversible error during the first round of jury selection, on the first day of a monthlong first-degree murder trial. Or so I thought.

I got up from my desk to get a glass of water and mull over the issue. While returning to my office, I saw my boss at the photocopying machine.

"How's DeLuca going?" Rich asked.

"My guy got screwed!" I replied, my voice filled with righteous anger. I explained to Rich how Justice Lake had refused to allow the defense attorneys to recall several prospective jurors for additional questioning, even though the judge apparently agreed that the jurors had said they could not be fair at some point during the voir dire.

After I finished outlining the issue, Rich looked at me wearily. "I'll paint the FREE DELUCA signs and meet you at the courthouse for the press conference."

"I'm serious," I proclaimed. "I don't know how I can lose this case."

"He killed a cop. You'll lose," Rich responded knowingly.

It is a measure of my naïveté that I thought he was kidding.

# COMING HOME

I went back to the office, closed the transcript, and put on my coat. It was close to 4:00 p.m., the time at my old law firm when we would just be putting in our afternoon coffee orders, hours away from dinner, never mind going home. The front of my dress was already damp. I had been unable to coordinate reviewing a first-degree murder transcript with working a breast pump. Walking toward the reception desk to sign out for the day, I felt slightly sheepish about my early departure. But I reminded myself that I had taken this job in part based on Rich's promise that I could keep flexible hours.

Inez, the receptionist, smiled at me warmly as I signed out.

"You kiss that baby for me when you get home," she instructed. "I'm so jealous."

"Let's chat at 4:00 a.m. when I'm feeding her for the fourth time tonight. That'll cure your jealousy."

"No, it won't. I remember those days. They go too fast, trust me," Inez said, laughing.

When I arrived home, Jessie was crying, but Marie was in good cheer. I wished Marie a pleasant evening, grabbed Jessie from her arms, and whisked her upstairs to the nursery. I sat down in the glider, surrounded by the room's baby blue, duckling yellow, and pale pink colors.

As Jessie nursed hungrily, I told her of my day. I explained that there was a person at work who needed my help, who was in serious trouble, who I did not think had been treated fairly. My first attempt of many to explain to Jessie what I do. As I spoke, Jessie moved her hands in circles. For the umpteenth time, I admired their perfection, the proportion of her fingers, long and tapered, each one topped with a tiny mother-of-pearl nail. People would actually stop me in the street and comment on her hands. It was the first feature upon which my mother remarked when she held Jessie minutes after her birth.

"Maybe you could sleep tonight?" I suggested to Jessie. "That would help a lot."

She regarded me seriously, as if considering my request but making no promises. When I woke bleary-eyed the next morning, I could not remember whether we had slept at all. The night was a blur of crying and feeding sessions.

After gulping down a mammoth-sized coffee on the train, I returned to the DeLuca transcript, which revealed another serious error. My client had asserted a justification defense. DeLuca claimed that he had killed Ruiz because he mistakenly, but understandably, believed that Ruiz was a drug dealer who was about to kill him and the others in the store. A person is entitled to use deadly physical force if he reasonably believes that force is necessary to defend his own life or the life of another person.

DeLuca had testified that he had shot Colombia when Colombia pointed his gun at Green. That testimony was supported by the autopsy results reflecting that the fatal gunshot wound had entered Ruiz's left arm and traveled through his lungs and heart. Ruiz could not have been facing DeLuca when the fatal shot was fired. So any claim that DeLuca had shot solely to protect himself was destined to fail, because it was refuted by the medical evidence. The trial prosecutor, in his closing argument to the jury, characterized the medical examiner's testimony as the "watershed" of the trial, because the autopsy results made it "so clear" that the gun that fired the fatal shot was positioned to Ruiz's left. Ruiz was facing Green and "didn't have a chance, not a chance to look at this defendant," the prosecutor argued.

Following the prosecutor's summation, Gross twice requested that Justice Lake make clear that Stephen DeLuca had the right to use deadly physical force not only to protect himself but to protect the lives of the other people in the store. Justice Lake had denied the defense requests, without explanation.

Another huge mistake. A defendant is entitled to have his jury instructed on a theory of defense if any reasonable view of the evidence could support it. In considering whether to instruct the jury on the defense theory, a trial court must consider the evidence in the light most favorable to the defense. In other words, Justice Lake had to assume that the jury would credit Stephen DeLuca's testimony that he shot Ruiz when Ruiz threatened Green with the gun. The judge's inexplicable failure to explain a theory of justification (the right to use deadly physical force to protect the life of another) presented yet another strong appellate issue.

DeLuca's jury had begun its deliberations during the afternoon of December 1, 1994. The jurors deliberated until 10:30 that evening but had been unable to reach a verdict. By lunchtime the next day, there was still no verdict. At 3:20 p.m., the jury announced its decision. Stephen DeLuca was convicted of the first-degree murder of Ruiz and the attempted first-degree murder of Neff. The jury acquitted him of two counts of attempted murder relating to Nevins and another member of the backup team. He was also convicted of second-degree weapon possession and criminal sale of marijuana in the first degree. Green was convicted of selling marijuana and two counts of selling a weapon.

On January 9, 1995, the parties appeared before Justice Lake for sentencing. The courtroom was packed, awash in a sea of blue uniforms. The press was also present. After braving the traffic from New Jersey into Lower Manhattan, my client's mother, Rosemary, had been unable to find a seat in the courtroom. She was forced to stand while awaiting the pronouncement of her only son's sentence.

Back in 1995, New York State had abolished the death penalty. The DeLuca case, involving a suburban white boy convicted of killing a Hispanic officer, provided an ideal platform from which local politicians and judges could rant about the need for the death penalty's reinstatement without raising the specter of racial injustice.

I cannot imagine how my client must have felt as he awaited sentence, seeing all those officers around him. And by now he knew that Justice Lake was unsympathetic to defendants in general and would be expected to impose the harshest available sentence. Stephen DeLuca was twenty-three years old at the time and had never served a day in prison before his arrest. He was about to see his entire future defined, years of prison announced, doled out like Monopoly money, in numbers too large for any young person to comprehend.

But Gross was not done performing, particularly with the press present. Despite its obvious futility, he made an impassioned plea for the court to set aside the verdict based on its failure to properly instruct the jury on DeLuca's justification defense.

Justice Lake was having none of it. In the middle of Gross's plea, he cut him off, declaring that the jury had not believed any of the defense's "bullshit." The courtroom exploded into raucous applause as the officers joined in the judge's display of contempt. When the courtroom quieted down, Stephen DeLuca was sentenced to fifty-five years to life in prison—the maximum permissible.

Reading the sentencing minutes infuriated me. It is not as if I don't curse regularly, but I try very hard not to do it in front of my parents or my children, and I have never done it in a court of law. There are certain places that demand respect. A judge about to dole out a life sentence has to appear above the passion of the moment and the mob's cry for vengeance. Without judicial dispassion, a sentencing proceeding appears as legitimate as a public flogging.

·····································

After reading the sentencing minutes, I was motivated to start writing. Good thing. Drafting an appellate brief is a painful and arduous process. All those pages of evidence and the legal issues have to be compressed into seventy pages or less.

Every lawyer approaches the task in a different manner. My approach involves four basic phases: (1) read the record and identify the issues; (2) take notes that condense the case's essential facts into a document that I can carry home on the train and read in bed after my children are asleep; (3) research the relevant case law; and (4) write, write, write.

It took me over three months to accomplish these steps in the DeLuca case. During that time, Jessie remained an exclusively breast-fed baby who continued to refuse to take a bottle in any form. So after working for seven hours straight on the brief, I would race home for the first feeding at 5 p.m. Then I would feed my daughter every three hours during the night: 8 p.m., 11 p.m., 2 a.m., 5 a.m., and 8 a.m., before leaving for work to write for the next seven hours.

By the time I had finished the DeLuca brief, I was convinced that I had developed some form of terminal illness. I made an appointment with the doctor for a full physical. He examined me briefly and asked me about my daily routine. As I described my three-quarter-mile walk to the train station, the commute into the city, the case I was working on, and the all-night feeding sessions, the doctor's expression morphed from concern to amusement. He sent me for blood work but told me he was pretty sure the tests would reveal nothing.

"You're a working mother," he told me. "You're tired. Get used to it."

After I got over the anger at my suffering being so easily dismissed, I did get used to it. Now I cannot remember how it feels to get a full seven hours of uninterrupted sleep. And I have stopped complaining of fatigue, except to other mothers and my husband—who has learned that he has to at least feign sympathy if there is to be any peace in our home.

But back when I was writing the DeLuca brief, I would find my head falling onto my computer keyboard. Writing briefs is primarily what appellate lawyers do. The time spent arguing cases is tiny compared with the amount of time spent writing.

Writing is work, but it is the only experience that allows me to forget everything else in my head. Before I get into the office, I might be worrying about the leaking roof, my child's sniffles, or that ever-growing credit card balance I am carrying. But when I really start to write, nothing else exists except for the case. By the time I look away from the screen, hours will have passed.

When the DeLuca brief was done, I sent it off to the client. I was pleased with how it had turned out. Despite my sleep deprivation and my months of maternity leave, I had managed to present the facts concisely and the legal arguments coherently. I was filled with relief.

My satisfaction was not shared by Stephen DeLuca, who was less than impressed with my efforts. He had several additional issues he wanted raised. I wrote to him, explaining why I thought his issues should not be included in the brief. He did not write back immediately; but a few weeks later, he agreed that the issues I had raised were the ones most likely to win on appeal.

With my client's approval, I filed the brief in February of 1998. Then I put the DeLuca file in a drawer and waited for the prosecution's response.

# CRYING FOUL

My four-year-old nephew is so sweet, so devoid of aggression, that when a playmate or one of my daughters pushes or slaps him, he immediately announces, "That's all right!" His mother has worked hard, with some success, to teach him to be less forgiving. He used to actually say "thank you" after taking a blow. My nephew does not have the makings of a criminal appellate attorney.

In my job, one cannot be too willing to excuse bad behavior (except, of course, one's clients'). If a prosecutor or judge acts badly, his errors must be explored in great detail, placed in constitutional context, and decried as violations of due process and fundamental fairness.

It is always an appellate lawyer's fantasy that the brief she writes will be so convincing, so irrefutable, so right, that the district attorney's office will throw up its hands, surrender, and concede that the conviction should be reversed. I have lived that fantasy in exactly one case in almost fifteen years of practice. Still, against my better judgment, in the months before I received the response in DeLuca, I began hoping for a concession. Instead, in the summer of 1998, I received a massive response, conceding absolutely nothing.

My opponent was Morris Stone, who was responsible for supervising all of the Manhattan district attorney's office's federal litigation. Stone's selection to handle the appeal should have signaled to me that the prosecution was prepared to fight me on DeLuca in any court, anywhere, anytime. But when I received Stone's brief, I remained confident that I was going to win the appeal in state court. There would be no need for federal court review.

The prosecution's brief argued that the record was inadequate to address the jury selection claims because Gross had failed to request recording of the first twelve prospective jurors' answers during the first round of voir dire. The prosecution barely mentioned Justice Lake's conduct in thwarting the defense from creating an adequate record once a dispute arose over the four challenged prospective jurors' comments.

Concerning DeLuca's claim that the trial court had erred in refusing to explain to the jury the prong of his justification defense relating to defense of another person, the prosecution argued that there was no reasonable view of the evidence to support the charge. DeLuca's shooting toward the front of the store endangered Green and Vently. The actions my client described during his testimony were not consistent with those of someone trying to save another's life.

By the time the oral argument was scheduled in September 1998, I was living with my in-laws, with a two-hour commute separating me from my office. Charlie and I had bought a decrepit old house, one with gaping holes in its ceilings caused by its ancient plumbing system. We were trying to make it habitable. I had been warned by friends that nothing can break your spirit like home renovation. But I was determined not to let the leaking plumbing, the peeling paint, the exposed asbestos, or the furry wallpaper defeat me. I commuted the two hours a day to work and two hours a day back to my in-laws' house so that I could live with the luxuries of running water and intact ceilings. Those luxuries did not prevent Jessie from contracting pinkeye or our car from repeatedly breaking down. But at least we could shower.

On the day of the DeLuca argument, I got to the train station at 5:00 a.m. and sat with the commuting investment bankers. I wanted to figure out for the fiftieth time exactly what I would say.

Even in cases with less profound consequences, where a client is not serving fifty-five years to life in prison, oral argument is a scary experience that I approach with dread. I am not particularly articulate, a serious flaw in any lawyer but terrible for an appellate one. I try to overcome my lack of natural eloquence with maniacal preparation, which often includes talking to myself as I role-play both the inquiring judge and the responding lawyer. I appear seriously schizophrenic to the people who see me walking to court.

In law school I had been on the moot court board, so I had experience with oral arguments even before I graduated or passed the bar. But moot court and real court have little in common. In moot court, the problems are set up so that each side has a strong argument in its favor, with some legal authority supporting its position. The moot court judges, who are usually law professors, serve up batting practice questions designed to show which participant is most prepared.

An example of a moot court question might be, "Counselor, what is the standard of review we are to use when analyzing the lower court's legal conclusions?" The well-prepared participant would answer, "The standard of review for issues of law on appeal is de novo." No problem. I was always prepared for moot court.

In real life, the appellate judges often believe my client is the devil himself and that I, as his advocate, am not much better. The questions I have been asked by real-life appellate judges are not meant to explore how well prepared I am. They are often meant to express disdain for me and my client. Some examples of "questions" have included: "Isn't your argument ridiculous?" (I think my answer to that was no.) "Are you in la-la land?" (I couldn't think of a good answer to that one. Charlie later suggested, "Is that what you call this place?") Another one of my favorites: "Aren't you here arguing this case just to get another notch on your belt?" (I'm pretty sure the answer to that one was no again.) Real court is not always the most intellectually stimulating experience.

Before my first oral argument, an experienced appellate attorney told me that every case involves three separate oral arguments: the one you prepare, the one you actually make, and the one you tell people you made after it's over. By the morning of the DeLuca argument, I had been preparing for a week. I had asked three of my office's most experienced attorneys to listen to my arguments and grill me with their hardest, meanest, and dumbest questions. Every once in a while, there is a judge on the panel who has not read the briefs but still feels qualified to dominate the debate. Despite all of my preparation, the argument was never really clear to me until I sat in the train station watching the sun rise.

I arrived at the Appellate Division, First Department, in Manhattan by 8:00 a.m. for a 10:00 a.m. argument. I am always worried that the train will break down and I'll miss an argument entirely. Whenever I arrive at a courthouse early, I breathe a sigh of relief and remind myself that, as Woody Allen said, eighty (or was it ninety?) percent of success is just showing up.

The DeLuca argument was on a Friday, usually my day off, but when the court schedules an argument for a particular date, you show up or lose your opportunity to argue. The scheduling clerk does not care if you are a working mother who doesn't have child care on Fridays. The court did not cancel arguments the afternoon of September 11, 2001, even as Lower Manhattan, including our office, was buried in dust.

The First Department's courtroom is designed to intimidate. I have never entered it without feeling awed. It is all dark wood and soaring arches. There is a domed ceiling, ornately painted, with the names of the court's former judges etched in gold. The bench upon which the five-judge panel sits is positioned high above the podium where the lawyers argue. It is always cold inside, as if they are trying to preserve the dark frescoes at the cost of everybody's comfort. Inevitably, I shiver as I am waiting for my case to be called. It is not unusual for lawyers who have never argued there before to remark on the court's beauty. Those comments always surprise me, because I dislike the place so much that I stopped noticing its beauty long ago.

On the day of the DeLuca argument, I picked up a copy of the court's calendar and filled out my notice of appearance to advise the court that I was present to argue the case. The names of the judges who would be hearing the arguments that day were written on top of the calendar, and the images those names evoked were not pretty.

When I first started arguing cases in the First Department, there were certain judges whose presence on a panel could fill me with relief. There were actually cases where I went into the argument expecting to lose and was rescued by a panel that by chance contained two sympathetic judges who persuaded the others to vote my way. But by the time of the DeLuca argument, those judges were long gone. I only had to read a single name on the top of the calendar to know that I was in for a long morning.

Justice Abraham Weiss would be presiding over DeLuca's case. Not long ago, I attended a funeral for a friend's husband, also a criminal defense attorney, at which a well-respected federal judge delivered a most beautiful eulogy. He described how there are attorneys who put judges at ease, there are ones who put them on edge, and there are ones who make a judge want to rule in the attorney's favor even if the judge shouldn't. My friend's husband was the type who made a judge want to rule for him.

I was the type of attorney who put Justice Weiss on edge. There were times when my arguments would actually make him turn a deep scarlet hue, like the time I argued that a client who had been convicted of a triple homicide deserved a new trial because the prosecution had failed to turn over a single police report. I would try to comfort myself by dismissing Weiss as a sexist, but there were plenty of women who argued in front of him to whom he was perfectly respectful. He just seemed to dislike me. To add to my concern, Weiss was smart and well respected and dominated every argument. He was not a good draw.

When DeLuca's case was called, I walked to the podium and began my argument. It's hard to describe a good oral argument. I have heard baseball players describe how a ball will almost stand still for a split second, and at that moment they just know they can hit it out of the park. A good argument feels something like that. There seems to be a lot of time between the questions, during which I can formulate my answers. It's like having a lively discussion at a dinner table with a group of relatives who really want to understand what you're trying to tell them. I feel at ease. I can just talk and explain my infinitely reasonable positions.

A bad argument is like getting stuck at a Christmas party talking to somebody's ultra-conservative investment banker boyfriend. I try to remain polite, but inevitably, within seconds, my voice becomes shrill. Everything I say seems to annoy the judge who asked the question. I am totally conscious of sounding like an idiot. There are times when I feel as if I'm almost watching the disaster unfold from outside my own body.

The DeLuca argument was a good one. I was able to convey to the court the outrageousness of Justice Lake's conduct, without any of the appellate judges becoming overtly offended. My tone seemed properly balanced, acknowledging the seriousness of my client's crime but emphasizing that when much is at stake, it is most important that everyone play by the well-established rules. A trial judge's refusing to allow a defense attorney to create an adequate record, while the attorney begged to do so, simply should not be condoned by an appellate court, I argued. To my astonishment, Justice Weiss seemed to agree with me. He accepted that the defense attorneys had done everything they could to create a record once the dispute arose over the four challenged jurors' comments.

But Justice Weiss was not prepared to reverse a cop killer's conviction over Justice Lake's idiocy.

"Can't we just order a hearing to reconstruct the proceedings?" Justice Weiss asked.

I knew that such a hearing would not benefit my client in any way, and I argued that four years after the original voir dire there was just no way to reconstruct the proceedings with the accuracy necessary to resolve the claim. In the four years between the original jury selection and the oral argument, Justice Lake, who would be expected to preside at such a hearing, had died. His recollections were gone. There was simply no precedent for ordering a reconstruction hearing where the parties disagreed about what had occurred moments after it transpired, I argued. But when the court's red light blinked, indicating that my time was up, I knew that I had not convinced a single judge to reverse Stephen DeLuca's conviction.

Until the DeLuca case, reconstruction hearings were ordered when minutes had been inadvertently lost or when the record was unclear because of ambiguities in the court reporter's note-taking practices, never when a judge had actively thwarted the creation of the record. Most often, they were used to determine whether the defendant had been present during a hearing or portions of the trial. The record of such a reconstruction proceeding usually looks something like this.

> THE COURT: I don't have a specific recollection of the defendant being present, but it is my invariable custom, policy, and practice not to conduct essential proceedings in the defendant's absence. Therefore, I am finding that the defendant was present.

End of hearing. Defendant loses. Basically, the judge reconstructing the record finds that he did nothing wrong that could warrant reversal of a conviction obtained on his watch. It's sort of like appointing the fox to investigate the burglary of the chicken coop.

By the end of the DeLuca argument, it was pretty clear that the First Department was going to order a reconstruction hearing so that the parties could attempt to re-create the prospective jurors' responses. Even though I had been unable to convince the court to reverse the conviction and order a new trial, I still felt good about the argument itself. It had been my first one since I had come back from maternity leave, and it had gone pretty well considering the nature of the case. In the past, when an appellate court had ordered a hearing of any kind, I had always been able to convince the prosecutor that we should forgo the hassle of the hearing, cut our losses, and make a deal that involved a reduced sentence for my client in return for our agreeing to withdraw the appeal.

But with DeLuca, there was not a lot of room to negotiate, because even a reduced sentence, twenty-five years to life, thirty years to life, would still mean that my client would most likely die in prison. The NYPD has a long memory. Whenever DeLuca would come up for parole, the department would petition the parole board to deny his release. For my client, a remand for further trial court proceedings appeared to offer little hope of improving his situation.

For me, the prospect of venturing back into the trial parts was unlikely to help me catch the 5:03 train home. From a time-management perspective, there is no worse place for an appellate attorney to be than back in the trial courts. Hearings ordered by the appellate courts are the stepchildren of every trial judge's calendar. Unlike trial lawyers, who can sign in to a part and then simply leave to handle another matter in another courtroom, I am stuck, at the mercy of an unhappy judge who does not know me and has no reason to do me any favors. For a while, every trial-level hearing I handled contained some variation of the following colloquy.

> THE COURT: I would like to work a little late this evening so that we can
> finish this hearing, as the Appellate Division ordered.
> ME: I can't. I have a child-care issue. My nanny has to leave early and
> my husband is traveling on business and my parents are out of town and
> my mother-in-law is getting a root canal.

Eventually, I learned to approach the bench so that I could share my personal life with the judge alone, without the court reporter incorporating my messy, conflicted schedule into the record.

The truth is that I always have a child-care issue. It's not because I don't have excellent child care and backup child care and backup, backup child care. The "issue" for me is getting home in time so that I can be the one caring for my children by dinnertime and certainly by bedtime. I am willing to sacrifice a lot for my job: sleep, a gym-toned body, clean closets, reading novels. But I will not happily miss supervising my children's homework or singing them to sleep because a judge cannot efficiently handle his calendar.

Once I heard a male attorney announce at 1:00 p.m. that he had to leave to pick up his children at school. Even though it was the middle of the court's workday, nobody said a word. No further explanation was required. Moreover, the man's tone reflected that the issue was nonnegotiable, not a matter of judicial dispensation. I have never been able to achieve such confidence, probably because unlike that father, I always feel that my requests to leave to care for my children are regarded as empirical evidence that mothers of young children should not be handling heavy cases that demand serious commitment.

So in December 1998, when the First Department sent the case back to the trial part for a hearing to reconstruct only two of the prospective jurors' responses, those of Karl Capp and Michael Bon, I was far from thrilled. Not only had I failed to win a case I believed to be a slam dunk on appeal, I now had to venture into hostile territory, trial court, to attempt to reconstruct a record four years after the original voir dire had taken place. It was a ridiculous remedy, a hollow attempt to provide a thin veneer of fairness to smooth over Justice Lake's corrosive misconduct.

"This is going to be fun," Rich remarked from my office's doorway, as he watched me reading the decision, my brow furrowed.

"For whom?" I asked.

"I'm sure you'll see to it that everybody has a good time," he replied.

Despite Rich's assurances that the DeLuca hearing was going to be fun for all, I had my reservations. It was the holiday season, the first one in which Jessie, now eighteen months, was old enough to fully participate. She would gather her stuffed animals around her to recount the story of Chanukah. I would stand outside her door eavesdropping in amazement. Other kids her age could barely string together a couple of sentences, but there was Jessie speaking of Judah Maccabee and the miracle of the oil. It's remarkable what a toddler can learn if you leave her in front of the television long enough. With the acquisition of speech, Jessie became more cheerful. I was enjoying her company more and more and felt increasingly eager to catch the early train home. The looming hearing promised to make that simple goal ever more elusive.

......................................

A few days after I received the DeLuca decision ordering the reconstruction hearing, a letter from Justice Margaret Kane landed on my desk explaining that due to Justice Lake's death, she would be conducting the hearing. The letter advised the parties to appear for a status conference within a few days.

Upon receiving the letter, the first thing I did was begin collecting intelligence reports. I knew that almost any judge had to be more sympathetic to my client than Justice Lake and was thankful for the small favor of not having to appear before him, but I had never heard of, never mind appeared before, Judge Kane. So I had to reach out to trial lawyers to learn her reputation.

The initial reports were not encouraging. "Humorless," "meddling," "a pain in the ass" were the words most often used by practicing defense attorneys to describe the judge. The one positive comment came from a former prosecutor whom I did not particularly like. "She's pretty fair, not a knee-jerk judge for either side," he explained. Of course, when an ex-prosecutor says a judge is fair, that usually means she's pro-prosecution.

I arrived for the status conference feeling desperate to strike a deal and not leave my client's fate to Justice Kane or the appellate court. All thoughts of that possibility came crashing down when the elevator doors opened onto the fifteenth floor of the courthouse at 100 Centre Street.

The hallways were filled with uniformed officers and undercover detectives milling around, awaiting the opening of Judge Kane's courtroom. At first, I thought there must be some massive trial going on that would require all those cops to testify, but common sense told me that officers would not materialize in those numbers to testify. I realized that the police were there to demonstrate their displeasure with the appellate court's remanding the case and to send a clear message to Justice Kane that her actions were being watched. As far as they were concerned, even a meaningless hearing was far more than Stephen DeLuca deserved.

I fought my way through the mass of officers and sat outside the courtroom waiting for it to open. To the uniformed throngs, I probably appeared to be a court reporter or a law student. They were expecting Herman Gross, DeLuca's media-courting trial attorney, to be outside the courtroom predicting victory in colorful prose. Only when Peter Brody, the assistant district attorney who would be handling the hearing for the prosecution, approached me to talk about the case did the police officers turn their hostile gazes in my direction. I could sense their collective relief. Surely, DeLuca had little chance of succeeding if his case was now being handled by a girl, especially one who was so clearly terrified.

Despite the conditions under which we were meeting, I liked Assistant District Attorney Brody almost immediately. First, he pronounced my name correctly, which showed that he had at least listened to me when I'd spoken to him on the phone the week before. Second, he brought the notes the trial prosecutors had taken during the original voir dire four years earlier and sought me out to hand them over. He was courteous, even nice to me, while the officers milled around glaring. But when I asked him whether there was any chance of our reaching a deal to avoid the necessity of the hearing, he made it clear that any relief for DeLuca would have to be imposed by the courts.

As anybody who watches *Law and Order* knows, when a crime is committed, the People of the State of New York are represented by two groups: the detectives who investigate the crimes and the district attorneys who prosecute them. If a defendant kills a decorated detective, he can expect little consideration from the prosecutor. If any consideration were extended to such a defendant, the police might stop showing up on time to testify in that prosecutor's cases. As I have said before, the police department has a long memory.

Soon after I had thanked Brody for the notes and thrust them into my "briefcase" (a worn-out Coach bag I had received as a college graduation present from my grandmother years before), the court officers opened the courtroom. Justice Kane took the bench and asked us to place our names on the record. Brody stood without hesitation and in a loud and calm voice declared, "Assistant District Attorney Peter Brody, for the People" and then "Good morning, Your Honor."

It was my turn. I said my name quickly, so anxious to sit down that I forgot to mention who I was representing.

Immediately, the court reporter asked me to repeat what I had just said. I was more used to reading records than making them. Add to that my nervousness at being at the center of this spectacle and it's understandable why an experienced court reporter could not understand a single word I had uttered.

Justice Kane looked down at me from the bench. She might have had a reputation for being humorless and a pain in the ass, but when she saw me she was smart enough to recognize a lawyer who was out of her element.

"You might want to speak more slowly, and it might be a good idea to mention who you are representing," she explained patiently.

I stood again, took a breath, and stated my name slowly and loudly, remembering to mention that I was appearing on behalf of Stephen DeLuca.

Police officers in the back of the courtroom laughed and hissed. Justice Kane ignored them.

"Counselor, your client has not yet been produced by the Department of Corrections. Do you waive his appearance for the purpose of these proceedings?" the judge asked. I had no idea what I was doing, but I answered, "Of course, Your Honor."

A moment later, the judge's law secretary, the person who helps her write decisions and research legal matters, approached the bench to ask to speak with her about another case. Justice Kane excused herself for a moment.

After the judge had left the bench, the court clerk, Raymond, called me over to his desk.

"Counselor, can I speak to you for a moment?" he asked. When I arrived at his desk, he leaned toward me and whispered, "You look scared. It's time to get your game face on."

"I am scared," I replied honestly. "And this is my game face."

Raymond's laughter, warm and genuine, filled the silent courtroom and instantly made me feel better.

Moments later, Justice Kane returned to the bench and invited the parties into her chambers to discuss scheduling. Once again, I felt grateful toward her, this time for getting me away from the heat of the hard gazes boring into my back.

In chambers, Justice Kane's familiarity with this inherited debacle impressed me. She was not a judge who waited to be told by the prosecution how the case should proceed. Instead, she informed both sides that she expected legal memoranda by the end of the week addressing the procedures to be followed during the hearing, including which side should bear the burden of proving what the prospective jurors had said four years earlier. The court's need for guidance was understandable, given the unusual nature of the hearing and the difficulty of the task before it. While trial attorneys might have considered Judge Kane's request annoying, I welcomed the task. It suggested that she was careful and actually interested in doing the right thing.

Before leaving her chambers, Judge Kane asked me to advise my client of all that we had discussed.

"Of course," I agreed.

"Do you have a corrections pass that will allow you to visit your client in the pens?" the judge asked me, referring to the holding cells where prisoners are kept when awaiting their court appearances.

"Uh, no, Your Honor, actually I don't," I replied, feeling like an absolute idiot. Without hesitation, Judge Kane wrote out an order directing the Department of Corrections to allow me into the cells located in the courthouse so that I could visit Stephen DeLuca.

Back in the courtroom, the crowd of officers had thinned, but there were still several sitting down. At the elevator bank, a few more were waiting for the painfully ancient elevators to arrive. As I approached, without speaking a word, each officer turned his back to me at the same time. That I could be an object of such a well-orchestrated display of scorn simultaneously frightened and flattered me.

When we got on the elevator, the officers began talking amongst themselves, expressing their outrage that the conviction was in danger of being reversed. It soon became apparent to me that none of them understood what was actually going on.

"Excuse me," I said softly to their backs, "but would you like me to explain what's happening?"

They turned toward me and seemed to see me for the first time. Looking into my face, they must have recognized that I was not some hotshot firm lawyer angling to make a name for myself. I spent the next five minutes talking to a small group of officers about the nature of the appellate claims. I explained that the appellate court was concerned that during the jury selection two jurors had expressed that they could not be fair to my client but that Justice Lake had refused to allow the defense attorneys to question those prospective jurors on the record to make sure they could be fair. We were back in the trial court to conduct a hearing during which we would try to figure out what the jurors had said years earlier in order to determine whether Justice Lake should have granted the defense challenges to those jurors. When I was through with my explanation, the police officers politely thanked me for taking the time to speak with them.

"Just out of curiosity," I asked, "what had you been told was going on?"

"Nothing," a young, plainclothes cop responded. "They just told us to go downtown to support Ronnie and so we came."

"Okay," I said. "Well now you know it's pretty boring stuff, so maybe you won't want to come next time." With those not-so-subtle words of discouragement, I smiled and waved good-bye.

I walked toward the entrance to the pens at the opposite end of the court-house. The locked door was thick metal and painted an awful metallic red. The guard who opened it looked at me with an amused grin and asked suggestively how he could help me. I smiled right back and said I would really appreciate it if he could help me figure out how to get in to see my client. After I handed him Justice Kane's order, the guard personally escorted me through another thick gate that locked behind me and into an elevator that stopped at the tenth floor. There he took me to another guard and told him to help me find my client.

The tenth floor guard was less helpful. "'Duh-Luca, Day-Luca, Dee-Luca," he repeated, searching the records of the inmates transported from Rikers Island into Centre Street that morning.

"He's not here," he told me.

"I think he is," I responded. "There was an order to produce him this morning to Justice Kane's courtroom. He must be here by now."

Rolling his eyes to let me know he was really going beyond the call of duty, the guard picked up the phone in front of him and called yet another floor.

"Hey Lopez, it's Haroldson. You got this guy DeLuca down there? Oh shit. Okay. Okay." Listening to the conversation, I knew there would be further hoops to jump through before I would be allowed to see my client.

"You were sent to give me problems. He's a red ID," Corrections Officer Haroldson informed me.

"What's that?" I asked. It sounded as if my client might have contracted the plague.

"Are you a lawyer?" Haroldson asked incredulously.

"I was the last time I checked," I answered, once again with a smile.

"It means, Counselor, that your guy is the highest possible security risk. You're going to have to go up to eleven to see him. That's where they're holding the red cards today."

"Thanks for all your help," I said cheerily.

There is simply never a reason to be nasty to corrections officers, court officers, court clerks, court reporters, or anybody else in the court system. Inevitably, any demonstration of pique will result in your waiting longer than if you simply grin and bear the delay.

Up on the eleventh floor, after waiting another half hour, I met Stephen DeLuca for the first time. Unfortunately, I meet only a small percentage of the clients I represent. Most of them are housed hundreds of miles away in upstate prisons, many located near the border of Canada. New York State's extensive prison system acts as an employment program for its impoverished upstate areas. If I took the time to meet every client spread across the state, I would have little time left over to work on any of their cases.

But I always regret not meeting all my clients, because something inevitably changes for me when I do meet them. The case transforms from an abstraction into a more personal struggle. It is fascinating to meet the person whose misdeeds have been so unflatteringly portrayed in the cold record. In real life, that person can never remain simply his crime.

Never has the difference between the record and the client struck me as hard as it did when I met Stephen DeLuca. In addition to the transcript, I had gotten my hands on the press clippings of the shooting and the trial. In the newspaper articles' pictures, DeLuca was depicted as a scowling, skinny punk, with dark greasy hair and a mustache.

The man being escorted toward me in leg and arm shackles, wearing gloves that looked like the kitchen mitts my mother regularly used to take pot roast out of the oven, looked entirely different. The first word that popped into my mind was "wholesome." DeLuca had a wide-open, clean-shaven face, a big-toothed grin, and short-cropped hair. Light freckles were scattered across his cheeks. He reminded me of a better-looking, dark-haired version of Howdy Doody. DeLuca had also apparently spent the past four years in prison lifting weights. There was nothing left of that scrawny kid depicted in the papers.

The corrections officer locked DeLuca into a room where I could sit across from him with bars separating us. The arrangement was not one particularly conducive to natural conversation.

"Mr. DeLuca? I'm glad to finally meet you," I said.

Obviously embarrassed by the circumstances under which we were meeting, Stephen was anxious to explain to me that he was not really a high security risk at all, but that the "red ID" measures had more to do with the nature of his conviction. It was hard for me to reconcile how anybody could consider Stephen DeLuca a security risk. He looked so harmless to me, so much like the boys I'd known throughout my own suburban upbringing.

As I watched my client attempting to find a less uncomfortable position to accommodate his elaborate shackles, I remembered the time I had been snooping around my oldest brother, Nate's, bedroom and discovered a brown paper bag filled with a huge chunk of pungent greenery. I must have been around eight years old, Nate a highly secretive fourteen. From the way the bag was stuffed deep into an underwear drawer, I knew that its contents were illicit, like the glossy pictures of naked women hidden less carefully under the mattress. My heart raced as I heard my mother's footsteps approach. I stuffed the bag back into the drawer and ran from the bedroom, terrified that my snooping might get my brother into trouble. Then, and over the ensuing years, he had proven highly skilled at getting there himself, without my help.

I forced the memory from my head and focused on my client. Apart from his Hannibal Lecter restraints, Stephen seemed perfectly ordinary. He had a quiet, respectful manner and was quick to smile. But in the eyes of the State, he was a first-degree murderer, and so there would be leg shackles, arm shackles, and oven mitts whenever we would meet in the future.

I explained to Stephen what had gone on in court that morning, about the judge's request for us to set forth how we believed the hearing should be conducted, and about the police officers who had come to demonstrate their support for Ruiz. Stephen listened intently to what I said, without interrupting. When I was through, he thanked me over and over again for all my work.

After we had spoken for fifteen minutes, I told him I wanted to get back to the office to start the memo the judge had requested. I would see him the following week in court when the actual hearing got underway. As I walked away, I knew that he continued to watch me, all his hopes for any future outside of prison vested in me.

Over the following years, as I would continue to represent Stephen DeLuca and refuse to let any potential avenue of relief go untested, I would grow to understand that not only my client, but his entire extended family, was counting on me. On several occasions while preparing for hearings, I would meet with his mother, Rosemary, in a local diner over breakfast to discuss the case. Invariably the conversation would turn toward stories from Stephen's childhood. I also spoke with great-uncles and sisters, cousins and friends, who regularly called in to check on the status of the DeLuca case and to offer their thanks and support.

I always struggle to maintain an air of professional detachment, to prevent the pained pleas of my clients' families from compromising my judgment. But despite my best efforts, my connection to Stephen DeLuca did become more than purely professional over the years. There is simply no way to easily describe our relationship. It was not really a friendship. We met under such strange circumstances, and but for our protracted case-related dealings, I would not have maintained contact with him.

But ours was not a purely professional relationship either. When Stephen's grandmother died, his family was busy making the funeral preparations and did not want to tell him about her death over the phone, with the prison authorities watching. So I went to deliver the news. I cried in my office before traveling to the prison to tell him, because I knew that his grandmother had meant a lot to him and I dreaded his reaction. When I told him, his eyes welled with tears, but he smiled and told me that he was thankful that I was the person from whom he had heard the news. On occasion, when Stephen did not have any money on his books to buy stuff from the jail's commissary, I made sure that he had at least a few dollars for essentials. On my birthday and on Mother's Day, he sent me lovely gifts, beautiful origami cards, a handmade pocketbook with my name stamped inside the strap, even a book about the Constitution. In the spring, his father brought me fresh lilacs from his garden.

I guess I simply liked Stephen DeLuca—his appreciative nature, his refusal to become embittered, his determination to make the best of a horrible situation. My client complained less than a lot of people I knew who were not facing the prospect of spending the rest of their lives behind bars. I truly believed that the system had dealt with him unfairly, that his trial had been conducted before an unsympathetic judge, in a politically charged environment, with tragic consequences. I never doubted that if he could get out of prison some day, he would never commit another crime. Collectively, these facts made me want to fight for him to the end. When colleagues would ask me how much time I intended to spend fighting the DeLuca case, I would respond that I had at least fifty-five years to try to get the conviction overturned.

# FINDING SOLACE IN UNLIKELY SOURCES

The week after our first meeting, Stephen and I were back in court to begin the reconstruction hearing. I had spent a lot of time addressing the issues Judge Kane had raised the previous week. I argued that although reconstruction hearings were usually informal proceedings during which the lawyers and judges simply placed their recollections on the record, the DeLuca hearing should be conducted like a trial, with each side giving sworn testimony under oath that would be subjected to cross-examination. I also argued that because Judge Lake had thwarted the defense's ability to create an appellate record, the prosecution should bear the burden of proving what the prospective jurors had said. I did not expect the judge to rule my way. But she did, on every issue.

As we started the evidentiary portion of the hearing, I was feeling pretty good. It would be up to the prosecution to prove that the two prospective jurors had stated they could be fair four years earlier and that Justice Lake had not committed reversible error by denying the defense for-cause challenges to them.

The prosecution's first witness was Anthony Burns, the prosecutor who had tried DeLuca's case. He testified with astonishing specificity about all of the prospective jurors' responses during the first round. Burns went so far as to describe in detail what several of the first twelve prospective jurors had been wearing four years earlier. These were people he had observed maybe for a couple of hours, most of whom never sat on DeLuca's jury. In the years between the DeLuca trial and the reconstruction hearing, Burns had selected many juries and probably questioned hundreds of prospective jurors. Still, he claimed to recall that prospective juror number twelve during the first round of the DeLuca trial wore her hair in a tightly pulled-back bun and had thin lips on which she wore brightly colored lipstick.

Most judges would have been impressed by Burns's vivid recollection and never would have entertained the notion that a senior prosecutor was fudging his sworn testimony, but as I'd by now discovered, Margaret Kane was not most judges. Pursing her own thin, brightly lipsticked lips, she looked down at Burns and queried:

"Mr. Burns, why is it that you remember this woman's lipstick and pulled-back hair, after all this time?"

"I just do," Burns replied, not used to having his word questioned.

"I see," Judge Kane remarked, unpersuaded.

According to Burns, none of the prospective jurors during the first round had admitted they could not be fair. If any had, Burns would have challenged them for cause himself, because he would never want an unfair juror sitting on a murder case.

But in his own notes, under the name of prospective juror number five, Karl Capp, Burns himself had written "couldn't be fair" and then crossed out the notation at some point. When Judge Kane asked him to decipher this aspect of his notes, Burns responded, "I couldn't hazard a guess." The judge did not seem pleased with that response either.

If Anthony Burns' memory was too good to be true, except when it was too bad to be true, Herman Gross's was consistently annoying. It was Gross's practice not to take any notes of the prospective jurors' responses, because he was too busy "connecting" with them—some might say performing for them. When Gross testified, it was plain from the frustration in his voice that the sting of losing DeLuca's trial had not faded over the years. At times, his testimony sounded more like a summation argument than a dispassionate response to questioning. According to Gross, Capp had definitely stated that he could not be fair at the DeLuca trial because he had a close relationship with an undercover narcotics detective. Michael Bon had made similar statements.

The one lawyer who testified in an absolutely convincing and credible manner was Howard Green's former attorney, Jake Ortiz. Because Green had never appealed his conviction, Ortiz had nothing to gain from the DeLuca hearing. As a private practitioner, every second Ortiz spent in court testifying in the DeLuca proceedings was a second he was not earning any money. Unsurprisingly, he had little desire to be involved. I must have called him ten times requesting his file without getting any response. Finally, as the date of the hearing approached, I had to actually ask Justice Kane to sign a subpoena threatening Ortiz with fines and other penalties if he failed to show up and bring his file. Only when that subpoena was served did I hear from him.

Fortunately for DeLuca, Ortiz had taken detailed notes of the prospective jurors' responses during the first round of the voir dire. Under Capp's name, Ortiz had noted that Capp had a friend who was an undercover officer and that Capp was "pro-prosecution." Ortiz had felt very strongly that the challenge to Capp should have been granted.

I asked Ortiz whether he believed Justice Lake had paid close attention to the jury selection proceedings. Ortiz laughed softly. "No. He actually slept through parts of them."

"He *slept?*" I repeated, genuinely surprised. I had not prepared Ortiz to testify at the DeLuca hearing.

"Yes. He did. He slept. And we all noticed, and we didn't say anything because we were afraid if we did, it would offend or embarrass him. It was going to be a long trial, and Judge Lake could make your life miserable if he felt you were trying to humiliate him," Ortiz responded softly, remembering the uncomfortable predicament created by the judge's somnolence.

Judge Kane was troubled. "How could you not say anything?" she asked incredulously.

Ortiz's response was direct. "Look, he's the judge. I don't like to offend. It could turn out very badly for my client. Everybody knew what Judge Lake was about. We had to play the hand we were dealt, the best we could."

Ortiz was the last lawyer to testify. The proceedings were adjourned.

After spending the day in court, I would return to the office to review the hearing testimony and consider whether it raised additional avenues of investigation to pursue. Upon receiving the prosecution's notes, I actually convinced Rich to send them to a former FBI document examiner in Quantico, Virginia, to see if he could bring up the crossed-out notations under Capp's name and date-test the inks to see when the notations had been crossed out. Apparently, the FBI can carbon-test ink samples and determine whether they had been made with the same pen. I figured if ADA Burns had crossed out the notations after the hearing had been ordered, I would have a strong argument that even the prosecution knew that Capp had said he could not be fair.

Unfortunately, my foray into forensic document analysis did not produce any compelling new evidence for the DeLuca hearing. The tests were inconclusive and did not clarify the prosecution's notes. My efforts served only to convince my boss that I was losing all perspective in the heat of the fight.

"Next you'll be seeking a court order to exhume Judge Lake to see if he was buried with any notes from the DeLuca trial," Rich grumbled.

He had laid out the cash for my forensic expert, whom I had persuaded to cut his usual fee in half.

"Hmmm. I hadn't thought of that. You think Judge Kane would order it?" Rich looked worried.

"I'm kidding," I said laughing. "But seriously, look at the notes under George Holmes. I want to do something about him."

George Holmes was the investment banker, prospective juror number two, during the first round, and the first juror the defense had challenged. The appellate court had not ordered a hearing to reconstruct his answers because when Gross said that Holmes had announced he could not be fair, Justice Lake had responded, "That is not so."

But both the prosecution's notes and those taken by Jake Ortiz showed that Holmes had made statements reflecting an inability to be fair. Ortiz had written that Holmes "could not be impartial" and that he had stated that "murder is never justified." Similarly, the prosecution's notes reflected that they expected a defense cause challenge to be lodged against Holmes.

"What can I do about this juror?" I asked Rich.

"That depends," he responded. "Do you really want the juror? Or do you just want to make trouble?"

"No. No. I really want the juror," I insisted.

"Then ask the Appellate Division to give him to you."

And so that night I drafted an application to the appellate court asking it to release George Holmes's confidential identifying information, namely his address and telephone number, to the reconstruction court. That information was maintained by the commissioner of jurors, and I could not get it unless the appellate court agreed that it should be released.

When we next appeared before Judge Kane, she was not pleased.

"I would have thought that before you went running off to the appellate court to ask to get information to call a witness, you would have wanted to hear from me to see if I would agree that his proposed testimony was relevant," she announced.

Ugh. I had bruised her ego by going over her head. Time to backpedal.

"I apologize, Your Honor. I just didn't want there to be any undue delay, so I thought I would get the contact information first and then address the relevancy issue," I explained.

The judge asked the prosecution to set forth its position with respect to my application. Apparently, the prosecutors were equally unhappy with my chosen course and announced that they intended to fight my application with full briefing. They considered it procedurally improper and an unjustified attempt to delay the proceedings. According to the prosecution, if I wanted to hear from George Holmes, I should have filed a separate motion. The prosecution's argument struck me as absurd, an attempt to make me leap through additional hoops like a trained poodle.

Judge Kane was not about to jump into the fray. I had asked the appellate court for relief, and if any relief were to come, it would have to be from there. However, the appellate court denied my application one week later without specifying the basis for the denial in any manner.

By that time, the day had come for Michael Bon and Karl Capp to testify. It amazed me that both prospective jurors were still in New York City. I always thought that people came and left the city on a regular basis. Based on the DeLuca reconstruction hearing, it seemed nobody ever leaves New York.

Michael Bon was the first person to testify. He was clean cut, dark haired, thin, and unremarkable. Strange to think that he had become such an important figure in my professional life; I could not take my eyes off him as I awaited his testimony and was ready to hang on his every word. Bon explained that he remembered being called as a prospective juror in the DeLuca trial. He remembered Gross, whom he found to be an interesting character. Bon admitted that he had a lot of friends at the "Four-O" and that his police friendships seemed to trouble the defense at DeLuca's trial.

Anybody who would describe the Fortieth Precinct as the Four-O is a cop wannabe. It is how the police themselves refer to the precincts from which they work, the Three-O, the Two-Eight. Nobody but cops speak that way. From that point on, I disliked Bon.

I was instantly transformed into a conspiracy theorist who believed that his friends at the Four-O had probably gotten word to him about how to testify at the hearing. I was not surprised when he ultimately insisted that, although he had indeed expressed an intense dislike of crimes involving guns and had explained that he had many close friends who were police officers, he had nonetheless promised to be fair to both sides during the original voir dire. This testimony pretty much sank our appellate claim that Justice Lake had wrongfully denied the for-cause challenge to Bon.

The futility of my efforts on behalf of Stephen DeLuca became all too clear in the moments it took Bon to get up from the witness stand and walk out of the courtroom. When Judge Kane announced the lunch recess, I turned to leave but did not make it outside the courtroom before I burst into tears. To make matters worse, Stephen DeLuca's family was there to see my outburst. As hard as I tried, I could not regain my composure.

"I'm so sorry," I said to his mother, between my sobs.

Stephen DeLuca's mother, Rosemary, had a flinty strength I had admired from the first time we had met. Unlike many of my clients' mothers, Rosemary never came to me crying or begging me to rescue her son. She knew I had small children. Having raised three kids herself, she understood the demands of mother-hood. She also intuited that the pressure of her son's case was placing heavy demands on my sanity.

"What do you possibly have to be sorry about?" Rosemary asked, placing her arm around my shoulder. "Pouring your heart and soul into trying to help my son? Is that why you're apologizing to me?"

Her strength shamed me. I was being comforted by the woman whose son was likely to spend the rest of his life in prison. I should have been the one doing the comforting.

"I'm okay now," I assured Rosemary. "I just need to get something to eat." When all else would fail, I blamed my emotional outbursts on low blood sugar. "I'll see you after lunch."

After the lunch break, it was time to hear from the second prospective juror, Karl Capp. He was Bon's polar opposite, heavyset, sloppily dressed, with messy hair. Capp recalled that at the time of the DeLuca trial he had a friend who was a police captain responsible for overseeing a narcotics unit. While Capp could not recall discussing this friendship during the jury selection, he testified at the hearing that if he had been questioned about it, he would have said that sitting on a case involving the death of a police officer would have made him uncomfortable.

"I have several friends who are police officers. I wouldn't want anybody to be involved. I wouldn't want the defendant to have any prejudice. Some people want to be on cases to convict people, but I don't think that's the right thing," Capp explained.

Hearing this testimony, I felt hope seeping back into my soul. There could be no doubt that Capp had been questioned about his relationships with police offi-cers. Ortiz's notes reflected that Capp had been questioned about the friendship and that Capp had responded he would favor the prosecution because of it. Those sentiments were also reflected by Gross's comments recorded during the original voir dire that Capp had "a close friend from Narcotics, he couldn't be fair. *That is what he actually said.*"

All I needed to prevail was to demonstrate that at least one of the chal-lenged jurors had represented during the original voir dire that he could not have been fair and that Judge Lake erroneously refused to grant the defense for-cause challenge to him. Based on Capp's testimony, I believed that any court would conclude that at least he had voiced concerns about his ability to sit impartially on DeLuca's trial.

Capp was the last witness to testify at the hearing. I spent the next month drafting proposed findings of fact, weaving together all the evidence and arguing that while Bon might have said he could be fair, Capp certainly had said he could not be. The prosecution, relying almost exclusively on prosecutor Burns's account of the jury selection, argued that Capp had never said he could not be fair.

Months later, in September 1999, six months pregnant with my second child, I was back at 100 Centre Street to receive Judge Kane's decision. She handed it over to me and the prosecution without saying a word. It was hefty, over fifty pages long. Making my way back from the courthouse, I was almost run over by several irate drivers as I walked blindly through intersections, reading intently. Charlie would have been furious if he had been watching. He was already frustrated by my refusal to slow down and take better care of myself during my second pregnancy.

By the time I got back to my office, I realized that the judge had adopted almost all of my arguments. She found that "the credible evidence has demonstrated that it is more likely than not that Capp stated, in substance, that he was uncomfortable serving on the jury due to his relationship with one or more police officers, and that such feelings might affect his ability to be fair and impartial in this case." She had rejected most of Burns's and Gross's accounts and had relied heavily upon Ortiz's notes and testimony.

I could not have asked for a better decision. The findings of a hearing court are routinely adopted by appellate courts, because a hearing court has the advantage of seeing and hearing the witnesses. A witness's credibility often turns on subtle cues, the expression on his face when he tells his story, his body language and demeanor. The nuances of a witness's account are lost on the cold record, because only his words are recorded.

After receiving Judge Kane's decision, I drafted yet another brief, asking the appellate court to adopt her reasoning, find that Judge Lake had improperly denied the defense for-cause challenge to Capp, and reverse Stephen DeLuca's conviction. For good measure, I also complained about being denied the opportunity to call George Holmes at the hearing.

The prosecution responded that Justice Kane had improperly rejected prosecutor Burns's account of the voir dire and that Capp himself had never said that he could not be fair, but only admitted that he might have been "uncomfortable." According to the prosecution, Capp's discomfort with sitting on a case involving the murder of a police officer did not mandate that Justice Lake grant the for-cause challenge. As far as Holmes was concerned, the prosecution insisted that I had never been prevented from calling him at the hearing, because I could have found him myself by calling every George Holmes in the New York City telephone directory.

I wrote my reply brief from home, too enormously pregnant to risk the train ride into work any longer. Rich sent me portions of the record and case law via Federal Express. I finished the reply brief and mailed it to him two days before my second daughter, Lila, was born.

.......................................

My second maternity leave, in comparison to my first, was blissful. If the demands of motherhood are like running a marathon, I had hit my stride by the time Lila came. I was used to going without sleep. I knew how to do everything from laundry to walking the dogs while simultaneously holding a baby on my hip.

As difficult as Jessie had been, Lila was easy. Maybe because she had to be. Dark, round, and rosy, Lila ate and slept well. She smiled almost from the moment she was born, like she was grateful just to be around.

And of course she had the advantage of having an older sister available for her constant entertainment. Jessie took her new responsibilities very seriously from the start. Although she was only two and a half, I would often hear Jessie lecturing the baby about the dangers of trying to play with the spigots on the bathtub or telling Lila not to put something in her mouth because it was "chokey." For the first time, laughter and motherhood flowed naturally together.

On my walks pushing the bulky double stroller I had bought at a local consignment shop, I would sometimes wonder whether the appellate court had issued its ruling in the DeLuca case. I was already counting DeLuca in my W(in) column. Judge Kane's reasoning seemed so strong to me, so intricately reasoned.

All criminal defense attorneys lose a lot of cases. Most trials result in convictions. And on appeal, only two to three percent of trial convictions are reversed. There have been years when the First Department's reversal rate in criminal cases has dipped below two percent.

I can remember every case that I have ever won. I keep each one in my mind, strung together like a collection of worry beads, and turn to them whenever my battered ego needs soothing. A win in DeLuca would be a valuable prize, capable of getting me over a lot of hard past and future losses.

My fantasy of winning DeLuca lasted until February 2000, when in a rare quiet moment I called to catch up with a friend whose husband was a judge in New York. My friend wasn't home, but her husband casually mentioned hearing about the DeLuca decision. My heart started to race.

"What decision?" I gasped.

"You haven't heard?" my friend's husband asked flatly, as if we were discussing something of absolutely no consequence. "You know, they reversed the hearing court's factual findings and affirmed the conviction." He actually sounded amused.

I could barely breathe.

"I've got to go," I said and hung up the phone.

I locked myself in the bathroom and once again wept. Moments later, Jessie was knocking on the door.

"Mommy, Lulu's crying," Jessie informed me. She could not pronounce Lila's name yet and we had all started calling the baby Lulu.

"Mommy needs a minute, honey," I explained, wiping my eyes and trying to regain my composure. "I'll be right out."

I opened the bathroom door, walked into the nursery, and picked up Lila, breathing in that magic smell that only newborn babies have for that brief time before they start eating real food. It's sort of like baking bread mixed with baby lotion. Almost instantly, Lila stopped crying and I felt better. Not good, but better.

When Rich mailed me the decision days later, I could not bring myself to open the envelope to read it. Instead, I kept it on my dresser, under a pile of magazines and unused baby formula coupons. Its presence felt toxic.

Weeks later, when I finally did open it, I learned that the appellate court had ruled that Judge Kane had mistakenly placed the burden of proof on the prosecution. According to the appellate court, "Here, it was defendant's burden to establish by a preponderance of the evidence that a juror expressed a bias that would have precluded him from rendering an impartial verdict. Independent review of the transcript of the reconstruction hearing reveals that defendant did not meet this burden." The appellate court also rejected the claim that Judge Lake had erroneously refused to instruct the jury about my client's right to use deadly force to defend the other people in the store, ruling that the omission was harmless. It could not have affected the trial's outcome.

Not only was I devastated that I lost the case, I was furious that I would have to spend the remainder of my maternity leave contemplating the best way to convince the court of appeals, New York State's highest court, to hear the DeLuca case. Unlike the appellate divisions, the intermediate appellate courts that have to hear every criminal defendant's appeal (like it or not), the court of appeals gets to decide which cases are important enough to warrant consideration. In a criminal case where the appellate division has unanimously affirmed a judgment, the chance of getting leave to the court of appeals is slim.

By April 2000, I had finished drafting the DeLuca leave application, begging the court of appeals to hear the case, to right the wrongs left unremedied by the appellate court. The object of any leave application is to make the issues presented appear "open," or unresolved, by the existing legal precedent and in need of resolution because they are of statewide importance. The problem was that the rulings in DeLuca's case were so unusual, it was hard to argue that the issues presented were likely to recur. Instead, it seemed to me that DeLuca had become a case where the usual rules did not apply. The only certainty was the outcome. We would lose, and Stephen DeLuca would spend the rest of his life in prison.

I simply could not accept that Stephen DeLuca would never get out of prison. In June 2000, when the certificate denying leave arrived on my desk, for once I did not cry. Instead, I started coldly considering my options.

One obvious choice was to take the case into federal court by filing a writ of habeas corpus. Habeas corpus roughly translates into "you should have the body." It was the ancient mechanism compelling the sovereign to produce a person before a court to investigate the propriety of the restraint on that person's liberty. If you listen carefully, you can almost hear the rattling of chains and the echo of the dungeon's doors when courts discuss the "great writ of habeas corpus."

Today in the United States, a state prisoner can still file a habeas corpus action alleging that he is being held in violation of his federal constitutional rights. So in DeLuca's case, we could march into federal court and argue that the state courts' bizarre series of rulings had thwarted my client's due process right to a fair appeal and that the trial court's refusal to instruct the jury on a theory of defense supported by the evidence was a further denial of due process.

But in 1996, the United States Congress passed the Antiterrorism and Effective Death Penalty Act (AEDPA). Its purpose was to make it more difficult for state prisoners to successfully lodge habeas petitions. The idea was to kill them first, and let God, rather than the federal courts, sort them out. AEDPA's existence made me anxious about going directly into federal court.

Before a state prisoner can successfully petition the federal courts for relief, he must "exhaust" his state court remedies. Traditionally, a prisoner exhausts his remedies by providing the state courts at every level one fair opportunity to address his constitutional claims. I certainly felt exhausted and believed that I had raised DeLuca's constitutional claims at every opportunity in the state proceedings. Nonetheless, the prosecution's arguments that I could have called George Holmes, that second juror, during the reconstruction hearing if only I had found him myself through the telephone book, bothered me. In my spare time, and without telling Rich, I started calling every Holmes in the New York City telephone directory.

Around the time I resolved to find Holmes, I was simultaneously planning Jessie's third birthday party, an undertaking that would further hone my telephone skills. After compiling a long list of options (tea parties, backyard carnivals, magicians) and conducting intensive fact-finding interviews, I settled on an animal theme. Not bunnies and ducklings, mind you. No, no, no. For my three-year-old there would be exotic animals gathered from around the globe. Blue-tongued skinks, boa constrictors, and chinchillas would be transported to my home.

I would convert my living room into a jungle of green streamers and plastic vines, inhabited by dozens of stuffed animals and reverberating with tropical bird calls pumped in with a noise machine. There would be an elaborately decorated jungle ice cream cake. The children would dress up in animal costumes. Three varieties of pizza and assorted juice boxes would be available. Yes, it would be an excessive, entirely inappropriate celebration of Jessie's birth.

When I watch the videotape of that party, I appear as a blur of constant motion in a jungle print dress, Lila clinging to me like a baby chimp. My father's joyful laughter can be heard in the background of every frame. On the rare occasions when the camera catches my face, my smile looks brittle. Two years later, for Lila's third birthday, we celebrated with just a cake, and my mirth equaled my father's.

The same maniacal energy that fueled my preparations for Jessie's party drove my search for George Holmes, who proved more difficult to track down than a blue-tongued skink. On President's Day in February 2001, I was in the office calling the Holmes homes to see if George was home. There were a lot of George Holmeses listed back then. Not to mention all the G. Holmeses. Then there was also the possibility that George was not listed under his own name, but rather under his wife's. I felt crazy making all those calls, and I remember being glad the office was empty that day so nobody would overhear me doing it again and again. I would call up some random Holmes number and explain that I was a lawyer working on a case and I needed to know if there was a George Holmes living at that address. If there wasn't—and there wasn't most of the time—I would move on to the next Holmes listing.

Finally, toward the end of the day, I spoke to a George Holmes who sounded just like he had been described in the transcript, an older, intelligent gentleman—I could tell just by how he said "hello." But when I asked him if he remembered being called to serve on a case involving the murder of a police officer, George Holmes insisted that he had never been called to serve on such a case. I thanked him for taking the time to speak with me and continued to cold-call some more Holmeses.

But something would not let me forget the man with whom I had spoken minutes earlier. It was just a feeling deep in my bones that he was the one for whom I was searching. He just sounded so right, so much like I had imagined he would.

I called him back and again apologized for bothering him. This time I had Jake Ortiz's notes in front of me, and I read off the details of Holmes's life that had been recorded years earlier—that he had been a retired investment banker from the Midwest who had previously served on a narcotics grand jury, that he had at that time recently fired his secretary. Before I had finished recounting this information, Holmes interrupted, explaining that after speaking with me he had remembered being called in a case involving drug dealing. He had been concerned about his ability to fairly evaluate the evidence given the nature of the case, he explained.

I did not want to talk to George Holmes in too much detail. If I wanted to call him as a witness, I did not want to be accused of creating false recollections by reading off Ortiz's notes to him. So I thanked Mr. Holmes and advised him that he might be hearing from me in the future. He was mystified as to how he could possibly have any information that would be relevant to my efforts to defend my client. It *was* mystifying that over six years after the trial I was still dealing with Judge Lake's refusal to spend five minutes allowing the defense to make a complete record of Holmes's remarks.

Having found Holmes, the question remained what to do with him. I could have done nothing and just proceeded into federal court. In the alternative, I needed to come up with a theory supporting a challenge back in the state trial court. The prosecution's suggestion that I file a new motion to raise a claim that Judge Lake had wrongfully denied the for-cause challenge to Holmes was easier said than done. The statute allowing a defendant to move to vacate a judgment back in the trial court only permits very specific types of claims to be raised. The wrongful denial of a for-cause challenge is not one of them.

To have any chance of prevailing, I would have to allege that misconduct had occurred off the record, which had resulted in prejudice to my client, or that the judgment had been procured in violation of my client's constitutional rights. The right to lodge a for-cause challenge is not a constitutional right; it is one created by New York State's statutes. If a biased juror had actually sat on DeLuca's jury, I could have argued that he had been denied his constitutional right to an impartial jury. But Holmes had been challenged peremptorily by the defense during the first round.

Then I saw the hook. Ortiz had said that Judge Lake had actually *slept* through portions of the jury selection process. That was certainly misconduct that was not reflected on the trial record. In New York State, the right to have the trial judge supervise the jury selection process is an integral component of the jury trial right. A few years earlier, the court of appeals had reversed a conviction because a trial judge left the bench to go to the bathroom during the voir dire, abdicating his supervisory responsibility. The mistake, the court of appeals ruled, had adversely impacted upon "the mode of proceedings."

A "mode of proceedings" error is appellate gold. Such errors are deemed so serious that they impede the integrity of the proceedings themselves. They do not need anyone to object to them. They cannot be waived. I would argue that Justice Lake, by falling asleep, had absented himself just as completely as the judge who left the courtroom to take a bathroom break. It was novel. It was creative. It could work.

But first I had to get it by Rich. Over the years, Rich and I have developed a set routine when I want to veer wildly off the obvious course of traditional appellate representation. I tell him what I'm planning to do. He listens intently, all the time looking at me like I have lost my mind. He then tells me why what I'm proposing won't work. I then tell him that I am going to do it anyway. He warns me against wasting too much time. I thank him for his support and proceed on my way. He never stops me from doing anything I really want to do. And I try not to present him with too many wild ideas until I have thoroughly thought them through.

Two months after my first phone call with George Holmes, I had drafted the motion to vacate the judgment and was back in front of Judge Kane. While during the reconstruction hearing the prosecution had espoused such a motion as the proper avenue for me to obtain review of any claim relating to the denial of the for-cause challenge to Holmes, now they argued that I was procedurally barred from pursuing it. Judge Kane decided not to reward the prosecution's contradictory positions.

In July 2001, she ordered a hearing on the motion. Getting anything done over the summer is almost impossible. The vacation schedules of attorneys and witnesses have to be accommodated. So we had only heard from a few witnesses by September 11, 2001, when all of Lower Manhattan exploded into chaos. My office, located only two blocks from the World Trade Center, became uninhabitable for the next three months. For weeks after the attacks, the courthouse was without a working telephone system. Everyone communicated by cell phone.

During that period I stayed home, unwilling to return to Lower Manhattan unless I actually had to appear in court. Judge Kane would call my house to schedule court dates and discuss which witnesses could appear and whose files were still intact. For some reason, whenever the court called for these discussions, I was giving the girls a bath or spooning apricots into Lila's mouth. Interrupting those activities seemed more likely to create a disruption than simply multitasking through the conference calls. So one second I was making choo-choo noises to convince Lila to take the last spoonful of food, and the next second I was discussing a witness's anticipated testimony. Those were some strange days.

But with Lower Manhattan still smoldering, the hearing went forward, and in December 2001, Judge Kane granted Stephen DeLuca's motion to vacate the judgment. After hearing from the same witnesses who had testified at the reconstruction hearing, and some additional ones I had scrounged up, including Rosemary DeLuca and Stephen himself, the court found that Holmes had made remarks during the voir dire that should have resulted in the defense for-cause challenge to him being granted. These included statements that "our society was too liberal in its approach to the criminal drug laws" and that "murder is never justified."

Justice Kane also found that Judge Lake had failed to adequately supervise the jury selection proceedings. "It is clear that the judge was inattentive during the questioning of prospective juror Holmes and consequently failed to hear his disqualifying answers," Justice Kane concluded. "The trial judge compounded his error by inexplicably refusing defense counsel's three separate pleas to recall Holmes to clarify his responses."

It was this decision that resulted in the heavy-breathing telephone calls to my house and the bagpipe dirge blaring into my answering machine. The Police Department's fury was stirred up further by articles in the *Daily News* and *New York Post*, blasting Justice Kane's decision. One *Daily News* article actually had a picture of Justice Lake snoozing on the bench accompanying its coverage of the decision. I'm sure even a few cops had to laugh at that one.

Before the ink was dry on the order vacating the decision, the prosecution announced its intent to appeal. The oral argument on that appeal was scheduled to be heard on February 28, 2003—another Friday I should have been home taking care of my children. When I asked the scheduling clerk why the DeLuca arguments always seemed to fall on Fridays, she explained that Fridays were traditionally light days on the court's calendar, and inevitably a lot of people expressed interest in attending the DeLuca arguments. The answer made my stomach turn.

# NO MORE TIME FOR TEARS

At the beginning of February 2003, I had been feeling particularly run-down. Over the previous three months, both of our dogs, whom Charlie and I had raised from puppies, had become terminally ill and died. The loss felt bigger than merely the absence of two beloved pets. It was as if a chunk of our youth had vanished. We walked around the house dazed, the silence deafening. Even the sounds of two little girls clomping around in plastic high heels and full princess regalia could not seem to fill the void created by the rapid loss of eight additional feet.

Unlike Charlie and me, the girls took the loss in stride and began immediately begging for a new puppy. Jessie would sit on the living room couch for hours leafing through *Simon and Schuster's Guide to Dogs*, trying to learn the names of every breed.

"How 'bout this one?" she would ask Charlie over and over, pointing to the

Borzois and Norsk Buhunds. Charlie would look at the pictures sadly and reply, "Let's wait a little bit, sweetie."

Adding to the weight of our mourning, Jessie was in kindergarten and I was still getting used to the demands of having a child in a suburban public school system. It seemed like every week there was a school breakfast or a class book reading or a school play, all of which I struggled to attend. Just emptying out her backpack, with its reams of PTA notices to be read and deciphered, felt overwhelming. On any typical evening, I would pull out four or five brightly colored pages reminding me to:

"Mark your calendars for the Ice Cream Social, Tuesday, March 6, 2003, 4:00–5:30 p.m."

"Don't forget the Spring Carnival Bake Sale; sign up now with your offering. We need full-course meals, not just sweets."

"Kindly contact Miss Penny, the school librarian. On October 10, 2002, your daughter borrowed *The Scrambled States of America* from the school library. That book is now seriously overdue."

The thought of cooking anything for the bake sale made me feel faintly nauseated. Even ice cream struck me as an unappealing option. Something was definitely wrong. I called the doctor, who took my blood and asked if there was any possibility I could be pregnant.

Ironically, the weekend before, I had been visiting my college roommate, who asked me if I planned on having any more children. I told her we were definitely done. Life with a five-year-old and a three-year-old was just starting to feel manageable. No more diapers or bottles. Enough room in the back of the Volvo station wagon for the kids and our stuff. Everybody was sleeping through the night, and I was even getting to the gym regularly before work.

But then the pregnancy test came back positive, and all of a sudden the gym seemed overrated. I realized that I had never given away my maternity clothes or the crib, that the car's back seat could accommodate three kids. We were definitely not done.

On February 28, 2003, when I arrived at the First Department an hour early for the DeLuca argument, the first thing I did was ask the clerk for the keys to the ladies' room. Once there, I threw up my breakfast, cleaned up my face, reapplied my lipstick, and went back upstairs to continue with my maniacal argument preparations.

The courtroom began to fill up with uniformed police officers and district attorneys. I approached a DA I vaguely knew. Trying to distract myself from watching the growing crowd, I asked him if he was there to argue a case.

"No," he answered, without any malice in his voice. "I knew Ronnie Ruiz. He was my friend. I'm here to watch the DeLuca argument."

That DA was not trying to rattle or upset me. He was not wearing a badge and putting on a show of loyalty for the cops. His quiet presence, more than anything else, conveyed to me how beloved Ronnie Ruiz had been, how much he continued to be missed. I could not find my voice to respond. I nodded and walked away.

When the courtroom finally opened, once again it was standing room only. As on the day of the original sentencing eight years earlier, there would be no seats for Stephen DeLuca's family. I surveyed the courtroom, my eyes returning again and again to the mass of undercover officers, their shields hanging around their necks. I could feel a sense of panic rising. My hands floated to the silver hearts hanging around my own neck.

The necklace had been a Mother's Day present from Jessie months earlier. She had explained in her usual thoughtful manner that there was a heart for Charlie, herself, and Lila. As I fiddled with the hearts, I reminded myself that none of the five men about to take the bench, none of the officers in the courtroom, not even my opponent, Morris Stone, had ever given birth to an eight-pound baby without a lick of anesthesia, as I had with Lila. The thought calmed me, and I was able to focus my attention on my argument notes with laserlike precision, to ignore the glinting steel of the police badges.

I have had many bad arguments in my career. There have been plenty of times where things have not turned out as I had hoped they would or where I have found my performance lacking. But nothing in my past experience had prepared me for the DeLuca argument.

It was not just that every judge on the court was tripping over himself to point out the weaknesses in my arguments, playing to the crowd and the reporters in the audience. Their attacks seemed particularly personal, an unrelenting barrage that I felt ill-equipped to meet. There seemed to be no time in between the questions for me to answer, maybe because the judges did not really want to hear anything I had to say.

They merely wanted to voice their displeasure over having to review a first-degree murder conviction they had already affirmed years earlier. I had waited too long to pursue the motion to vacate the judgment, several suggested. My efforts to expand the scope of the reconstruction hearing to include Holmes years earlier had been procedurally improper. Judge Kane should never have ordered a hearing in the first place, they announced. Every judge who spoke expressed utter contempt for my actions. According to their comments, I had disgracefully manipulated the system, waiting until poor Judge Lake had died to allege he had slept through the proceedings when he could no longer defend himself.

I sat down twenty minutes later and felt as if I had been physically battered. I was dazed as Morris Stone stood for his rebuttal argument. Within a minute, it was over, and the presiding judge called the next case, without even according me the pro forma "thank you" routinely bestowed on an arguing attorney.

I picked up my papers and ran from the courtroom. I made it only to the adjacent attorneys' coat room before collapsing onto a chair and breaking down once again. Several attorneys from my office had come to watch the argument. They followed me into the coat room and formed a human wall to shield me from the hordes of police officers shuffling past. I think even the cops felt sorry for me after witnessing the whipping I had taken. They were strangely quiet.

"Only lawyers are allowed in the coat room," Jonathan, one of my colleagues, hissed at them.

Jon had spent a lot of time defending people who had been arrested while protesting the impending war in Iraq. He had his own issues with the cops.

"Just keep moving along," he warned them. "Nothing to see here." His enthusiastic efforts at cop crowd control made me laugh through my tears.

When I got back to the office, I couldn't bring myself to call Charlie to recount my drubbing. "How'd it go?" he e-mailed me. "The WORST," I typed back, unable to summon up the energy to describe the experience further.

I spent the rest of the day in my office with the door closed, mostly staring out the window and feeling sorry for myself. I would wait until Monday to write Stephen. I was sure his family would let him know how it went before he would get my letter. What was there to say anyway?

Dear Mr. DeLuca:

You're fucked. Get used to it. I am tired and nauseous.

Very truly yours,

........................................

When I worked for the Criminal Appeals Bureau of the Legal Aid Society early in my career, I would occasionally second seat, or assist with, trials to help preserve the appellate record in case the client was convicted. I never second seat now because unlike the Legal Aid Society, my office does not represent clients at the trial level.

In one of those early trial cases, the jury stayed out for four days. During the deliberations, the prosecutors became nervous and offered our client a plea to time served. Our client could have pleaded guilty and walked out of the courtroom that day. Instead, he took his chances with the jury and was convicted on the top robbery count. He ultimately was sentenced to twenty-five years in prison.

Devastated, I asked the trial attorney how he could stand working under such stressful conditions, making decisions that had such enormous consequences day in and day out. The attorney was several years older than I. Unlike me, he had built up some level of immunity for his psyche over the years of hard losses, kind of like a snake handler bitten so many times that he has grown immune to the venom. He looked at me sympathetically and explained, "You have to remember that at the end of every day, no matter what happens, you're going to go home."

On that February day in 2003, waiting for the time to pass after the DeLuca argument until I could leave at a respectable hour, I tried to take solace in that advice and looked forward to getting home. I did not know that my day would only get worse.

When I walked through the door, Marie was in a rush to get to her regular Friday evening job. I paid her for the overtime and started thinking about dinner.

The first hour I am home from work is usually the hardest of my day. Inevitably, the kids have a lot of emotional energy they have saved up. They rush in to inform me of their unresolved disputes.

An example of a recent debate that greeted me:

"Jessie called me stupid because I didn't know that fairies breathe fire," Lila complained.

"I didn't know fairies breathe fire either," I responded seriously.

"See!" Lila declared. "Mommy didn't know either."

"I never said fairies breathe fire. I said dragons breathe fire. You little twit," Jessie countered, her tone simultaneously conveying contempt and frustration.

On the Friday of the DeLuca argument I immediately walked into a dispute about computer games. Jessie wanted to play one before dinner. Knowing it would be hard to drag her away from the screen and hoping to prepare a quick meal, I told her that she could play one after she had eaten.

Jessie is usually a pretty reasonable kid, not subject to tantrums. But she is also a kid wedded to routine, and when I have to work on Fridays, she is particularly on edge. She announced that she was going to play a computer game and turned defiantly toward the living room where the computer was located.

"No, You Are Not!" I replied from the kitchen, in my lowest, most serious mommy voice.

Jessie ran into the bathroom screaming, "YES I AM!!" She slammed the bathroom door loudly. As the bathroom door slammed, Charlie, just home from work, walked through the back hall into the kitchen.

Jessie was really screaming now, loud, high-pitched wails emanating from the bathroom.

"What's going on?" Charlie asked, looking simultaneously exhausted and concerned.

"She's having a meltdown because she wants to play a computer game," I explained.

Charlie, blessed with reserves of patience I do not share, went to try to calm down Jessie. Almost immediately, he was running back to the kitchen, his face pale.

"She's hurt," he said. "Her hand's bleeding."

"Huh? What did she do?" I asked, following him back toward the bathroom. Jessie was standing there staring, stunned and wide-eyed at her upraised hand, blood running down her arm. There was so much, I could not make out where it was coming from.

Watching Jessie scream, I felt an irrational urge to laugh. For a split second, watching the scene from outside my own body, I simply could not believe the day I was having. An eerie sense of clear-eyed calm followed. I ran back into the kitchen, grabbed a newly laundered towel and wrapped it around Jessie's hand. "Put Lila in the car," I told Charlie. "We're going to the emergency room."

While Charlie strapped Lila into her car seat, I got into the back seat of our Volvo and lifted Jessie onto my lap.

"It hurts! It hurts! It hurts! I *hurt*!" Jessie screamed over and over again.

"I know it hurts, baby. We're going to make it better. The doctors will fix you right up. It's going to be fine," I assured Jessie, trying to believe my own words.

As Charlie sped to the ER five minutes away, I felt like I was in an army jeep driving through a combat zone. There seemed to be blood everywhere. The towel I had taken from the kitchen minutes earlier was almost all red now. Jessie looked pale and sweaty. Her skin was cool to the touch. I was worried she was going to go into shock. Upon arriving at the hospital, I lifted Jessie over my shoulder and ran to the ER entrance.

The doctor running the ER's triage contacted a plastic surgeon to try to repair Jessie's hand. Once the blood was cleaned up, it became clear that she had severed the top of her middle finger when she caught it in the door. The ER doctor ordered x-rays to assess the damage to the bones in her fingers. If they had been crushed beyond repair, reconstruction of the finger might prove impossible.

I went with Jessie to the radiology wing while Charlie stayed with Lila, waiting to speak with the plastic surgeon.

"Is there any chance you could be pregnant?" the x-ray technician asked me as I leaned over Jessie, trying to comfort her as a nurse straightened out her hand.

"Actually, I am pregnant," I answered. I had temporarily forgotten and had walked passed the signs warning pregnant women not to enter the area.

"You'll have to leave her here," the technician told me.

"We'll bring her back to the ER when she's through," the nurse promised.

I went back to find Charlie and tell him what was going on. I found him talking to the plastic surgeon, Dr. Mahoubian. The surgeon explained to us that his first choice to repair the damage to Jessie's finger would be to find the severed tip and reattach it. Charlie rushed home with Lila, assigned the macabre task of searching for a piece of his five-year-old daughter on the bathroom floor. I would stay to be with Jessie during the surgery.

"Usually, in these types of procedures, we have to put the child under general sedation," the doctor explained in thickly accented English. I would later learn he was from Lebanon, a place where I'm sure he had encountered his fair share of disfiguring injuries to small children.

"Is there any way to avoid that?" I asked. Jessie had already been so traumatized. The thought of putting such a small child under general anesthesia scared me. I also knew that putting her under would prolong her hospital stay. I wanted her back home as soon as possible. She would be more comfortable there, in her own bed, beneath her special patchwork quilt, away from the noise, antiseptic smells, and anxious rush of the hospital.

"It's hard," The doctor replied. "It's rare that a child can stay still enough during the surgery."

"Can we at least try it?" I begged.

He agreed, with the understanding that if it proved too difficult, Jessie would be given general and the operation would proceed in an operating room, without me being there. I was determined not to let that happen.

By the time they wheeled Jessie back from radiology, Charlie had called his cell phone, which I had borrowed, to tell me he could not find the fingertip. Dr. Mahoubian would therefore have to reconstruct Jessie's finger by grafting a portion of skin from her palm onto her fingertip, a more complicated and difficult procedure than simply reattaching the severed tip.

The nurse began laying out the surgeon's instruments on the table: hypodermic needles, gauze, sutures, and finally the scalpel, its blade gleaming. The orderlies placed Jessie in a straitjacket. She looked panicked. The sense of calm that had taken over me hours earlier was still there. I looked directly into Jessie's eyes, which seemed to have grown unusually large. When I spoke, there was no fear in my voice.

"Listen to me, Jessie," I told her, "and look only at me. I'm going to tell you a story about a princess and her puppies."

Jessie still looked scared, but the promised story immediately captured her attention. I continued in my most soothing, steady voice.

"Once upon a time, there was a princess, who lived in a beautiful kingdom by the sea. The princess had everything she wanted, but she was lonely and wanted a puppy to keep her company. So she bought a beautiful puppy named Anna, who had long, white, soft fur, pointy ears, a black nose, and the scratchiest pink tongue, which she used to lick the princess whenever she wanted to get her attention. But there was a problem with Anna. She had a huge appetite. She would eat everything in sight. All day long, the princess would feed her, and still Anna would be hungry. Then Anna started eating the princess's shoes. Well, that was it. The princess had had enough. She sent Anna to live on a farm, where there would always be plenty of food for her to eat. But without Anna, the princess was lonely, and so she got another puppy, Bella. . . ."

On and on the story went, through all the letters of the alphabet, each flawed puppy vexing the princess, who simply could not cope. By the time we got to the letter Z, Jessie's finger had countless stitches reconstructing its tip, and her arm was bandaged above her elbow. She had stayed impossibly still and focused.

"You did good," Dr. Mahoubian said when he had finished wrapping the final set of bandages around Jessie's arm. "Both of you."

Charlie was there to take us home. Marie had come back to watch Lila. By the time we got home, it was close to 3:00 a.m. I put Jessie in bed while Charlie went back out to get her codeine for the pain and antibiotics to prevent infection. I curled up at the foot of her bed and fell immediately into a deep sleep. The DeLuca argument, for which I had awakened twenty-four hours earlier, was part of a different life, someone else's life.

Somewhere near the border of Canada, Stephen DeLuca remains in an upstate prison. His fate is now in the hands of the federal courts. I spent the months immediately following my third maternity leave drafting a habeas petition that was over a hundred pages long, recounting all the twists and turns the case had taken through the state court system. I had been so disheartened by the final loss—which basically set forth in written form the themes struck during the oral argument blitz—that there were times I actually considered giving up. It was Rich who urged me on, with civics lectures explaining how habeas corpus was invented for cases like DeLuca's—cases where the state courts simply could not do the right thing because of political pressures.

It will take years before the final chapters of the DeLuca case are written. I fervently hope that when the last decision is issued, Stephen DeLuca will get a new trial that will be overseen by a competent judge and his fate will be decided by a properly selected jury. I hope that I will live to see the day when Stephen DeLuca walks out of prison.

But if I do not live to see either of those things, I'll still remember to be grateful for every day that my children are healthy. And I know that no matter what that final decision says, I will not weep when I read it. Since February 28, 2003, I find I have fewer tears to shed.

I tell myself that my transformation into an "other" makes me a better lawyer, more clearheaded, cleaner thinking. But in the middle of the night, when I lie awake thinking about something that I have failed to do on a case, some avenue I have not pursued, I wonder if my former weeper self would have been so careless. In the morning, I awaken to the voices of three little girls, clamoring for my attention, all thoughts of my former and present self vanquished by their need for breakfast.

*part 2*

# The Importance of Being Charming

In May 2004, I was back on the fifteenth floor of 100 Centre Street, standing at the elevator banks. I was only pretending to wait for an elevator. More accurately, I was lying in wait for the prosecutor who was handling the case on which I had just appeared.

My client, Janet Flores, had been convicted in 1995 of felony murder for taking part in a very poorly planned heist, carelessly executed by a group of mostly teenaged conspirators. Often in felony murder cases, my clients have not pulled the trigger or even gone near the victim. Janet was just such a client and a first offender to boot. Still, her initial encounter with the criminal justice system meant that she would potentially spend the rest of her life in prison.

Janet had also been convicted mainly on the statements of accomplices who never ended up testifying at her trial. I had filed a motion to vacate her conviction based on a recent landmark Supreme Court ruling that the introduction of such out-of-court testimonial statements violated a defendant's Sixth Amendment right to confront the witnesses against her.

By the time I filed that motion, Janet had already served nine years in prison. While there, she had learned to speak English and then had begun racking up credits toward her college degree, with a major in social work. She had started a program to educate Hispanic women on domestic violence. She'd also worked in the prison's day-care center and helped to arrange special events such as a Mother's Day carnival for the children whose mothers were imprisoned, financing these programs by selling snacks to her fellow inmates. In short, Janet Flores had accomplished more in the past nine years than a lot of people I knew who had not spent that time behind bars.

The strength of the motion's legal arguments and the impressiveness of Flores's achievements made me hopeful that the prosecutor would be easily convinced to be reasonable and perhaps voluntarily vacate my client's conviction. My hopes rose further when I saw that my opponent was Martin Whalen.

Whalen was high up in the homicide bureau in the Manhattan district attorney's office. When I first saw him in court that day, he reminded me of the mustached man on the playing cards in Monopoly. "Go to Jail. Go directly to Jail. Do not pass Go. Do not collect $200."

My negotiations with older men usually go well, which I have come to attribute to my wide-eyed, earnest manner. I find that men often enjoy explaining the ways of the world to younger women. It makes them feel sophisticated instead of old; wise instead of weathered. If that younger woman happens to be attractive, all the better.

So I expected Martin Whalen to be putty in my hands. When he rounded the elevator banks, I pounced, subtly.

"Mr. Whalen?" I asked. They love it when you call them Mister—more power and respect. "Would you be willing to speak with me about your response in the Flores case?"

Whalen looked at me coldly. "Your motion was filled with lies, misrepresentations, and half-truths," he spat.

"Lies, misrepresentations, and half-truths?" I echoed, stunned into sounding like Dorothy on her journey through the haunted forest to visit the wonderful wizard. ("Lions and tigers and bears! Oh, my!")

An elevator appeared, as if on cue. Whalen stepped inside.

"You'll have my response in a week," he snapped.

I was too off balance to think of joining him in the elevator. The doors slammed shut with a loud thunk. I was so flustered that instead of waiting for the next elevator, I walked down fourteen flights. By the time I reached the lobby, I had come to a horrible realization. "I'm losing my charm," I whispered to myself.

Outside, the late spring day had turned rainy and unseasonably cold. Trudging through the puddles, without the benefit of an umbrella, I fumed. *The arrogant prick wouldn't even give me the courtesy of hearing me out,* I ranted to myself as water seeped through the soles of my shoes.

I had calmed down considerably by the time I got back to the office. I would just have to figure out a different way to make Martin Whalen be reasonable and do things my way.

......................................

From the time I got my braces off at age fourteen, until the time I had my third daughter over two decades later, I was considered a pretty girl—not beautiful, but pretty. There is a difference between the two. My grandmother was beautiful. She died when she was ninety-two, but even at that age, people still turned to look at her when she entered a room. I am not yet forty, but I can already feel the creep of my future invisibility.

My grandmother was the matriarch of a large clan in Baltimore, where people still talk about her beauty. Looks have always been very important in my family. At every family gathering, I can be sure that the first words of greeting will be a status report on my appearance. Hopefully, my uncle Earl will come up to me and say, "You look good, kid." Last time, on the occasion of my grandmother's funeral, Earl took the opportunity to tell my husband, "You look like you gained some weight there, Charles."

In addition to my family's legacy of appearance obsession, in the Westchester suburb of my youth, most every nose, male and female, was "fixed" before its bearer reached sixteen. Only in rare cases of familial restraint would the nose job be postponed until the summer before freshman year of college. Liposuction had barely been invented when I was a teen, but at least one girl I knew back then had already had her tummy flattened.

Newly minted adolescent prettiness can prove to be a dangerous instrument. It can cut through the hearts of geeky boys like Jay Greenblum sitting next to you in physics class, cut so quickly that the wounds will be invisible, until an unexpected prom invitation is issued in the spring and you wonder how he ever misconstrued your interest in studying together.

And then there were the job troubles. When I was fifteen, I went to work for an Upper East Side couple as a mother's helper. They had one child, a two-year-old son named Sam. Neither one of them seemed to work. With my aid and that of their chauffeur, they were attempting to tackle the daunting task of summering in the Hamptons.

The Upper East Side mother was one of those women who had come to motherhood late in life. She must have been almost forty when she hired me. She seemed particularly clueless about how to play with a two-year-old boy. I wowed her during the interview by spitting out and catching an ice cube over and over again. Sam thought that was a great trick and broke into monkey-like laughter every time I did it.

On my first day watching Sam at the country club swimming pool, I overheard a conversation between my employer and one of her friends.

"How could you hire something that looks like *that*?" the friend bemoaned in an exaggerated whisper. "She looks like she walked out of a Botticelli painting."

At that moment, squeezed into my sky blue bikini, my waist-length brown hair whipping around my face in the ocean breeze, I was too busy trying to simultaneously watch Sam and the cute, tanned lifeguard to catch Upper East Side's response. Later that night, my job description miraculously changed to include the glamorous task of cleaning the summer home's four bathrooms. I was gone by the end of the month.

But by senior year, I had honed the use of my looks to the point where I could wield them with a samurai's precision. I might wear oversized sweatshirts and baggy jeans to study hall, but when I was waiting tables, for example, I knew that the shorter my skirt and the more I smiled and laughed, the larger my tips would be—from both men and women.

As the mother of three daughters, I often think about the message I want to send about our society's obsession with the female appearance. There are times when a stranger will approach me at the grocery store or at the video shop to comment on the beauty of one or all of my girls.

Many mothers I know rebuff such comments. "And she's *smart*, too," these mothers will retort, hoping to impress upon their small daughters that smart trumps pretty.

I never respond that way though. I think it's more important to teach my girls to accept a compliment with grace, and so I simply say "thank you." I have no worries that any of my daughters will grow up to be empty-headed twits, more concerned about their clothes and makeup than their potential contributions to the world. But if they do, it will not be because I failed to offend an old lady by insisting that she also acknowledge my toddler's intelligence.

In my efforts to help my clients, my appearance remains an important weapon. I simply do not look like anybody's idea of a seasoned criminal defense attorney. I dress far more conservatively than most free-spirited defense types and lack their easy confidence. As a result, nobody sees me coming. When a recalcitrant witness has to be persuaded to cooperate, Rich often sends me off with no more than an order to "charm him."

I can usually accomplish this. One of my greatest advantages as an advocate is that people naturally want to help me, probably because I have mastered the art of appearing in desperate need of help. If I need someone to search through four years of accumulated records, and if I ask nicely and in person, generally those records will be reviewed and turned over in short order.

I recently wandered into a restricted area of a maximum security prison by mistake after meeting with a client inside. Fortunately, rather than sounding the alarm or firing warning shots, the guard came down from the watch tower to ask me if I needed help and then escorted me to my car. If I had been born a man, I would have been shot dead long ago.

But lately my confidence in my ability to charm has diminished as my waist has expanded to carry twenty extra pounds and as my hair has begun to turn what I can't help viewing as a witch's shade of gray. I know plenty of working mothers who wake to go to the gym at 6:00 a.m. and regularly get their hair cut and colored, but it seems I am just not one of them. I have not even been able to give up Pop-Tarts.

Fortunately though, it turns out that when charm fails, a woman can resort to other means of persuasion. I was to learn that lesson firsthand from the Flores case.

# WHEN IT RAINS, IT POURS

I came to represent Janet Flores late into her case. Like Stephen DeLuca, Janet had been one of the office's first clients, and like DeLuca, she had been convicted of murder. Janet had not killed a cop. Instead, during a poorly planned plot to rip off the drug money counting house where she had been working, the spot's manager wound up dead. Before Janet had reached the age at which she could legally drink, she found herself facing a felony murder charge.

Rich had originally handled the state court direct appeal. In 1999, when the appellate court refused to reverse the conviction and grant a new trial, he made the call that the case should proceed to federal court. Taking a case federal by filing a habeas corpus petition alleging that a defendant's conviction was obtained in viola-tion of her federal constitutional rights is considered a plum assignment by younger, less experienced attorneys. The conventional wisdom holds that federal judges are smarter and treat constitutional issues with greater care than do state court judges. But indigent defendants are not entitled to the representation of counsel on such "collateral" attacks. Therefore, if my office commits to taking a client's case into federal court, there has to be a pretty strong claim—for the simple reason that we are not paid to do it.

The attorney who'd originally filed Flores's habeas petition in April 2000 had accepted the assignment and then proceeded to leave the office a year later. Then the thick file, filled with the original briefs, our habeas petition, the State's response to that petition, and our response to their response, was transferred to my office.

When I balked at the size of the file, Rich assured me that there was nothing

I needed to do on the case at that point but wait. And wait I did. Through all of 2001, 2002, and 2003, the file sat on my office windowsill, untouched by me, except when I had to write to Janet and tell her that there was absolutely nothing to report on her case and nothing that I could do to speed up the proceedings. The federal courts take their own sweet time addressing the steady deluge of habeas corpus petitions filed by state prisoners, most of whom are challenging their convictions in garbled prose without the aid of an attorney.

In March 2004, I had returned to work, way too quickly, after the birth of my third daughter, Maya. There is an unwritten rule that governs the lives of female lawyers. A woman can have one child and still be regarded as a committed professional. If she has two children, she is pushing the tolerance of the profession. If she has the audacity to have three children, she has crossed over the line into Mia Farrow territory and can be expected to cut and run at any moment to adopt another one from Cambodia.

The commitment of such women must be tested over and over again. My first day back from my third maternity leave was a Wednesday, and I was in court arguing a complex series of appeals and cross-appeals. I could barely focus on the court's questions, my breasts hurt so much from the afternoon's missed feeding session.

Ironically, my pain had the effect of mellowing me, keeping me from crossing the line into shrill and abrasive. It is hard to get angry at a group of cranky judges when your main concern is getting out of court without spurting breast milk on anyone. I won those cases and made it home in time for an early evening feeding.

On Thursday, my second day back, I started reviewing the DeLuca file again. There were looming deadlines that had to be met for filing that habeas petition. If I missed them, my client would be shut out of federal court for good. Deadlines are a serious business in my line of work, not something with which to be trifled.

By Friday, I had made it through my first half-week back, and I was at home with Maya while my other two girls were in school. Jessie was struggling with the demands of first grade, already faithfully charting the books she was reading, keeping a weekly journal of her thoughts, stressing about returning her homework on time. Lila was in her last year of preschool, refusing to wear anything but pajamas, a fashion statement with which I refused to interfere despite the consternation of her teachers.

As I walked through the door after dropping off Lila, the phone was ringing. The caller ID—a feature acquired on my home phone as a result of the DeLuca case and the heavy breather—showed that it was my office calling. A Friday morning phone call from my office is not necessarily a problem. Mine is a small, close-knit workplace, and my best friend there, Zoe Berg, will regularly call me at home just to check in and chat.

I picked up the phone without any dread, expecting to hear Zoe. Instead it was my boss's voice on the other end. Not good. In all the years I had worked for him, Rich had never called me at home on a Friday. He is a boss who totally respects my boundaries. It is one of the reasons I have been able to work for him for so long.

"What's up?" I asked, with mounting dread.

"When it rains, it pours," he responded. That did not sound good. "The magistrate in Flores issued his report and recommendation denying habeas relief. Apparently, all those hearsay statements we thought were so damaging, the ones saying our client saw the gun, turns out they didn't really matter."

I could not believe my bad luck. The case had lain fallow for almost four years. Now my first week back from maternity leave, with the DeLuca habeas to deal with, I had to worry about Flores as well.

On the other end of the line, Rich was taking my silence as an invitation to explain the decision further. But my head felt fuzzy, and I could not fully focus on his words. On Friday mornings, I usually think mostly about making beds and getting everybody to school on time.

"There's a whole section in there about the Supreme Court's new *Crawford* case and whether it should retroactively apply to cases pending on habeas," Rich continued.

He could have been speaking Swahili for all I knew about the new Supreme Court decision or retroactivity analysis. Still, I figured it was time to say something brilliant and insightful.

"Ugh. Retroactivity analysis. The worst. Does anybody really understand that stuff?" was the best I could come up with.

"You will in ten days," Rich quipped. "That's when our objections to the report are due to the district court judge. Make that seven days. We were served today, so our response will be due a week from Monday."

If I had not given up crying over work by that time, I definitely would have wept. Seven days to master a new groundbreaking Supreme Court case and the retroactivity doctrine, which I had never understood because it is among the most impenetrable areas of appellate practice.

"I'm sure I will," I said, sarcastically.

"It'll all be fine," Rich assured me. "Just enjoy your weekend and be prepared to dive in on Monday. I'm reviewing the report myself this weekend, so by then I'll be on top of it. I'll meet you at the office early; how's 8:00 sound?"

"Sounds good to me. See you then," I promised, trying to sound confident. I hung up the phone feeling anything but.

Like the maiden in the fairy tale facing a room full of straw she would have to spin into gold, the task looming before me did not seem possible. I did not even remember any of the facts of the Flores case. The last time I had looked at the briefs had been more than three years earlier, when the monstrous file had been transferred to my office.

But at least I still had an entire weekend of mothering before me. Maya had fallen asleep in my arms while I had been talking to Rich on the phone. Looking down at her sleeping face, feeling the warm weight of her, the office seemed far away. Holding a sleeping four-month-old is one of life's greatest simple pleasures, like a good cup of coffee and a piece of buttered toast first thing in the morning. I vowed not to think about work.

But on Sunday night, I could not sleep and was out of bed before the dawn cracked (and not because of a crying baby). I wanted to get to work and read through all the briefs in the Flores file before meeting with Rich to discuss the magistrate's report. I tiptoed into each girl's room to kiss her before I left. Leaving before my daughters awaken is another one of those practices—like missing dinner or bedtime—that I loathe. But sometimes it cannot be helped, and in fact I always feel puritanically virtuous on those occasions when I have to walk to the train station before the sun rises.

Upon my arrival at my still-darkened office, a copy of the magistrate's report, sixty pages thick, was sitting on my chair. In a habeas action, the district judge can refer the case to a magistrate, who can recommend a certain outcome but not issue a binding decision. The party aggrieved by the magistrate's report then has ten days to write to the district judge with her objections, listing all the mistakes and problems with the report. Any error or issue not contested is deemed waived. I live in constant fear of waiving issues.

The magistrate who had issued the Flores report had been a Legal Aid appeals lawyer before becoming a federal magistrate. Often it is the former defense lawyers who are the worst for my clients once they cross over to the judge's side of the bench. It's as if they are out to prove they hate the defendants even more than the former prosecutors do.

But the Flores magistrate, Jim Kates, was not one of those. I had never met him, but he had a reputation for combining decency with intelligence. If we had not convinced Kates of the rightness of our cause, the Flores habeas petition looked like a pretty hopeless battle. Unfortunately, now Janet Flores's case was my hopeless battle to fight.

........................................

I sat in my desk chair just staring at the reams of paper, stacked in rows, that comprised the file. *One, two, three, four, five, six* piles, I counted, before getting up the nerve to pull the first down off the radiator shelf. I fished out Rich's original brief and started reading. One thing about my boss, he tells a great story.

The vivid writing transported me back to a June night in 1995 at about 1:00 a.m., when the police received a radio run to respond to a dicey address in the Washington Heights section of northern Manhattan. Washington Heights is now a neighborhood that people flock to, seeking refuge from the stratospheric real estate costs of the Upper West Side, where a studio apartment can run half a million dollars. But in the mid 1990s, the neighborhood was still mostly made up of recent immigrants from the Dominican Republic.

Once the police arrived at the apartment building, they took the elevator to the seventh floor, where they found a man, later determined to be Angelo Peres, aka

Catora, sitting in the hallway in front of the elevator. Catora was naked except for a sheet covering his lower body. He had been shot in the chest but was still breathing.

A path of blood led into the bedroom of nearby apartment 7H. Inside that apartment, there was a large bloodstain on the bed's sheets. There were also bullet holes, shells, and casings left from a rampaging nine-millimeter semiautomatic Luger, but no gun was found in the apartment, and no one else was there.

The second, rear bedroom also had a story to tell. There was a table with a money counter on top, a briefcase full of drug records and cash, lots and lots of cash—over $55,000, as accounted for by the police.

Whether the $55,000 the police had found was the actual amount that had originally been there was, as always, open to debate. That would depend on the honesty of the responding officers and their ability to withstand temptation. It is not as if they were responding to the scene of a bank robbery, where every dollar's serial number would have been recorded. Over the years, I have heard enough complaints from my clients about vanishing money to believe that some gets skimmed.

Despite the huge amounts of cold cash in open display, the apartment had no safe or security system. There was no alarm and no weapons.

As the responding officers were still inspecting the apartment, EMS paramedics arrived to attend to Catora. By this time, he was going into shock. In the ambulance, his condition continued going downhill to the point where his blood pressure could not be recorded.

At the hospital, Catora was revived sufficiently to answer questions. When a paramedic asked him who was responsible for his present situation, Catora responded, "Eva and Mary." Mary was the middle name of Janet Flores—a bad fact for the defense.

Then Catora died. The cause of death was described by the coroner as the result of two gunshot wounds, each entering the back and exiting the abdomen. The coroner's report, which I dug out of the file, reflected that one of the shots had been fired from less than one and a half feet away—an up close and personal shot.

With Catora's death, the police now had a homicide investigation to pursue, and the case would be picked up by the most experienced detectives. They started with those boxes of drug records, which reflected that the operation was being run from prison by Ray Merana, who was serving time, not surprisingly, for selling drugs. Merana was brought from prison to the Thirty-fourth Precinct. He gave the investigators an address in Yonkers where they could find "Eva" and "Mary."

Officers drove to that address to wait. Merana then called the women and told them to turn themselves in "or else." Three individuals soon left the Yonkers apartment: Eva Rosa, Janet Mary Flores, and Janet's brother, Pedro. The three were immediately nabbed by the awaiting officers and taken to separate interrogation rooms at the Thirty-fourth Precinct.

It was after midnight when the interrogations began. By 5:00 a.m., the seasoned detectives had proven no match for the two girls, who kept insisting that they knew nothing about the incident. Eva eventually wrote a note to Janet in Spanish asking, "Should we tell the truth?" Janet checked the "yes" box on the note, and the interrogators brought the women together so that Eva could confirm that it was Janet who had actually checked the box. During this brief meeting, the two women giggled together.

After the gigglefest, Janet wrote out a statement. In it she explained that she lived in an apartment with her brother, Pedro, and Eva Rosa. She and Eva worked for Catora counting money. Pedro had called a friend, Derrick, in Miami so that Derrick could come up and help them rip off the counting house. On the appointed day, Janet and Eva had gone to work accompanied by Derrick and Pedro. The women had gone inside apartment 7H while their two accomplices waited for them in the hallway.

The plan was for Eva, an apparent charmer, to keep Catora "busy" in the bedroom, while Janet, a plain Jane, was to open the door to let Derrick and Pedro into the apartment so the two men could take the money. After Eva had been busy with Catora in the bedroom for about ten minutes, Janet opened the door and let the men in. Pedro grabbed a box full of cash. But Derrick entered Catora's bedroom. Janet heard three shots and Catora pleading, "Eva, why you do this?" By this time, Pedro had already left with the money. Janet, Eva, and Derrick took a cab back to their apartment to meet up with Pedro there. The conspirators, apparently nervous about keeping the money in their own apartment, decided to let Derrick take the cash and the gun to a nearby motel.

Janet admitted that the gun belonged to her and Eva but explained that she did not know how Derrick had gotten it before going to the counting house. She had certainly never given it to him to use during the planned theft. According to Janet, the plan had only involved sneaking in and stealing the money but not killing Catora. However, even if Janet had not shot Catora personally, her participation in the robbery and the victim's resulting death would support a conviction for felony murder.

After obtaining Janet's and Eva's statements, the police recovered $144,741 from the cab driver, who regularly drove Eva Rosa wherever she needed to go. Eva had promised to buy him a new car if he held on to the money until she got back from Puerto Rico, and the driver had somehow been persuaded enough by Eva's charms to agree to do so. When Eva called him from the precinct and told him that detectives would be coming to pick up the cash, the driver surrendered it to them per her instructions.

With Janet, Eva, and Pedro, three of the four conspirators, in custody, the police started looking frantically for the fourth, Derrick Fabio. They quickly learned that he was on a bus heading back to Miami. The New York police alerted the Florida authorities, who arrested Derrick as soon as he got off the bus, recovering about $45,000 cash from him.

Derrick was taken to the Metro-Dade police department's homicide office for interrogation. He was only seventeen years old, and the police allowed him to speak with his mother and uncle before he gave a recorded statement, under oath.

Derrick's story was very different from Janet's. According to his confession, sometime in June he'd received a phone call while in Miami inviting him to fly to New York to be part of the robbery. He'd flown into Kennedy Airport, bringing no weapon with him.

Once in New York, he'd met up with Pedro, Janet, and Eva at their apartment and a few hours later took a cab to Catora's apartment. Derrick had hidden a fake gun in his waistband. But he knew that Eva was armed with a real one. According to Derrick's statement, the gun had been openly displayed among the robbery participants, and he had even at one point held the black, six-inch semiautomatic. Derrick admitted knowing that Catora would probably have to be killed. The four had even discussed putting a pillowcase over Catora's head so that he could not see his assailants. But that aspect of the plan had been rejected for some unspecified reason.

The four had arrived at Catora's apartment at 1:00 a.m. Derrick had waited in the stairwell with Pedro while the women had gone inside. After ten minutes, Janet opened the apartment door. The plan had been for Derrick to threaten Catora with the phony gun. He pointed the fake gun at Catora, announced a robbery, and ordered Catora to raise his hands and to lie facedown on the bed. But unexpectedly, Eva Rosa pulled out a real gun from under the bed. Catora said, "Eva, why are you doing this to me?" Eva grabbed a pillow, put it in front of the gun, and opened fire, shooting three times. Catora was hit but continued to scream, "Eva, no!"

Everyone left. According to Derrick, they had together taken the money in a cab to a motel. Eva threw the gun out the cab window. They divided up the money, and Derrick took his share, $45,000.

By the time of Janet's trial, Eva Rosa had pleaded guilty to second-degree murder in exchange for a reduced sentence of fifteen years to life in prison. When pleading guilty, she admitted that the gun used to kill Catora had been her own but insisted that she had given it to Derrick Fabio, who then used it to shoot Catora.

Three statements, from three different people, describing the same incident in three different ways. That is what the police interrogators got from Janet, Derrick, and Eva. According to Derrick, the plan had always been to forcefully rob Catora, the gun had openly been displayed, and Eva had murdered Catora in cold blood. Eva insisted that she gave the gun to Derrick and that it was he who had shot Catora.

But according to Janet, the plan was one of stealth, not violence. The idea was for Eva to keep Catora busy while Janet opened the door and the men snuck in to steal the money. Unlike Derrick and Eva, Janet claimed that she did not know anybody had taken the gun to the counting house that evening. She never participated in any discussions about harming the victim or placing a hood over his head. The thought that Catora would be killed during the incident had never entered her mind.

Who was telling the truth? Even Martin Whalen, the seasoned homicide prosecutor, admitted outside the jury's presence he hadn't a clue.

······························

The prosecution did not really need to figure out the truth to charge all four conspirators with felony murder and robbery. According to their own statements, all the defendants had agreed to participate in the plot during which Catora had been killed. The evidence was sufficient to support second-degree murder charges. Janet, Eva, Pedro, and Derrick were swiftly indicted and their cases prepared for separate trials.

While the prosecution did not fret over the three different versions of the same crime given by each of its participants, to me the participants' statements were like a hypothetical question on a criminal procedure exam from hell. For our purposes in reviewing the case on appeal, the ultimate evidentiary issue that had to be decided at Janet's trial was: Whose statements would be admissible and why?

There was no question that Janet's own statement would be admissible. It was an admission to prove that she had participated in the shooting.

Assuming that proper interrogation procedures are used—no whipping with rubber hoses or electrical shocks are allowed *yet* in interrogations occurring within the fifty-nifty United States—the prosecution can always introduce a defendant's custodial statements against her at a criminal trial. But what about Derrick's statements describing the plot and attributing the shooting to Eva; and Eva's statements describing the incident and attributing the shooting to Derrick?

At Janet's trial, the prosecution did not want to call either Derrick or Eva to testify against Janet. To secure their cooperation, the prosecution would have to cut each one a break, a reduction in sentence, and there would be no reason to do that if the prosecution could just introduce their out-of-court statements. That is where the complex confrontation clause analysis comes into our real-life law school hypothetical.

The confrontation clause of the Sixth Amendment to the United States

Constitution provides that in every criminal trial, the accused has the right to "confront the witnesses against him." The purpose and genius of the confrontation clause can be appreciated by anyone who has survived the high school rumor mill. It was always so easy to swear that you knew Beth Franklin did it with Brian Kaplan in the backseat of Brian's rust-colored Mustang last Saturday night. Such knowledge, shared in whispers in the school hallways, was always uttered behind the backs of Beth and Brian, of course. Nobody would ever say it to their faces.

Suppose that instead of merely being grounded for life and forbidden from seeing each other if their parents learned of their alleged misdeeds, Beth and Brian could be convicted of heresy and each one burned at the stake. In Merry Old England, the authorities could have rounded up the high school gossipers and asked them to swear that they knew of Beth's and Brian's foul actions. The Crown could then introduce those sworn statements against both Beth and Brian at trial to prove their guilt. Poor Beth and Brian would never have had the opportunity to question the gossipers or look them in their lying eyes before being roasted.

By drafting the confrontation clause, our Founding Fathers hoped to avoid the tyrannical practice of trial by government-procured affidavit. Before the State condemns Beth or Brian, our Constitution guarantees them that they will have at least one opportunity to face down their accusers, to force them to come into the courtroom, look both Beth and Brian in the eye, and repeat their allegations. Beth and Brian will then have the right to cross-examine or question them about how exactly they learned about that backseat business.

Legal scholars often refer to cross-examination as the greatest engine ever devised for uncovering the truth. Any parent would agree. When you find your new living room couch redecorated with green flowers, you do not start dusting for fingerprints or considering who favors that particular shade of indelible marker. You immediately gather the usual suspects and start posing some very pointed questions while crouching down to meet their guilty little gazes. No parent would want to surrender the right to cross-examine.

Nor would any criminal defendant. But the right to confrontation, like any rule, has its exceptions. And in the years before 2004, those exceptions had started to eat away at the confrontation clause's fundamental protection and promise. At

Janet Flores's trial, the most important exception involved "statements against penal interest."

The idea behind this exception is that people do not usually falsely implicate themselves in wrongdoing; when they admit to something for which they can be seriously punished, those statements must be true. If I ask my three girls who has tracked dirt across my newly mopped kitchen floor, and by some miracle Lila admits that she has done it, that admission would undoubtedly be true. Lila is quick to rat out her sisters or to blame the dog for her misdeeds.

The problem with the exception is that it simultaneously takes an overly cynical and overly simplistic view of human nature. If Jessie were to take responsibility for the dirty floor, I could not trust the admission—my eldest daughter is surprisingly willing to brave my wrath to protect her little sisters. And an admission of guilt from Maya would be meaningless. At two, she could have simply misunderstood the question or failed to comprehend that an admission would lead to a minute or two on the naughty step.

Whatever the wisdom of allowing statements against penal interest to be introduced against criminal defendants, by the time of Janet's trial in March 1997, the courts regularly admitted them. It therefore was not surprising that the prosecutor sought to introduce both Derrick Fabio's custodial confession and Eva Rosa's admissions during her plea bargain. Martin Whalen argued that both Derrick's and Eva's statements, although they both sought to shift and spread the blame away from themselves for actually shooting Catora, were sufficiently self-inculpatory to qualify for admission.

The defense vehemently opposed the introduction of Derrick's and Eva's statements on the grounds that they were unreliable. Those statements, if credited by the jury, would be fatal to Janet's defense to the felony murder charges.

Under the felony murder doctrine, if a person takes part in a violent felony, such as a robbery, and a nonparticipant is killed, she still is guilty of murder, even if, like Janet, she never went near the victim. At trial, Janet intended to admit that she had taken part in the plot that resulted in Catora's death, but she would raise an affirmative defense to the charges, arguing that she had not done the shooting herself and did not know that violence would be used or that any of the plot participants were armed. If the jury found that Janet had not shot Catora, had not seen the gun, had not known that anybody had taken it to the counting house, and that she had no reason to believe that Catora would be harmed, Janet would be acquitted of the murder charge and get out from under a life sentence.

Derrick's statements—with his detailed descriptions of the gun being handed around and discussions of hooding Catora during the crime—were particularly harmful to this affirmative defense. The reliability of statements made by a person in police custody, without the benefit of counsel, has always been viewed with suspicion by the law. During interrogations, suspects are often trying to talk their way out of the situation by spreading blame onto others. It was unlikely that before talking to a lawyer, the seventeen-year-old Derrick really understood that by confessing to his part in the robbery, but denying the shooting, he had nonetheless confessed to a murder.

To overcome this potential defense argument, prosecutor Whalen argued that Derrick's confession was not the typical one, because it had been recorded under formal circumstances, with a court reporter present, and only after Derrick had sworn out an oath promising to tell the truth. In the end, the judge at Janet's trial let in both Derrick's and Eva's statements.

The jurors had to decide whose version of events to credit, Janet's, Derrick's, or Eva's. They had to make that determination without hearing from any of the witnesses. Janet never took the stand in her own defense. For the defense, it could not get any better than the statement Janet gave at the precinct in which she admitted taking part in the plot, but had described it as one involving stealth rather than violence. Putting a defendant on the stand to be cross-examined by an experienced prosecutor is a risky proposition. Almost always the accused is nervous. She is often also inarticulate and easily confused. The combination can be fatal to mounting a successful defense.

In order to introduce Derrick's and Eva's statements, the prosecution had to show that neither was available to testify. When called to the stand, Derrick and Eva asserted their Fifth Amendment rights against self-incrimination and opted to remain silent. While they were present in court, they were still deemed legally "unavailable," because they were unwilling to discuss the incident.

Understandably, the jurors struggled to reach a verdict. Determining the true nature of the plot by reviewing conflicting accounts in police-recorded statements without the benefit of live testimony proved tricky. The jury began deliberating in the afternoon of March 12, 1997, and deliberated throughout the day before being sequestered overnight. The next morning, the deliberations continued well into the evening before the jury convicted Janet of all the charges: felony murder in the second degree, robbery in the first degree, and robbery in the second degree.

A month later in April 1997, the court sentenced Janet to nineteen years to life imprisonment. Janet was twenty-two years old at that time. Even assuming she was a model prisoner and earned every second of good time possible, she could not get a shot at parole for over fifteen years.

On the direct appeal, we had primarily argued that the introduction of Derrick's and Eva's statements against Janet had violated her Sixth Amendment confrontation rights. Rich argued that those statements, because they were blame shifting and spreading, were not sufficiently reliable to qualify as statements against penal interest. Their erroneous introduction warranted reversing Janet's murder conviction and ordering a new trial at which the jury would not be permitted to consider the accomplices' statements.

The appellate court agreed that the portions of Derrick's statement blaming Eva for the shooting and Eva's statement blaming Derrick for it should not have been admitted into evidence. But because those aspects of the statements said nothing about Janet, and the prosecution never argued that Janet was the shooter, their introduction did not undermine Janet's defense. The remaining portions of the statements were considered sufficiently against Derrick's and Eva's own penal interests to qualify for admission. The appellate court therefore affirmed the conviction in April 1999, and the court of appeals denied Janet the right to appeal the case any further two months later.

We repeated our arguments in the habeas petition, and the prosecution adopted the Appellate Division's reasoning. The prosecutor admitted that the blame-shifting portions of Derrick's and Eva's statements should not have been admitted at Janet's trial but argued that their admission did not harm Janet's defense.

Then on March 8, 2004, almost four years after we had filed the habeas petition, the Supreme Court of the United States decided *Crawford v. Washington*, dramatically altering the legal landscape surrounding the confrontation clause. Under *Crawford*, any statement that could be deemed testimonial in nature would be inadmissible, even if it could be considered totally reliable. "The only indicium of reliability sufficient to satisfy constitutional demands is the one the Constitution actually prescribes: confrontation," the *Crawford* court emphatically declared. Under *Crawford's* reasoning, neither Derrick's nor Eva's out-of-court statements could have been admitted at Janet's trial. The ruling seemed to open the doors to Janet's prison cell a crack, if only I could figure out how to argue successfully that she deserved to benefit from it.

## AND THAT'S FINAL! OR IS IT?

If Janet had been tried on March 8, 2004, or any time thereafter, neither Derrick's nor Eva's out-of-court statements could have been introduced at her trial. If this new rule applied to Janet's habeas petition, she would be entitled to a new trial, the magistrate's report and recommendation recognized. But the magistrate determined that the new rule should not apply "retroactively" to Janet's petition, analyzed the propriety of introducing the accomplices' statements under the rules in place during the state court trial, and denied relief.

The doctrine of retroactivity can be byzantine in its application, and thinking about it has always left me with a headache. In order to understand it, even on a basic level, it is important to address the two competing concerns the rules are designed to serve—finality and fairness.

On one side of the equation is the notion of finality. When I was six years old, my family took a cross-country vacation for four weeks. My father, a psychiatrist, took all of August off in accordance with the mandates of his profession. We flew to Las Vegas and rented a car, probably some larger version of the Ford Pinto.

My parents threw my oldest brother, Nate, in the far back, right over the exploding gas tank. My middle brother, Harrison, and I shared the middle seat, unrestrained by seat belts.

Harry and I started fighting as soon as the car pulled off Vegas's main strip. We argued over who had encroached on the other's side of the car, who hit whom first, who spit on whom first, and who had flicked the first booger. About five hours into this battle, my mother warned us to stay on our own respective sides and to just ignore each other. But that did nothing to quell us. We were so busy arguing that we didn't notice that my mother had leaned over into the back seat, wielding her black Goody hairbrush. The "thwack" of the brush on the tops of our squabbling heads stunned and ultimately silenced us.

Finality is like that smack of my mom's hairbrush. At some point in a criminal case, the justice system says enough is enough. The case has to end. If the defendant was tried under rules we now recognize to be wrong or unfair, so be it.

The point when the case becomes final—when the hairbrush falls—is when a defendant has gone through one round of direct appellate court procedures. So shortly after Janet was denied leave by New York's court of appeals in 1999, it was as if her case became frozen in time, and her claims would be judged by the law that existed at that time, not by the rule announced in *Crawford*.

But after my mom so uncharacteristically whacked Harry and me upside the head, she must have felt that inevitable, creeping motherly guilt. That feeling that you have done something so unfair that your kids will still be talking about it with their therapists thirty years in the future.

The concern that a tremendous unfairness has been perpetrated by the authorities is the other side of the retroactivity equation. Therefore, if a new rule is announced that is really central to the process, a prisoner will be entitled to its benefit even if her conviction became final before the new rule was announced. The language the Supreme Court has used is that the new rule must change a "bedrock procedural element" and impact "the fundamental fairness and accuracy of the trial."

While Magistrate Kates had deemed *Crawford* not to be this type of new rule, he had come to that conclusion without the benefit of briefing by either side;

the briefs had been submitted years before *Crawford* had been decided. A quick computer search revealed an important case from years earlier that, like *Crawford,* had also involved a dramatic change in the Supreme Court's interpretation of the confrontation clause. The new rule announced in that earlier case had been held to qualify for retroactive application. The report and recommendation did not mention this case or attempt to distinguish it.

By the time I had discovered that first morning that Magistrate Kates might have overlooked some important legal authority, Rich had arrived in the office with a thick pad of comments relating to the magistrate's report. I told him I was contemplating putting together a motion for reconsideration, citing the legal authority I had found. Rich agreed that was an appropriate course to take, so I went back to my office to more carefully review the habeas briefs submitted by each side. Now, hours after reviewing the briefs, I had a vague, unsettling feeling that I had missed something important in my rush to read over the papers the first time around.

# READING THE FOOTNOTES

I did not need to read our briefs again. By that point, I was pretty familiar with our arguments. I quickly refreshed my mind on the case's details by reading Rich's original brief. But I had never thoroughly read through the prosecution's response, and so now I turned my full attention to their papers.

Appellate prosecutors in New York City are like gamblers who all have the same tell. If there are facts that are particularly thorny for them to deal with, something they want to downplay, those facts will always be buried in a footnote. So I have learned to pay close attention to the footnotes.

Sure enough, footnote three raised the hair on the back of my neck. In that footnote, the prosecutor set forth the dates of Derrick's trial and sentence. While Derrick's trial had preceded Janet's by a month, he had not been sentenced until the very day Janet's jury returned its guilty verdict. The timing seemed too precise to be a coincidence. *Why had the prosecution waited until Janet was convicted before moving forward with Derrick's sentencing?* I wondered.

Most attorneys probably would not have spent too much time worrying about the dates in footnote three, but I could not stop thinking about the fortuitous timing by a prosecutor who seemed so very methodical. Something was wrong.

Zoe Berg has been one of my best friends since we started sharing an office nine years ago. Since then, we've each had plenty of opportunities to acquire our own separate offices. And while I spend more time with Zoe than with anyone else in my life, pretty much eight hours a day, four days a week, I never tire of hearing her insights, legal and otherwise. Pound for pound, I would guess that she is the best appellate lawyer practicing in New York. She weighs about 96 pounds, but you would never notice when she's arguing a case because she's such a force. On the personal front, there is no issue too small or large to broach: childbirth, taxes, death, divorce, spinach ziti, pot roast, nannies versus day care, amniocentesis versus CVS, sons versus daughters. We've pretty much touched on everything. Zoe makes fun of me when I start saying things are wrong with my cases and likens me to the kid in *The Sixth Sense* who sees dead people.

"You see innocent people . . . everywhere," Zoe whispers in a horrified tone, as if I am suffering visions or speaking in tongues.

But the truth is, I do notice things other people miss. Shortly after Charlie and I were married, I planned a vacation to Deer Isle, Maine. I had only been to Maine once or twice before, and I selected a not-too-rustic inn with gourmet food overlooking a beautiful inlet for our stay. Charlie hated it right away because he had been going to Maine since he was a boy and his family always stayed in cottages without electricity and looked into tide pools for entertainment. To him, Maine and foie gras were an unholy union. We arrived at the inn just in time for afternoon tea, another abomination in Charlie's eyes, and sat down to chat with some of the other guests.

A couple, Michael and Rachel, who were maybe fifteen years older than we were, had been there for a few days, and we started asking them about how they had spent their time so far. As we talked, Michael drank his tea hungrily and played with the ice cubes by shaking them against the side of his glass. We talked for around fifteen minutes before Charlie and I returned to our room.

"They seemed nice," Charlie remarked casually, trying to hide his seething hatred for the inn, which was only revealed days later during a particularly nasty spat after our car broke down in Acadia National Park.

"Yeah, I wonder how long Michael has been in recovery?" I responded.

"What are you talking about?" Charlie asked, confused.

Our conversation with Michael and Rachel had never veered into personal territory. We had only spoken about the local bike routes and where to rent kayaks. It was not as if Michael had been abstaining from alcohol while the rest of us indulged in happy hour cocktails. Everyone was eating cookies and sipping tea.

"I could just tell. It was something about the way he drank his tea, as if he was used to finding comfort in a glass," I explained, not really knowing myself how I knew.

Charlie looked at me then how Zoe looks at me now when I start talking about my weird notions and ideas. But sure enough, that night at the inn on Deer Isle, when Michael and Rachel joined us for dinner, neither one of them ordered a drink. They declined our offer to split a good bottle of wine. A few days later, Michael explained that he had not had any alcohol in five years, because he had struggled with alcoholism throughout his life. From across the table, Charlie looked at me as if I had pulled a rabbit from the napkin on my lap.

Just as I suspected Michael was an alcoholic from watching him slurp his tea, I knew that the prosecution had waited to sentence Derrick Fabio because they did not want him to testify at Janet Flores's trial. Derrick would be less likely to testify if he were awaiting sentence, because the prosecutor could use anything he might say to argue for a longer sentence. Any defense attorney would tell a client who had not yet been sentenced not to testify about the events underlying his conviction, unless of course he were given some benefit for his testimony. Once the prosecution won the battle over the admission of Derrick's police statement, they had no reason to call him to testify. *But what about the defense? Did Derrick have something to say that could have helped Janet's defense?* I wondered.

The prosecution was trying to hide something, but what? I put the brief down and punched in "Derrick Fabio" as a search term on my computer's legal database. Derrick's case had been upheld by the appellate court six months earlier. The main issue on appeal: a claim that his pretrial custodial confession, the one used against Janet, had been inaccurately translated and was entirely false.

I could not tell from the reported decision whether Derrick had testified at his own trial and recanted his custodial confession under oath—the same statement the prosecution had argued was particularly reliable because it had been given under oath at the police precinct. Fortunately, I knew the attorney who had represented Derrick on appeal and who would have the answers to my questions. I needed him to send me the records from Derrick Fabio's case, fast.

I dialed Nick Robleski's number from memory, but he was not in his office yet. Like me, Nick has three kids, and he has to drop each off at a different school before coming to work.

There is a lot that sucks about being a public defender. If you want respect or glory or admiration or appreciation, public defense is not for you. Clients generally believe that you get what you pay for, and because my services are free, they expect me to be less than mediocre. Judges generally assume that lawyers who have any real talent go into private practice once they have gotten over their youthful ideas of saving the world. The money is horrible. A twenty-five-year-old law school graduate who has yet to pass the bar but has the common sense to join a large New York firm will make more than twice what I will this year.

But one of the best things about being a public defender is getting to work with and know other public defenders. Not the ones just out of law school, passing through to get "client contact." But the ones who have been fighting the battle for years, without getting burned out. The ones you call when you have suffered a crushing loss or been on the receiving end of an outburst from a client's family or racked up an unexpected win. They will know exactly how you feel, because not too long ago they experienced a similar loss or outburst or win.

I have never trusted group dynamics. I never joined a sorority in college or associated with a particular clique in high school. I cannot even bring myself to join a synagogue. But I would go out of my way to help a fellow public defender in the same way someone else would a fraternity brother. I have fielded phone calls from maternity leaves and vacations to provide insights I might have, and I am always glad to do it.

Nick Robleski is the type of public defender I love. When I call him with a serious problem, he inevitably forces me to lighten up by telling me a similar disaster he has suffered and survived. Within minutes of my leaving a message, he called me back.

"Hey, hey," Nick practically sang. "What's up with you?"

"I need something," I replied, too focused on Janet's case to share in Nick's levity this morning. "You got a guy, Derrick Fabio, I need the record in his case, like now."

"You're in luck," Nick announced, as if I had won a frozen turkey. "I have the record right in front of me. The court of appeals just agreed to review Fabio's case, lucky guy."

"You've got to be kidding me. Why?" I asked, praying New York's highest court had not granted leave to consider an issue that we could have raised—but failed to—in Janet's appeal.

"It was something about the trial court changing the scope of its ruling about the crimes Fabio could be asked about when he testified. The court made the ruling without Fabio being present. I don't even remember what I said in my leave application, to tell you the truth, except of course that it was a stunning denial of due process. The court sat on it forever," Nick explained.

"So he did testify at trial!?!" I said, a little too loudly for polite conversation.

"Yeah, he testified. I don't recall exactly what he said at the moment, but he did testify." Probably in the months Nick had been waiting for a decision on his leave application, he had worked on twenty other cases.

"Just send me the transcript, as soon as possible, okay?" I pleaded.

"You'll have it by this afternoon, on your desk. I'll messenger it down," Nick promised.

"You're the greatest," I said and hung up the phone. Two hours later, the entire transcript of Derrick Fabio's trial arrived at my office, and I knew what the prosecution was hiding.

At his own trial, Derrick Fabio had testified under oath that the statement he had given to the police had been false, because it was the product of a botched translation. According to Fabio's sworn trial account, in June 1995, his childhood friend Pedro Flores called to ask if he would travel to New York to pick up some money. Pedro wanted Derrick to then return to Miami to buy drugs at reduced Florida prices and bring them back to New York to sell them at a markup. Derrick agreed to be part of this scheme and flew to New York. Pedro picked him up at the airport and brought him to Janet's apartment, where Derrick stayed alone while Pedro went to conduct some business. Upon Pedro's return to the apartment, Pedro had a box filled with money and a lighter that looked like a gun. Derrick had no idea where Pedro had gotten either item.

Only after this robbery had been completed did Pedro tell Derrick about the plan to rob the counting house. The plan was for Eva to go to bed with Catora and for Janet to open the door to the apartment to allow Pedro to enter; but the plan was botched because Eva had gotten nervous and brought out a real gun, which she shot three times. According to Derrick's trial account, he hadn't been aware of the gun, hadn't held it, contrary to his previously documented police statement. He took the money from Pedro in order to buy the drugs in Miami.

Derrick also testified that his police statement—the one the prosecution would seek to introduce two weeks later at Janet's trial—had been written in English, a language that he did not speak or read, and that he did not understand what he had been signing. Derrick denied that he had provided the police with any of the information contained in his statement.

In other words, Derrick had testified under oath that his police statement was inaccurate, and prosecutor Whalen had failed to disclose those facts to Janet's defense attorney or trial judge. Instead, Whalen argued that the custodial statement to the police was reliable because it had been given under oath, all the while knowing that it was later recanted under oath.

Derrick's trial testimony was potentially helpful to Janet's defense in two distinct ways. First, the defense could have argued that Derrick's police statement was unreliable because Derrick himself had stated it was the product of a botched translation, and by the time of Janet's trial, he had formally recanted his previous statement. These factors would have strengthened the defense arguments that Derrick's police statement was too unreliable to be placed before Janet's jury. Second, if the court had nonetheless still admitted Derrick's police statement, the defense could have introduced the record of Derrick's contradictory trial testimony in order to argue to Janet's jury that Derrick's police statement was unreliable. Either way, Derrick's trial testimony was the type of evidence any defense attorney fighting a felony murder case would want to have.

The failure to disclose it was not exactly behavior consistent with the prosecution's mandate to see that justice is done and not to convict at all costs. The prosecution is required to disclose any evidence that might be helpful to the defense either because it is inconsistent with evidence the prosecution is presenting or because it is consistent with the defendant's position. This prosecutorial obligation, grounded in concepts of basic fairness, had been long established by the time of Janet's trial. The seminal case on this principle, *Brady v. Maryland*, had been decided in 1963. It's amazing how often prosecutors in the heat of battle conveniently forget to disclose *Brady* material.

I wanted to make sure that Janet's trial attorney had not known about Derrick's recantation and just chosen not to mention it for some inexplicable reason. Calling trial attorneys long after they have lost a client's case is one of my least favorite tasks. They always assume that I am looking to prove that their ineffectiveness was the reason my client lost in the first place. In reality, most of the time I am only trying to figure out something that is not clear from the record or I am looking for a lost motion or exhibit.

I did not know Janet's trial attorney, Bill Edwards. When I called the number listed in the file, his secretary answered. I introduced myself to her and told her that I needed to speak with Edwards about the Janet Flores case. To my amazement, moments later Edwards himself picked up the phone.

"This is Bill Edwards," he announced, in a deep, slightly gruff voice that I am sure resonated in a courtroom but seemed out of place on the phone, like an opera singer giving a full-voiced recital in a small elementary school auditorium.

"Hi. Thanks for taking my call. We've never spoken, but my office represents Janet Flores. I don't know if you remember the case? It was from a long time ago," I rattled away.

"I remember Janet well," Edwards replied sincerely. "She was a good kid who got mixed up in some stupid stuff. How's she doing?"

"She's okay. Could be better. We just got a bad report and recommendation from the magistrate in our habeas petition, and in the middle of it all, I learned that Derrick Fabio recanted his custodial confession two weeks before Janet's trial, and from what I can tell, the prosecutor never told you about the recantation. Do you remember that?" I asked, shamelessly leading Edwards to recall the facts the way I hoped he would.

"I remember that Whalen turned over Fabio's statement right when the trial was starting and that it sort of caught me off guard and that I argued it should not come in because it was unreliable. Did I mention that it had been recanted?" Edwards asked.

"No. You mentioned it was unreliable but not because it had been recanted," I explained.

"Then he never told me it was recanted. I would have used *that* if I knew about it," Edwards assured me.

"Will you sign an affirmation saying so?" I asked. In my experience, trial attorneys will say a lot of helpful things on the phone, fewer helpful things in a sworn written statement, and too often downright harmful things once they take the stand to testify at a hearing. But Bill Edwards surprised me.

"Of course, I'll sign an affirmation," he bellowed. "It's the truth. I'll do whatever I can to help Janet. Let her know that when you see her, okay?"

"I will," I promised. "Thanks so much for your help. I'll send you a draft this afternoon. Let me know if there's anything that's wrong with it. If it's okay, just sign it and fax it back."

"Will do," Edwards agreed and hung up without saying good-bye. Even the most cooperative trial attorneys have little time for conversational pleasantries.

By April 2004, when I learned about Derrick Fabio's recantation of his police statement during his own trial, Janet Flores had been incarcerated for almost nine years,
since the warm June night of Catora's shooting. In addition to preparing Edwards'
sworn statement, drafting the motion to vacate Janet's conviction would take several additional weeks of combing through the records of both her and Derrick
Fabio's trials. I did not want to wait until I was finished to visit Janet. After so many
years of nothing being done for her, now I was fighting on all fronts, and I was
excited to have something to report.

Bedford Hills Correctional Facility is one of two maximum security prisons
lodging female prisoners in New York State. The other one, Albion, is located too
far away to even think about visiting. But Bedford Hills is located in a wealthy
enclave in Westchester County, close to where I grew up.

There is a different feeling at Bedford than at other maximum security facilities. The visiting room looks like a day-care center, with toys and books available
for the inmates' children. There is a sense there that the ideal of rehabilitating
people—by teaching them skills, addressing psychological or substance abuse problems, and rewarding progress—is not some quaint or naive notion. I have been told
that a recent change in superintendents has made Bedford a less humane place to
be, but compared with some of the men's facilities I regularly visit, it still seems
pretty good.

When Janet walked into the visiting room, I recognized her right away,
even though I had never met her or seen her picture. She looked just as I had
imagined, like someone you would trust to count your money or keep your books.
Janet was petite, with a pale complexion and thin-lashed brown eyes behind her
glasses. She wore her brown hair pulled back in a no-nonsense bun. A small gold
cross hung around her neck. But for her prison jumpsuit, she could have been
sitting behind the desk at any public library explaining how to negotiate the
Dewey Decimal System.

Before I finished introducing myself, Janet thanked me for coming to see her.
She spoke in the measured cadences of a person who was consciously working to
improve her English. I told her about Derrick Fabio's recantation, my conversations with her trial attorney, and my decision to write to the magistrate and ask him

to reconsider his recommendation to deny the habeas petition. I assured Janet that after waiting so long for a decision from the magistrate, I would push hard to make sure that we would not get bogged down in state court. Janet was smart and seemed to understand the issues that we discussed. It felt good to be really working on her case at last.

Over the next few weeks, my professional life revolved entirely around Janet's case. I drafted the state court motion to vacate her conviction and prepared a motion for reconsideration to Magistrate Kates, asking him to look again at his determination that Janet should not get the benefit of *Crawford's* new rule and advising him of my discovery of Derrick Fabio's recantation. I asked Kates to withdraw his original opinion and not reissue a new one until I had gotten an answer on my state court motion to vacate Janet's judgment. Just in case Magistrate Kates denied that application, I also had to draft my formal objections to his report. Fortunately, Kates granted my request to withdraw the original report and agreed to refrain from issuing a new one until the state courts had addressed my additional *Brady* claim.

After drafting the state court motion to vacate, accusing the prosecution of deep-sixing the recantation and arguing that under the state constitution *Crawford* should apply retroactively to Janet's case, I asked Rich to call the district attorney's appeals bureau and speak to one of his contacts there. I wanted to send them the motion before filing it, in the hopes that they would advise the trial bureau to voluntarily vacate the conviction. If prosecutors in the appeals bureau believed the legal issues in my motion were likely to result in Janet's conviction being overturned at some point, they could try to persuade Whalen to agree that a new trial should be ordered. Together we could come up with a neutral legal theory warranting relief if the prosecutor's office did not want to admit any wrongdoing.

When I believe that I have a very strong legal claim, I always give my adversary a preview. Particularly where I am making serious allegations that a prosecutor has acted improperly, I try to operate under the assumption that an honest mistake has been made. If the prosecutor can save face and do right by my client, great. I have no personal stake in publicly shaming anyone, although sometimes that too can be satisfying.

We sent the motion to the district attorney's appeals bureau before filing it. The message came back that the homicide bureau had a no-surrender policy when it came to murder cases. The bureau would fight hard to uphold the conviction. I filed the motion and skulked around the courthouse elevators still hoping to charm prosecutor Whalen into a concession. His scornful promise to answer my papers within the week proved a difficult one for him to keep. A month later, I still did not have a response.

While ADA Whalen struggled to answer my claims, my eldest daughter was struggling to make friends in first grade. Jessie never told me that she was having a hard time. When it comes to complaining, Jessie has a weird system. If her bath is a degree too warm or I buy the wrong ham at the grocery store, I will hear about it immediately. But when she accidentally severed the tip of her finger by slamming it in the bathroom door, she never complained in all the months of doctors' appointments, even during the painful process of having dozens of stitches removed.

It is when she is not complaining that I have learned to be on high alert. I first learned about her trouble adjusting at school one evening when she was getting herself ready for bed. As she pulled off her shirt to put on her pajama top, I realized that I could see every single one of her ribs. She had lost weight, a lot of weight, right in front of me, without my realizing it. I felt the cold grip of fear creeping into my own chest. She had been eating breakfast and dinner, so the only possible change in her eating habits had to be at lunch.

"Jessie, have you been eating the lunch that we're packing for you?" I asked casually.

"No. I don't like to eat in the cafeteria. It smells funny and I have nobody who wants to sit with me," Jessie responded flatly, as if this information would not matter to me in the least.

Now my heart was racing. I pictured Jessie, sitting alone, with nobody to talk to, starving but unable to eat, day after day.

"What about Lauren or Victoria or Eve?" I asked, listing the names of her best friends from kindergarten.

"None of them are in my class now, and they don't want to play with me anymore," Jessie explained.

"What about the girls in your class now? Isn't there anyone you like?"

"Not really," Jessie said, looking down, with a slight shrug of her shoulders.

I scooped her up into my arms and held her. She felt as small and light as a bird.

"Don't worry," I assured her. "It'll just take some time to find a new friend. You're so great, anybody would be lucky to be friends with you. I love you tons and tons." I kissed Jessie good-night, shut off her light, and walked down the hall to my bedroom.

There I contemplated the social dynamics of first grade girls. It was not an issue into which I had any deep insights. I was raised with two older brothers, and boys have always seemed easier to understand. Boys run around. They punch each other. They fall down and get hurt. They eat a lot. No great mysteries there.

My childhood friendships with girls tended to be limited. I could only manage one friend at a time. Inevitably that friendship was unnaturally intense. My best friend in first grade, Alex Wexler, was so mean that when I would sleep at her house, she would not let me drink from her family's cups. She believed that my lips were too thick and that I would somehow impart my cooties onto their glasses. I accepted this slight unquestioningly without advising her mother or my own of the prohibition. It took me years to learn that friends let friends use their stemware.

If I could go back to first grade with the wisdom that I have acquired, I would look for a girl like Jessie to sit next to in the school cafeteria. Jessie is wise beyond her years. She is loyal and kind—never one to forsake a friend. If she were a candy, she would be a dark chocolate truffle. Unfortunately, the tastes of first grade girls run toward purple Ring Pops and neon blue Fruit Roll-Ups. Jessie is not the type to watch the coolest TV shows or insist on particular clothes. She tends to tuck her shirt too far into her pants, which she then hikes up too high so that her ankles show.

The consummate first-born child, Jessie takes life seriously. Used to being the boss of her siblings at home, she will not simply follow the group. In contrast, I was the youngest child, a natural-born follower.

Jessie came home one day from first grade and told me her entire class had gotten mad at her because she had told the gym teacher that somebody had forgotten to change into his sneakers. As a result, her classmates lost bonus points they needed to earn a treat at the end of the month. I used the occasion to teach Jessie that unless there is a real safety issue involved, like somebody is playing with fire, it's usually a good rule of thumb not to rat out your associates. It felt funny having to impart that lesson. I learned not to snitch the hard way, at an early age, from my brothers' fists.

I had little other useful advice to offer that year. I did not want to tell Jessie to just go along with the crowd. I admired her independence. I was not even in her school often enough to have a sense of which girls might be likely friendship candidates.

After taking Jessie to the doctor to make sure there was nothing physically wrong, I started eating up my vacation days so that I could meet her for lunch once or twice a week. I am fortunate in that I get a lot of vacation time, usually more than I can use and still get all my work done. But that spring, I spent a lot of time at home, using vacation time to work on the Flores case, while still being around for lunch with Jessie. Some days, I would take her out to eat. Some days, I would just go sit with her in the school cafeteria. Slowly, she put the weight back on. By the end of the year, she had made one good friend, Miriam, and the crisis had passed. Just in time for me to receive the prosecution's response in the Flores case.

## CATCHING FLIES WITH VINEGAR

There was nothing conciliatory about the prosecution's papers. According to them, any failure by Janet's defense to learn of Derrick Fabio's recantation was the defense's own fault. After all, ADA Whalen argued, it was certainly no secret that Derrick had gone to trial and been convicted weeks before Janet's trial began. It was equally obvious that at his trial, Derrick would have no choice but to deny the accuracy of his confession if he was going to beat the murder rap. The prosecution was equally dismissive of any claim that Janet was entitled to *Crawford's* new rule, arguing that it was not the type of bedrock principle that undermined the essential fairness or reliability of the trial's outcome.

In reply papers, I attempted to neutralize the prosecution's claims by arguing that it was obvious that the defense did not know about Derrick's recantation; if they had, they would have used it. Therefore, regardless of whether Janet's attorney should have known about it, the prosecution's reliance on Derrick's first statement because it was made under oath, without revealing that it had also been recanted under oath, was misleading and dishonest, and violated basic notions of fair play. There are many ways for a defendant to challenge the reliability of a confession, I argued, without taking the stand and swearing that it is false.

It was not long before we heard from the state trial court considering the motion. Within days of filing the response, I received a telephone call from the judge's law secretary, Theodore Wynn. I had met Ted a lifetime earlier, before I was married. His office was two doors down from mine at Legal Aid. He was the type of guy who always had an impolitic remark about a supervisor or colleague, which he would issue in a wry tone, with one eyebrow raised. His riffs always made me laugh, but I had a sneaking suspicion that similar riffs about me had been played for the amusement of others.

By the time of the Flores motion, Ted had long since left Legal Aid to go work for the judge who had presided over Janet's trial, the Honorable Thomas Manchester. Judge Manchester, a former narcotics prosecutor, had spent much of his judicial career presiding over serious narcotics offenses. It seemed that at some point in every trial he would declare "drugs are death," his version of "just say no" or "beauty is truth."

He had shown Janet little sympathy at her trial. Eva Rosa, who had probably fired the gun that killed Catora, had been sentenced as a result of her plea bargain to fifteen years to life in prison. She had admitted her guilt, had forgone a trial, and was rewarded with the minimum permissible sentence for the murder charge. On the other hand, Janet, who had merely opened the door to the apartment, had been sentenced to nineteen years to life.

To Manchester, Janet was a key worker in a multimillion-dollar drug ring, who had gotten greedy and actively participated in a scheme that resulted in the murder of her boss. My job was to make him see not only the legal merits of my motion but the responsible and accomplished woman into which Janet had matured while in prison.

"The judge is requesting the pleasure of your company next week. He wants to ask you and trial counsel a few questions," Ted advised with mock formality.

"Sounds lovely. Is the judge ordering a hearing or just a conference?"

The answer would determine the kind of week I would have. A hearing would require me to prepare an examination and be prepared to offer evidence in accordance with set rules. For a conference, I would need to do little more than show up.

"Not a hearing," Ted assured me. "Just a friendly chat."

Ted and I spoke for a few more minutes about possible dates for the conference. Afterward, I called Bill Edwards to make sure he was available.

The following week, we were all in court on Janet's case, ready to address whatever concerns the judge voiced. While prosecutor Whalen and Edwards exchanged pleasantries, I sat in stony silence, unable to even look at Whalen. I don't know if I disliked him so intensely because I believed he was being overly rigid or whether his unexpected failure to respond to my initial overture at the elevators had shaken me on a deeper level.

When Judge Manchester took the bench, he looked down coldly at both Janet and me. Apparently, he held convicted murderers and appeals attorneys in equal esteem.

"Well, Counselor, this is your motion, so why don't you call your witness and start your examination?" the judge demanded.

I was caught entirely off guard. I thought Ted had assured me only days earlier that the judge was not ordering a formal hearing, that we would just be getting together for an informal conference. I glanced over at Ted, hoping he would bail me out and explain why I was unprepared. Instead, he merely stood next to the judge.

Time to stall. "Your honor, the first thing I would like to do is introduce approximately fifteen pages of records from Bedford Hills Correctional Facility, demonstrating Ms. Flores's impressive rehabilitative efforts while in prison. I would ask that they be annexed as Exhibit C to my original motion.

"What *possible* relevance could those records have to this motion?" the judge asked. His clipped words made clear that he expected me to stop wasting his time and to concede that the records had no possible relevance.

I wanted the judge to review the records because they painted a picture of Janet I wanted him to see: a responsible, hardworking, intelligent woman, very different from the girl who had giggled in the holding cells when being interrogated about a murder. Apparently, Justice Manchester didn't really care what had happened to Janet in prison.

Fortunately, the prosecution had argued that Janet's motion should be denied in the "interest of justice," which gave me an opening to argue that the judge should consider Janet's rehabilitation when deciding the motion. I reminded the judge that even if *he* did not consider the evidence of Janet's rehabilitation to be relevant to the exercise of his discretion, the appellate court could substitute its own discretion for that of the trial judge. The higher court might consider the records relevant. I tried to keep my tone respectful, but I hoped the message was clear: Don't fuck with me. I'm going over your head if you do.

To his credit, Justice Manchester did not. "I hadn't thought of that. Of course, we'll make the records part of your motion, and I will review them later. Now please proceed with your witness, Counselor."

I did. Without any prepared questions, I took Edwards through his representation of Janet, the arguments over the admission of Derrick Fabio's statement, Edwards's assessment of the damage its introduction had wreaked on Janet's defense, and most important, how knowing about the recantation would have changed his approach to the case. Edwards explained that he would have argued that the recantation rendered Derrick's custodial confession too unreliable to be admitted as evidence against Janet. If the judge had still admitted the confession, Edwards explained, the defense would have admitted the recantation and argued that Derrick was a liar, to whom an oath meant nothing and who would say anything, anytime, if he believed doing so would benefit him.

Prosecutor Whalen questioned Edwards about how he could have failed to find out that Derrick had recanted his confession. By the end of the cross-examination, it was clear that the two men had disliked each other during the original trial, and their feelings had not changed in the nine years since.

At the close of the hearing, I said good-bye to Edwards and walked briskly out of the courtroom to the stairs. No more skulking around elevators for me hoping to win Whalen over.

It took Justice Manchester months to decide the motion. During that time, I reconciled myself to the grim reality that we would lose. I just wanted the decision sooner rather than later so that I could get back to federal court and continue the fight.

When Ted Wynn called me to tell me he was going to fax me the court's decision, I did not even bother to ask about the outcome. Instead, I mechanically read off the fax number from our letterhead, baffled that I still could not recall it automatically after all these years.

"Don't you want to know what we decided?" Ted asked, amazed at my robotic response.

"Okay, I'll bite. What did you decide?"

"The murder conviction's vacated, but the robbery conviction stands."

"*What?*" I asked incredulously, part of me believing that Ted was setting me up for someone else's lunchtime amusement.

"Murder vacated. Life sentence vacated. New trial ordered," Ted said seriously.

"Oh my god. That's such great news!"

I was ecstatic. Without the murder conviction in place, Janet would be up for immediate parole. Her sentence on the highest remaining count, the robbery in the first degree, was eight and one-third to twenty-five years, and she had already served almost ten years in prison.

"That sounds more like you," Ted laughed.

"No seriously, Ted, thank you."

I suspected Ted must have played a key role in the decision; Justice Manchester would not have gone out on a limb on his own to vacate the conviction of a player in the drug trade. I ran to the fax machine, waiting to read what they had written.

Rich was already there pulling the pages from the machine to read them.

"You're not going to like it," he warned.

His reaction baffled me. Like hot fudge sundaes, there is no such thing as a bad win for an appellate lawyer. There are just so few of them.

"Why not?" I asked incredulously, ripping the pages from his hands. I hate it when he reads one of my decisions before I do. It's like struggling through hours of painful labor and not being the first one to see the baby.

The problem was apparent from the first paragraph. The court had rejected all our claims about Derrick's recantation, finding that the defense should have known about it.

The murder conviction was vacated based on the new *Crawford* decision, which the court held should apply retroactively even to those cases that had become final years earlier. Such a broad ruling, which could impact hundreds of cases beyond Janet's, guaranteed an appeal by the prosecution and created a real danger of reversal by the appellate court. Any ruling that can open the floodgates of litigation and upset cases put to rest decades earlier is deemed dangerous to the system.

Sure enough, by that afternoon, I had received the People's notice of appeal. I called Whalen to see if we could strike a deal. He was out of the office and did not return my call right away. Without a plea bargain, the People's appeal could tie us up in state court for another two years. Then we would have to continue the slog through the federal courts.

We needed to make a deal, which the prosecution had no incentive to make. Time was on their side. As we fought, Janet would most likely remain in jail on the murder count; judges seldom grant bail in murder cases, and none had been set the first time around.

"They'll never strike a deal based on that decision," Rich predicted.

"Probably not," I agreed. "But I still have to try. I just haven't figured out a way to get to the prosecutor."

But to my surprise, when Whalen returned my call later in the week, he seemed open to negotiations.

"I don't see why we can't reach some sort of agreement."

Just as I could feel my hopes for Janet rising, Whalen's next statement brought them crashing down. "If your client pleads to murder two, we'll offer fifteen years to life. That's what Eva Rosa got before trial."

"Eva Rosa shot the guy. My client never went near him. We won't agree to murder or any sentence that carries life." While my words were strong, my voice sounded high and tinny in my own ears.

"Well, we won't offer manslaughter because then the highest sentence would be eight and one-third to twenty-five. That's not enough. Maybe we could run the robbery sentence consecutive to the manslaughter count. Fifteen to forty-five, or something like that? But I don't know if consecutive sentences would even be legal under these circumstances."

"I'll run it by my client, but that still sounds too high," I said.

When I got off the phone with Whalen, I called Janet at Bedford Hills and conveyed the prosecution's offers, fifteen to life for murder two, or fifteen to forty-five by running the robbery and manslaughter sentences consecutively to each other. Neither offer sounded particularly good to Janet. She believed that despite her excellent prison record, she would be forced to serve out the maximum sentence.

"I'll keep after the prosecutor," I promised. "Maybe I can bring him down." But even as I promised to try, I had little faith in my chances to succeed.

My first order of business was to convince Whalen that imposing consecutive sentences in some form would be legal. I researched the issue and determined such a deal was permissible under the sentencing laws.

I reached out to an appeals attorney in Whalen's own office to convince Whalen to go forward with the plea negotiations. David Morgan was high up in the Manhattan district attorney's office appeals bureau. He had been there forever, and I had dealt with him over the years when particularly thorny problems had arisen. While Morgan's written prose was often harsh and acerbic, he was always reasonable and decent when we spoke.

"Listen, David, I'm trying to save you guys a lot of time and effort on this Flores case, but you have to help me out here."

"Our only concern is that any plea bargain be legal, so that your client can't come back years from now and say she wants out of the deal," Morgan replied.

"I've got some cases for you that show it's all good." I recited some case cites supporting my position.

Morgan promised to look them up and get back to me. An hour later, he called me back, agreeing that any deal involving consecutive sentences would be kosher. He would call Whalen to tell him that there was no legal barrier to the deal. But it would be up to me to convince Whalen to be reasonable.

To live with three little girls fortunate enough to have a doting father is to be constantly reminded of the diversity of means available to coax and persuade. Each daughter has honed her own method of wrapping her father around her little finger.

Jessie, for example, is a master of reverse psychology. She'll casually mention that she has just finished reading a book or eating a box of chocolates that her dad has previously given her, thank him again for the gift, and deny that she could ever enjoy another book or chocolate as much as the ones she just finished. Pretty soon, her dad will be dashing to the store trying to find something that she will equally enjoy.

Lila, however, takes an entirely different approach. When she wants something from her dad—most often the batteries changed in a toy or glue to bond one of her inventions—she'll pepper Charlie endlessly with her requests. In no time, he's getting up from his dinner to find those batteries.

Maya has not yet settled on any one approach. She'll ask sweetly for a cookie, start screaming demands within a matter of seconds, and moments later crumple into sobs on the floor if her terms are not met. She has us all pretty well trained by now; we start searching for that cookie within nanoseconds of her uttering that first request.

Over the several months of my plea negotiations in Janet's case, I pretty much tried all these methods, short of sobbing at Martin Whalen's feet, to coax him into offering a more reasonable deal. I even tracked down the superintendent of Bedford Hills while she was getting her hair done at a local salon and begged her to speak to Whalen on Janet's behalf. She was willing to help and called Whalen to tell him what a model prisoner Janet had been.

I spoke to people at Janet's school programs and asked them to call Whalen, and they also agreed to help. I gathered up more certificates from the prison outlining Janet's achievements. I wrote to Whalen about Janet's commitment to helping her fellow inmates' children and described all the programs she had worked on to better their lives.

"My client is a young woman who is anxious to help others and to have a family of her own," I wrote. "Forcing her to spend additional years in prison may very well prevent her from fulfilling these most basic human desires." I hoped that maybe Whalen had a soft spot for kids I had not yet hit.

After each effort, I would call Whalen back and ask for a new number. We had gotten down to fourteen to forty-two by the summer of 2005, when I called him back to ask again for less time. By this time, we had been negotiating for over six months. Janet remained in prison because Judge Manchester had refused to set any bail. The prosecution had not perfected its appeal. I wanted the case over.

I called Whalen on a hot day early in July with another possibility. The prosecution could agree to vacate Janet's robbery conviction, she could then plead guilty to an armed felony, which would carry a minimum sentence half as great as the maximum, and then we could run a manslaughter conviction concurrent to the robbery.

Whalen listened and then declared, "I don't think any deal is possible. David Morgan told me he had concerns about the legality of the sentences running consecutively."

Hearing Whalen put me off with excuses about his appeals bureau standing in the way, when I had spoken to David Morgan myself months earlier to clear the deal, literally made me see red, then black, then bright flashes of light. I spoke before I regained my composure.

"Look," I said. My voice was unrecognizable. It was deep, hard metal, without a trace of any sweetness. "I don't care if you want the deal or you don't. But stop jerking me around. I cleared the deal with Morgan myself months ago. If you don't want to deal then just say so. It's time for you to step up and be a man."

There was silence on the other end of the phone. While ordinarily I would have nervously tried to fill it with laughter or a joke, I was too stunned to say anything.

After a long pause, Whalen said, "I'll call you back," and hung up.

My moment of demonic possession passed, I turned around to see if my office mate, Zoe, had overheard the conversation.

She was sitting at her desk, wide-eyed. "What was *that* about?" she asked, then started to laugh.

"I think I just told the head of homicide to be a man," I responded, dazed. I expected there would be blowback, complaints to Rich, apologies that would have to be made.

Instead, Whalen called me back ten minutes later. "Twelve and a half to twenty-five," was all he said. "That's my final offer."

"I'll pass it by my client," I said and hung up without saying good-bye.

Janet agreed to take the offer. By the time she pleaded guilty, she had served over ten years in prison. The bargain meant she would be eligible for parole in eighteen months because of her excellent prison record and the "good time" credit she had earned. Even if she missed her first opportunity at parole, there was a good chance she would get out on her second or third try. Most likely, she would be paroled by the time she had served fourteen years—significantly less time than she would have served under her original sentence.

........................................

Sometime in the near future, Janet Flores will walk out of the prison doors a free woman. She will leave better educated and wiser than when she went there. I feel great optimism about her future. Janet has developed a network of devoted supporters enthusiastic about helping her to succeed on the outside.

As Janet struggles to make a new life outside the prison walls, I have three daughters whom I must school in the gray arts of charm and persuasion. Not everyone will be as eager to please them as their father. I will teach them the practical: to accept an honest compliment with a simple "thank you" rather than deflecting it with humor or sarcasm; that in this age of cell phones, e-mail, and text messaging, sometimes the best way to get what you want is to look a person in the eye and simply ask for it; that unless you are a swimsuit model, wearing a bikini to work is probably never a good idea; and that true friendship is a rare gift worth waiting for even if there are times when you have to sit alone in the school cafeteria.

But I will also try to teach my daughters the mystical, so that each will become attuned to her own sixth sense and recognize the importance of life's subtle clues and footnotes. I hope that my girls, like me, will learn to notice what others might miss.

And I will teach them what it has taken me almost forty years to learn: That while it is true that you catch more flies with honey than with vinegar, there are times, when all else fails, when a woman should not be afraid to take the gun out from beneath the bed . . . and blast away. Figuratively, of course.

*part 3*

# Into the
# Self-Cleaning Oven

The reception center at Rikers Island Correctional Facility is how I envision the gateways of hell. There is no fire and brimstone—only soul-crushing bureaucracy. While Rikers is technically located in Bronx County, in order to get there by land you must work your way through the purgatory of Queens. It is not a place that attorneys willingly visit for any reason—doing so can cost you the entire day.

For a person like me, stricken with directional dyslexia, the arrival at the first Rikers' checkpoint is always an accomplishment in and of itself. At this first station, you must display your lawyer's corrections pass, demonstrating that you have submitted to a full security background check. Only then are you allowed to cross over the bridge onto the island, to proceed to the second security gate.

It is at this second checkpoint that the true hell begins. There you must join the endless, snaking line of visitors being processed through. While lawyers are supposed to be processed more quickly than regular visitors, Rikers is one of those places where the rules and reality rarely meet.

Inevitably, no matter what the time of year, it is hot, either from the ancient heating system in the winter or the nonexistent air-conditioning in the summer. Inevitably, it is smelly, as the masses seeking admittance sweat under the heat. Body odor mixes with the underlying odor of decay wafting off the water: a truly pungent cocktail. The unmistakable scent of desperation also perfumes the air, for Rikers Island is where criminal defendants awaiting trial in New York City are housed while they are being shuttled back and forth to court.

Once through the second gate, there is more waiting, this time for a shuttle bus to arrive and transport you to the individual housing unit you are seeking to visit. Once at the individual unit, you must submit to additional metal detectors and surrender all personal possessions.

By April 23, 2001, I had not yet become used to the routine. I did not know that I would spend more time on Rikers that spring than in all the previous years of my career combined. My client, Eric Eastman, had been convicted of committing a crime on cell block C-74. And that day, I was there to visit the crime scene.

Earlier in the week, I had spoken with somebody at the Department of Corrections Legal Department, who had put me in touch with Rikers' assistant deputy warden for security, Joe Freeman.

The ease with which I had been able to arrange the crime scene visit should have given me pause. I had heard that Corrections would not allow a defense attorney back into the cell block without a court order. But my request had been granted without question.

When I arrived at the cell block, Deputy Warden Freeman was nowhere to be found. An assistant informed me that he was out sick. Having just spent three hours traveling and clearing security, I was not about to accept being told to come back another day.

"I want to speak to somebody in the legal department now," I demanded, my rude tone born of sweating in a dark suit that included a skirt a full size too small around the waist.

Freeman's associate was unimpressed. "I'll call Legal right now, Counselor, but it's not gonna do you any good," he assured me.

He went into a small office to use the phone. When he returned ten minutes later, there was a smug look on his face that told me I would not be getting anywhere that afternoon.

"Legal says the crime scene viewing was yesterday and you missed it."

"What are you talking about?" I said. "You must be confused. I'm the only lawyer working on this case."

"There was a whole group of lawyers here viewing the scene," the assistant informed me. "If you got questions, you have to call Rhoda Levine at Legal." He then retreated to his office and closed the door. There would be no further discussion between us.

I was left outside, just a few feet away from my intended destination. Standing there feeling only frustration, I did not know that my failure to get into hell would prove to be my client's salvation.

......................................

Around the family dinner table of my childhood, my father taught us that God did not exist. Religion was for the intellectually lazy, people who could be persuaded to believe that the world was flat or that the sun revolved around the earth.

My father's orthodox atheism was the result of his rearing by observant Jewish parents. His own father had been particularly authoritarian in religious matters. The eldest of seven brothers, my grandfather left school at thirteen to help support his family after the death of his own father. Despite his lack of formal education, or maybe because of it, my grandfather was a force that commanded reckoning. He made and lost more money during his lifetime than most people will ever see. When he was not making or losing a fortune, he was playing piano like a virtuoso, or chess like a Russian master, or riding horses like a Kentucky blueblood. When the United States entered the Second World War, although not eligible to be drafted due to his age and family obligations, my grandfather volunteered for the navy. He spent several years in the South Pacific on an aircraft carrier.

No personal hardship, loss of fortune, or wartime atrocity could shake the intensity of my grandfather's faith. When he had money, he gave much of it to the synagogue. When my father contracted polio during the year of his bar mitzvah studies and could not leave his bed for weeks, my grandfather tutored him at his bedside, ensuring that my father would not miss his formal Jewish passage into manhood.

But my father found no answers to the questions of his youth in the Torah. He flew through high school, college, and medical school in Maryland before making his way to New York just as soon as he could manage the journey. Although my grandfather had the money to pay for my father's schooling, he refused to do so, insisting that my father make his own way.

As a medical resident in New York City, my father met my mother, who was also a refugee from an Orthodox Jewish upbringing. When she left her family home in New England, her own father sat shivah, the Jewish ritual for mourning the dead. But his threats to cut her off were short lived, because he simply missed her too much to deny her existence. I was born shortly after his death and named in his memory.

In my childhood home, every mystery in the universe could be answered by referencing either Freud or Darwin. I learned the principles of dream analysis and evolution before I entered kindergarten.

But despite the absence of God, ours was not a secular home. Thanks to my mother, we were all forced to attend religious school from the age of five. By the time I was eleven, I was spending three afternoons a week studying Hebrew, learning to cook traditional Jewish meals, and attending ethics classes. While my brothers complained bitterly about my parents' hypocrisy, I never questioned it.

Sure, I complained about Hebrew school because it was uncool to like it, but I never dreaded going. All my friends were Jewish, and we would gossip and pass notes during class. Judaism's teachings resonated with me: the emphasis on performing acts of kindness, the command to try to heal the world, the attention to practical minutiae such as feeding your animals before you, yourself, eat, or paying a person his wages on the day he performs his labor.

There was also the long shadow the Holocaust cast over my childhood. I cannot remember a time before I knew that distant kin had been killed simply for being Jewish. Rejecting a Jewish identity, when millions had died because of it, seemed impossible.

And so I embraced it. I marched to support the rights of Soviet Jews. I marched to support Israel's right to exist. I spent a summer in Israel, helping to build a gathering place for elderly Holocaust survivors.

My father supported these activities because none of them overtly had anything to do with God. I never told him that there were times, outside of Hebrew school, when he and my mother were late to arrive home, that I prayed for their safe return. I still do. For while I was taught that God did not exist, even my father recognized that there are no atheists in foxholes.

As an adult, there are days when my world seems like one large foxhole. Nothing can drive you deep into the trenches of despair like motherhood.

Shortly after my grandmother died of pneumonia, my youngest daughter contracted it. Maya was only seven weeks old, and she was to spend the next two months battling various respiratory infections. The doctors did not know exactly what was causing Maya's illness. Cystic fibrosis was suspected. I spent my days in doctors' offices and my nights ministering to Maya with humidifiers, nebulizers, antibiotics, decongestants, saline drops, trips into the steamy bathroom, all in a futile attempt to clear her tiny, wheezing lungs. The medications made her limbs jerky and her sleep fretful. I would rock her and pray all night long.

"Please, please, please, just let her breathe better," I would whisper to the empty room.

When the morning came, I would go back to the specialists to report on Maya's status, what seemed to be helping or not. They would measure the oxygen in her blood, listen to her chest, suggest that I see another doctor. This routine went on until the spring, when Maya turned four months old and miraculously improved. I don't actually believe that my prayers helped cure my youngest daughter, but they helped me maintain my strength during that difficult time.

My work can also feel like entering a war zone. And not merely because my office looks like a bomb exploded in it, randomly strewing papers everywhere. It is because the stakes are high, as is the potential for despair.

And so I will find myself sitting in my backyard, looking up at the stars in the night sky, and whispering, "Please, please, please, just let this one come out right." That is how I survived working on the case of the People of the State of New York against Eric Eastman.

## DO YOU WANT IT?

In August 2000, I was finding the return to work following Lila's birth difficult. Whereas I had been anxious to get back to the workplace after five months at home with Jessie, and was able to quickly immerse myself in the DeLuca case, I had greater ambivalence about returning the second time around. From Jessie I had learned that babies do grow up quickly, that you can blink and an entire season will have passed. I was pretty sure Lila would be my last baby, and I wanted to savor the experience.

I also felt that I had barely been handling the demands of working with one child. How I was going to manage working with an infant and a three-year-old was anybody's guess. As the June date slotted for my return to work approached, my anxiety grew. I delayed as long as I could, toyed with the idea of quitting altogether to work at Starbucks, and then dragged myself onto the 8:05 train to New York, figuring that I could always quit later. Starbucks would probably still be there.

Fortunately, Rich, sensing my ambivalence, allowed me to cut back my hours and to commute in to the city only three days a week. For the first time in my career, I was actively looking for cases that would not challenge me. I wanted to coast.

Rich walked into my office one afternoon with a case that seemed to fit my new career trajectory. As opposed to the DeLuca transcript, the over-three-thousand-page record that had greeted me on my return from my first maternity leave, the file Rich held fit easily under his arm.

"I think I have something perfect for you," Rich announced. "It's a disgusting crime, but the record is short because only one witness testified. The client might be challenging, but nothing you can't handle."

I was immediately intrigued, not only by the size of the transcript, but by Rich's description of the crime. Rich and I have known each other for a long time. We have worked together and discussed endless numbers of heinous cases involving random acts of violence against a host of sympathetic victims. Our office has represented parents convicted of murdering their children, men convicted of raping their daughters, youths convicted of crime sprees that have left multiple victims dead in their wake. In all that time, I could not recall Rich ever describing a case as "disgusting."

"What did he do?" I asked.

"He led a gang rape against a fellow prisoner," Rich explained. "Nasty stuff."

"That's it?" I asked, somewhat let down. "That's the disgusting crime? How is that any more disgusting than if he had raped a woman?"

Rich was not interested in discussing the sexual politics of rape at that moment.

"Do you want the case or not?" he asked, obviously annoyed.

"There was only one witness? Just the complainant? They couldn't come up with anyone else? That's weird," I observed, trying to talk my way back into Rich's good graces. I would need to be there if I was to have any hope in my new coasting ambitions.

"I don't think this prosecution was exactly a high priority for the district attorney's office. There's nothing to it, just an argument that the complainant was unbelievable as a matter of law. You can do it in a week," Rich predicted.

Under my new reduced work schedule, I would only be expected to complete eight briefs during the entire year. The prospect of finishing one of those briefs in a week was too appealing to pass up.

"I'll take it," I announced enthusiastically.

"Sold." Rich smiled and dropped the file onto my desk.

Despite the shortness of the transcript, the file itself was filled with letters. Eric Eastman had been writing to the office a lot, enclosing stacks of papers, newspaper articles, and letters, lots and lots of letters, many written in all capitals. "BULLSHIT!" "RAILROADED!" and the most dreaded of all, "INNOCENT"; like flares fired from a sinking ship, these words soared off the pages, over and over again.

Appellate lawyers take different approaches to their clients' pleas of innocence. As awful as it sounds, many ignore them. In the eyes of the law, everyone convicted after a trial by jury or judge is guilty. Only in a tiny fraction of cases will an appellate court deem the trial evidence legally inadequate to support a conviction. To prevail on an appellate claim of legally insufficient evidence, a defendant must prove that no rational juror could have found him guilty beyond a reasonable doubt. Convincing an appellate court that twelve civic-minded citizens who devoted days or weeks to listening to the witnesses ultimately came to an irrational conclusion is almost impossible.

Even where a person is legally guilty because he has been convicted of a crime based on legally sufficient evidence, that does not mean he actually, *factually* did it. That has been the lesson taught over and over again by DNA exonerations. In hundreds of cases, it has been irrefutably proven that defendants convicted of heinous crimes on the basis of eyewitness identifications, false confessions, faulty scientific evidence, or lying witnesses were actually innocent and did not commit the crimes for which they had been found guilty by perfectly rational jurors.

But there would be no DNA evidence exonerating Eric Eastman. I knew that because Rich had not mentioned any testimony about the DNA analysis. If any DNA evidence had been recovered, the medical examiner would have been called as a witness during the trial to explain its relevance. In sexual assault cases, DNA evidence is the big ticket item for the prosecution. Recovering a suspect's DNA from a victim precludes almost any viable defense other than that the sex was consensual or that the lab botched the analysis.

I also knew from quickly perusing the file that the stacks of papers Eric Eastman had been sending to the office would all relate to what had happened at his trial. I could not begin to address his concerns if I was not familiar with the proceedings. I decided to ignore Eastman's pleas entirely for the moment, until I familiarized myself with his case.

. . . . . . . . . . . . . . . . . . . . . . . . . . . . . .

The transcript bore an enormous red "CONFIDENTIAL" stamp across its front, the scarlet letters worn by all sex offense cases. The truth is, I don't like sex cases. There. I said it. As coldly analytical as I am supposed to be when considering my clients' crimes, I am always unsettled by the ones involving allegations of sexual abuse. As a result, I tend to work twice as hard on them, in order to convince myself that I am not shortchanging anybody.

My fundamental discomfort with sexual assaults is that I do not understand them at all. Murder, I get. There have been times when I have been so angry at someone—a particular ex-boyfriend comes to mind—that the thought of his untimely and violent death appealed to me. Stealing, I understand. I have coveted things I could not afford and have entertained thoughts of slipping them into my pocket before the salesperson noticed. Selling drugs, sure. Anybody who has worked at a fast-food restaurant or scooped ice cream for a summer at minimum wage should understand that the idea of some faster money might appeal. But I just do not get the urge to intimately violate somebody at gunpoint. Maybe it's a guy thing. I know the stock answer is that rape is about violence, not sex. I still don't get it.

As Rich had promised, the case against Eric Eastman and his co-defendant, Brian Michaels, was a simple one. David Johnson was the sole witness called on behalf of the prosecution at trial.

Unsurprisingly for a person spending time on Rikers Island, Johnson had a criminal record. Forgery, larceny, and drugs seemed to be Johnson's crimes of choice. His record stretched back to the late 1980s.

In November 1997, Johnson had been arrested for robbery and taken to Rikers. By January 1998, he had worn out his welcome on his original cell block, and after being beaten senseless by some fellow prisoners, he had been transferred to cell block C-74.

There Johnson met and became friendly with Eric Eastman and Brian Michaels. Johnson denied ever having any problems with Eastman until February 1998, when one evening Eastman was propping open the door to his cell with a bucket and summoned Johnson.

When Johnson went over to see what Eastman wanted, Michaels dragged him into the cell and Eastman threw him on the bed, causing Johnson to hit his head on the wall with such great force that his forehead was noticeably bruised. There were two other men in the cell, Drey Monroe and Andrew Zimmer. Eastman ordered Johnson to "suck Michaels's dick," and Michaels put a pillow over Johnson's head when he tried to scream. Then Johnson felt his pants being pulled down and liquid being poured over his rear end.

I did not need to read the transcript closely to know what came next. Johnson described being penetrated by Eastman's penis while Michaels held a scalpel to his throat. Another inmate, Brad Waters, entered the cell and ordered Eastman to "get the fuck off." Waters's attempts at heroism were short-lived, however, as Michaels threatened to kill Waters with the scalpel. Eastman also threatened to kill Waters if he interfered in Eastman's "business" again. While this confrontation was going on, Johnson was able to jump off the bed and run into his own cell, lucky number 13.

The cell, which remained locked shut for most of the day, was open at that time because it was "option" on the cell block, meaning that the inmates had the option to go into their cells for a short period of time. Waters followed Johnson into the cell to see if he was hurt.

Johnson was crying hysterically after the attack when a female corrections officer found him and Waters together in his cell. Although it was forbidden for two men to be in the cell together, this female officer saw the tears on Johnson's face and knew that something was wrong.

After Waters and Johnson were removed from the cell, the female corrections officer walked back toward the security bubble, located at the other end of the block. In the corridor, Waters and Johnson again encountered Michaels and Eastman. Another angry confrontation ensued, with more threats and Michaels brandishing the scalpel. Eastman and Michaels then told another inmate, Bill Reynolds, that Johnson was cheating on him with Waters.

It was the defense's theory that Johnson's complicated love life was the reason he fabricated the attack in the first place. Both the prosecution and the defense agreed that Johnson had been found in his cell with Waters on the night of the incident. According to the defense, Johnson had been cheating on Reynolds with Waters and needed an excuse for being caught in the act. According to the prosecution, Waters was in the cell trying to help Johnson after the gang rape. At trial, Johnson admitted that he had been romantically involved with Reynolds. But he emphatically denied that he had ever been interested in Brad Waters and insisted Waters had merely been attempting to help him after the vicious assault.

Following the confrontation in the corridor, Johnson approached a male corrections officer, John Alder, to tell him that "something severe just happened in the back." Johnson requested to speak with a captain, but no one ever came to speak with him about his complaint.

The next morning, Eastman and Michaels were back to their old tricks, threatening Waters with the scalpel. Only when Eastman was called out to go to court did Johnson feel secure enough to report the incident in detail to the captain on duty, Jason Bridges.

Johnson was subsequently taken to the clinic on Rikers Island for medical attention. While he insisted that there were noticeable bruises on his head and back, no medical records from the clinic were admitted into evidence.

Johnson was then transported to Bellevue Hospital for further treatment, and a rape kit was prepared by taking swabs from his penis, mouth, and anus. No medical records were introduced from Bellevue Hospital. No DNA evidence was recovered.

The trial prosecutor concluded his direct examination of Johnson by eliciting that he had not wanted to transfer off the cell block before the incident and that he had not filed a lawsuit against the Department of Corrections seeking to recover any damages for the rape.

The defense rested with neither Eastman nor Michaels testifying in his own behalf—each man believing that Johnson's testimony was so inherently implausible that no jury would credit it. Eastman's counsel, Bruce Pucci, argued aggressively on summation that Johnson was a liar with his own agenda. The allegations arose, said Pucci, because Johnson had been caught in his cell with Waters and was angry at Eastman for interfering with his intimate relationships with both Waters and Reynolds.

The prosecutor, Ron Rivera, acknowledged that his entire case came down to whether the jury believed David Johnson. But according to the prosecution, Johnson had no reason to lie about being raped. Before the incident, he had no gripe with Eastman or Michaels. He wasn't trying to scam the system by filing a lawsuit. "He's not one of those guys trying to make a dime on the citizens of New York," the prosecutor assured the jurors.

"I'm asking you, ladies and gentlemen, think about it. What does he have to gain? He was humiliated on the stand by the defense attorneys. Humiliated. He was humiliated when this happened to him, and he was humiliated when he testified before this jury about what happened in that cell. If you believe him, I want you to come back here with a verdict of guilty, but if you don't believe him, then come back here and acquit these defendants," prosecutor Rivera beseeched the jurors.

The jurors apparently believed Johnson, because they convicted both Eastman and Michaels of sodomy in the first degree. Eastman had been convicted of two burglaries in the past. The sodomy conviction was his third strike. The minimum sentence he could receive was twenty years to life in prison.

Toward the end of 1999, just days before Christmas, the parties appeared in court for the sentencing. Pucci asked the judge to set aside the verdict because Johnson was not a credible witness. The trial judge, Stanley Davis, was unmoved. Issues of credibility were for the jury, he observed, and promptly denied the motion.

Then Eric Eastman stood to address the court. Pucci's efforts seemed anemic next to those of his client. Eastman handed up his phone records from Rikers, which reflected that Johnson had repeatedly called his home on Eastman's account. Eastman explained that Johnson had taken money from him to buy drugs, which Johnson then failed to deliver.

Eastman also handed up a note from David Johnson that read, "East. Yo. I respect the game. But I am really in love with Brad." In the note, Johnson blamed Eastman for interfering with his relationship with Brad Waters.

Eastman warned that he was innocent and that the judge would be sentencing two men for a crime they did not commit. The trial judge refused to consider the evidence Eastman offered since it was not relevant at the sentencing proceedings and could have been offered at trial.

Judge Davis then imposed the minimum possible sentence—twenty years to life in prison. Eastman was forty-four years old. He suffered from seizures and high blood pressure. If I could not help him, there was a good chance he would not live to see the parole board. Michaels fared better because he had fewer prior felony convictions. He was sentenced to fifteen years.

· · · · · · · · · · · · · · · · · · · · · · · · · · · ·

I closed the transcript and sighed loudly.

"What's up?" Zoe asked from across the office, sensing even before I did that something was bothering me.

"It's a T-One," I responded, using our shared Legal Aid jargon for a dead case. At Legal Aid, where I had met Zoe years earlier, we filled out filing forms that reflected whether the brief involved a trial, hearing, or plea and the number of issues being raised. A T-One was a trial case where you had found only a single issue.

"So, that's what you want. You're coasting, remember?"

"But I think he's lying."

"Who, your client?" Zoe asked, not quite sensing the problem yet.

"No, the complainant. I think the complainant's lying. Something's wrong."

"Why don't you call the trial attorney? Maybe there was more going on here than what's on the record. Maybe the fix was in or something and the client just couldn't bring himself to plead guilty so they did a sort of fake trial and the judge gave him the minimum afterward. Sort of a long guilty plea. That goes on a lot up in the Bronx," Zoe suggested.

Zoe's husband had worked for a judge in the Bronx for years. She understood the clubby atmosphere in the courthouse that sometimes led to deals being struck that would never appear on any official record.

Taking Zoe's advice, I dialed Bruce Pucci's Long Island office from the number listed on the file papers. When Pucci answered the phone, I introduced myself and asked him if he remembered the Eastman case. He said he remembered it well. Pucci naturally spoke in a tough, combative tone, which he had honed through years of cross-examining witnesses. While I'm sure it worked for him at trial, it brought out the worst in me.

"So tell me, how did you lose this piece-of-shit case?" I asked, too focused on getting the answer to worry about offending him.

Pucci did not offend easily. "Have you met your new client yet?" he asked snidely.

"No. I just got the case, so tell me everything I need to know."

"There was a strange aura about the case. Eastman's this huge, tough older guy, and you could just tell that Michaels was his boy. They, like, joked around with each other throughout the trial in a very weird way, if you get my meaning. And the victim came off really believable. I thought I would be able to rip him apart on the stand, but he admitted that he was gay and that he was having a relationship with another inmate. He just came off as having nothing to hide. And Eastman is an angry guy. I wouldn't recommend your going to see him without a bodyguard. It was really a disgusting case."

Disgusting. There was that word again. I was starting to understand that the "aura" permeating this case was a dark cloud of homophobia. The prosecutor, defense attorneys, and judge had all been men. Nobody had wanted to examine the allegations too closely.

I had little patience after that for Pucci's insights, and so I thanked him and told him I would call him if I had any more questions. Then I turned my attention to the stacks of papers Eastman had sent, newspaper articles about prisoners wrongly convicted of crimes they did not commit and additional copies of court papers I already had.

But included in Eastman's correspondence was something that had not been sent to me by the court. It was the original, handwritten note that Eastman had referred to at his sentencing, the one Johnson had allegedly written to him, admitting his love for Brad Waters. It read:

> East. Yo. I respect the game. But I am really in love with Brad. And it's your fault that he played with my feelings. Now say fuck him. Let him suffer. Don't buy him shit tomorrow. Don't do shit for him. And when we come out, we will call your wife and my sister and do our power moves. We will try to get you and Drey down tomorrow. Let's keep shit REAL. Me and you. Okay. Peace.

The unsigned note seemed to support Eastman's statements during the sentencing that Johnson was angry at him for interfering with his relationship with Brad Waters; the note also suggested that Johnson and Eastman were doing some sort of illegal deal together.

But from a legal perspective, the note was useless. Even assuming I could prove that Johnson had written it, the defense had known about it at trial and had decided not to use it for some unspecified reason. We were stuck with that decision now, even if it had proven to be a bad one in retrospect. Defendants are not permitted to sit on evidence during the trial and then allege that it is "newly discovered" after the verdict, warranting reversal of the conviction. If that type of gamesmanship were permitted, the system would cease to function. So it would take more than the note to save Eastman.

I was hesitant to write to Eric Eastman, because I knew that as soon as he knew my name, I would become the focus of his frustrations. I have given countless lectures to fellow attorneys and law students addressing the best manner in which to handle difficult clients. But by the time I began representing Eric Eastman, I felt that I was losing my touch. My natural ability to find the right words—to strike the right tone at the right time—had vanished.

It was as if something about raising small children had thrown off my internal timer, causing me to singe both clients and casseroles alike. A sense of patience and understanding no longer permeated every line I addressed to my clients, as it once had. All too often, there was an unintended brusqueness to my tone.

With my cooking, I would take the time to shop for organic vegetables, intricately assemble a vegetarian lasagna, put it in the oven, and then forget it until the blaring of the kitchen's smoke detector summoned me. All too often, we had to eat our family meals on the basement steps or outside in order to avoid smoke inhalation. "Smells bad" was among Lila's first word couplings.

Aware of these recently acquired limitations, I spent extra time crafting my introductory letter to Eastman. I wanted him to know that I was on his side but also to convey that I did not want him to overwhelm me with demands. I promised that I would incorporate many of the points he had set forth in his letters to demonstrate that David Johnson was a liar.

Within the week, I had drafted the brief, arguing that Johnson's entirely uncorroborated testimony was not the stuff that supported a finding of proof beyond a reasonable doubt. The jury had simply gotten it wrong.

I had a lot of material with which to work. Johnson was a criminal with a long history of committing offenses that reflected a propensity for dishonesty. There just aren't too many honest forgery convicts out there. The prosecution had offered no evidence of Johnson's alleged injuries, such as the medical records from the facilities where he had been examined. His account of the attack was not corroborated by another witness, although it allegedly took place on a crowded cell block. There was no DNA evidence supporting the rape claims.

But there were a lot of factors that would favor the prosecution on appeal. First, under the governing standards of review, the appellate court had to consider the evidence in the light most favorable to the People. Second, Eastman had been convicted by a Bronx jury. Conventional wisdom holds that it is almost impossible to convince a Bronx jury to convict anyone. Third, Johnson's account of prison rape comported with popular notions about Rikers Island. Thunder and lightning. Smoke and fire. Rikers and rape. Some phenomena just seem to fit together naturally.

And of course, there was the ultimate question, the one that the prosecutor had asked over and over on summation: Why would David Johnson lie about being raped if it wasn't true? The answer suggested by the defense, that Johnson was angry at Eastman and Michaels for interfering with his romance with Brad Waters, seemed thin.

In all the years I had been practicing, the Eastman case was the only prosecution for a prison rape I had encountered. Not only had I not seen another, I had never had any client complain to me about being raped. There is just such a stigma surrounding it. Why would Johnson lie about suffering such a humiliating ordeal?

Within days of sending off my first letter to Eastman, I received a response.

> Dear Counsel,
>
> I understand that you are going to be the attorney representing me on my appeal and I know that you probably have a lot of clients. But I am not like your other clients. I am AN INNOCENT MAN. As God is my witness, I never touched that MOTHERFUCKER Johnson. Why do you think the prosecution could not get a single witness to testify other than Johnson? Because he is lying. NOTHING HAPPENED. You can ask anybody who was there. They'll all tell you the same thing.
>
> Listen up, the second you catch me lying, you can turn your back on me and quit my case but I am telling you the truth. PLEASE HELP ME!!!
>
> Peace Out. East.

The letter made me feel queasy. I had almost finished writing the brief in Eastman's case. I would be expected to file it within the month. In my soul, I knew it would lose.

I could have drafted the losing opinion myself. "Appellant's guilt was proven beyond a reasonable doubt and is not against the weight of the evidence. The jury, which had the advantage of seeing and hearing the complainant, chose to credit his account of the incident. Viewing the evidence in the light most favorable to the People, the evidence was sufficient to support appellant's conviction of sodomy in the first degree."

I could file the brief and move on to the next case, or I could actually try to help Eric Eastman. I looked down at the letter in my hand. "PLEASE HELP ME!!!" shot off the page.

I got up and walked into Rich's office and stood silently in his doorway, letter in hand, not knowing what I was going to say.

Rich looked up from a pile of papers on his desk.

"What would I have to do to convince you that Eric Eastman is innocent?"

Rich looked puzzled.

"You think he's actually innocent? That he didn't do anything?"

Standing there, in the hard light of Rich's office, I was unwilling to admit that. It felt like admitting that I believed in Santa Claus or the Easter Bunny, like declaring "Jesus saves!" in the middle of one of my father's lectures about Freud's theories on the human need to create a deity.

"I know the complainant's lying. I just know it. Maybe my client did something, but the complainant's lying. I want to know what it would take to convince you of *that?*" I asked, changing my original question.

Rich thought for a moment. "Maybe if you could get a signed, sworn statement from Brad Waters saying that Johnson made the whole thing up."

"Waters? The one Eastman and Michaels threatened to kill? The one who interrupted the attack?"

"Yeah, him." Rich smiled. He was setting me up for an impossible task.

"Okay then. I'll have to find Brad Waters," I thought aloud.

"Fine. But you know that we can't hold off filing forever while you're looking for Waters. The court is not going to accept that."

Rich was done joking. The appellate court's order assigning our office to the case specified that we were to file the brief within 120 days of receiving a complete record. If we did not file in the prescribed time, we would be called upon to explain the reason for the delay.

"Technically, I don't even have a complete record yet. I'm still missing a few pages from a pretrial hearing. The court can't make me file an appeal without a complete record," I offered.

"I'm just saying there are limits," Rich warned.

"Limits, I understand, limits. I'll keep that in mind," I promised, feeling annoyed at Rich's focus on bureaucratic minutiae when I was trying to make him see the big picture.

Back at my desk, I called around to try to find the best investigator willing to work at the reduced rates my office could pay. Roy Swain had worked for attorneys in my office before, so I knew he had been willing in the past.

Roy was a retired housing police detective. He had spent his career policing New York City's housing projects and knew the territory well. If Brad Waters wasn't in prison, he was probably staying with someone in some project somewhere. I called Roy and told him briefly about the Eastman case. He was interested, and so I sent him all the information I had on Brad Waters.

Then I waited, while my client's desperation mounted.

## YOU ARE MY SUNSHINE

Dear Counsel:

I know that MOTHERFUCKER Johnson filed a lawsuit. He's probably going to get rich off this case while I rot in prison. I am dying in here. There is no sunlight, only darkness. The only thing that keeps me going is knowing that you are on my side. YOU ARE MY SUN-SHINE!!!

TRUTH. East.

Such letters made me feel guilty and useless. Coincidentally, I had been singing "You are my sunshine, my only sunshine" to both Jessie and Lila from the time they were born. By January 2001, when I received Eastman's letter advising me that I had become *his* sunshine, the song was inextricably intertwined with my girls' bedtime routines. I tried substituting other lullabies, but inevitably they would beg me to "sing *Sunshine*," with their sleepy little voices, as soon as I turned out the light. Singing in the dark, I had to force my client's letters from my mind.

When Lila or Jessie would wake up in the middle of the night, needing a glass of water or reassurance from a bad dream, I could not fall back to sleep. My thoughts would turn to Eastman, alone in his cell, locked down twenty-three hours a day in a super-maximum-security prison because his seething rage rendered him unpredictable.

"Please, please, please, help me see my way through this," I'd plead silently inside my head.

But apart from my occasional bouts of insomnia, I was finding managing work with two kids surprisingly easy. Before Lila's birth, Jessie made endless demands on my attention, but with Lila around, Jessie had a constant companion, a source of entertainment, an ever-willing audience and sidekick. They would play together for hours, Lila's innate silliness balancing Jessie's earnestness. At other times, Jessie's quiet focus would help Lila settle down. Their easy camaraderie reminded me of our dogs.

During our third year of law school, Charlie and I decided to buy a puppy, figuring on some level that if we could raise a dog together maybe we could transfer those skills onto children someday. We bought a boxer puppy, Sunny, and moved into an apartment on Bleecker Street that allowed pets. We devoted endless time and energy to raising Sunny, believing that we had already learned everything we needed by the end of our second year of law school; the third year was obviously just the university's attempt to needlessly extract even more money from our already depleted bank accounts.

But no matter how much time and energy we devoted to the puppy, she never seemed truly happy. We would play tug-of-war with her chew toys, have catches with her in the park, cook her gourmet meals, and let her sleep on our bed. The only time she seemed content was when she was at the Washington Square Park dog run, around other dogs.

And so we bought another puppy, Elvis. The moment we brought him home, Sunny was a new animal, happier than we had ever seen her before. She immediately went up to Elvis, who was six months her junior, and sat on him. From that day on, they were inseparable. They would die twelve years later within weeks of each other.

While having two dogs was more work in certain respects, in other ways it was easier than having just one. Sunny didn't want to sleep on our bed anymore. She preferred to sleep next to Elvis on her dog bed. We didn't have to play tug-of-war with her chew toys. She played that game with Elvis instead.

Similarly, once Lila came around, Jessie no longer looked to me to be her playmate. She could play dress-up and tea party with Lila instead. I could be a mommy, not another princess or teatime companion. It was just easier.

............................................

It was lucky that I was finding motherhood easier, because by March 2001, my frustration in the Eastman case was reaching a high point. I had received the final pages of the record; the brief had been written since September 2000; and my investigation was going nowhere. Roy Swain had not found Waters. I had found no evidence of Johnson's filing a civil lawsuit, which would have shown that Johnson had a financial motivation to make up the attack. No rape, no recovery.

Then in April 2001, I got a call from Roy Swain.

"I hope you have some good news for me, Roy, because things are looking pretty bleak here," I admitted.

"I do indeed. I found him. Brad Waters is in Odyssey House on Ward's Island, part of a drug program he got into to try to keep his sorry ass out of prison. That's why we were having such a hard time finding him. Those treatment places keep their records pretty confidential," Roy explained.

"Will he talk to you?" I asked.

"Already has. Told me that Johnson made the whole thing up. He didn't even know Eastman and Michaels had been sent away."

"I've got to see him. Can we go tomorrow morning? Before he gets out and leaves us hanging? I need a signed statement from him."

Roy and I agreed to meet early the next morning. I hung up the phone feeling more hopeful than I had in months. In reality, a signed statement from Waters could accomplish little. He was a named witness who had been at a known location, in prison, during the trial. Neither side had chosen to call him. Any testimony he could offer, even if he had not been a convicted felon, would not have been sufficient to overturn the conviction. But I knew that the signed statement would convince Rich that I was on to something and buy me more time to investigate.

The following morning, the trip to Ward's Island, located in northern Manhattan, was slow as I sat next to Roy and we inched our way uptown through rush-hour traffic. Gaining admittance to Odyssey House was even slower. The culture of rehabilitation centers is skeptical of lawyers. Understandably, drug counselors do not want people coming in, upsetting their patients, importing troubles from the outside world, setting the vulnerable up for relapse.

When Brad Waters walked into the room, I could tell he was working the system. Maybe he had a drug problem, but he was plainly at Odyssey House simply to avoid prison. His entire being broadcast contempt for the program.

Waters was incredibly young and thin in a small-boned way. I remembered my conversation with Pucci describing Eastman as a huge, tough guy. The man sitting before me looked as if I could break him in two. He also did not look like the type to risk death for the sake of another. Johnson's casting Waters as the white knight of his encounter with Eastman and Michaels struck me as pure romantic fiction.

I knew that Roy had built up some rapport with Waters, and I did not want to take the lead during the interview. When we sat down, Roy greeted Waters warmly.

"Hey man, how you doin' in here? You makin' out okay?" Roy asked, as Waters straddled a chair and sat down silently. "This here is Eastman's lawyer I was telling you about the other day. I want you to just tell her everything that you told me."

Waters was obviously uncomfortable with the prospect of telling me everything. It was one thing to talk about shit with a brother, but with a white girl around, you just did not go there. I had to figure out a way to break through his reserve.

"Brad, I understand that you don't know me, but the only reason I'm here is to help Eric Eastman. If you don't help, there's a good chance that he's going to spend the rest of his life in prison for something you told Roy never happened. I need your help," I pleaded, looking straight at him.

Waters looked at the linoleum floor as he started to tell me his story.

"It's like this—a bunch of corrections officers came at me the day after Johnson and me had been found in the cell together, and they told me Johnson was going around saying he'd been raped."

Waters looked up and met my eyes. I silently willed him to keep going, nodding my head understandingly.

"I was afraid they was going to blame me for it, so when the officers told me he was saying it was other guys, I just went along with it and agreed with everything they said. Later, Johnson came to me and was like, 'Yo, man. We can get rich if you got my back on this.' I was like, 'Fuck that shit, leave me out of it.' After that, I didn't speak about it, not to the DA, nobody. I just wanted to stay the fuck out of it," Waters explained.

"Okay. I understand. But you can't stay out of it anymore. Let's go over it again, from the beginning. What was going on in the cell when you and Johnson were in there?" I asked.

Big mistake. Waters looked up from the floor with eyes turned cold.

"Nothin'. We was just talking." He sounded like me in high school when my mother would come home and find me and a boyfriend "just talking" in my room with the door closed. Not wanting him to end our conversation, I changed the subject quickly.

"Okay. But you never saw my client attacking Johnson. You never saw him or Michaels threaten you or Johnson. You said you'd seen the attack so that you wouldn't be accused of it yourself. Is that totally accurate?"

"Yeah, you got it."

"And you would be willing to sign a sworn statement right now saying that's the truth?" I asked.

"I don't really want to get involved," Waters demurred.

"And Eric Eastman doesn't really want to spend twenty-three hours a day in lockdown for the next twenty years. We all got it tough here. You can help. You *have* to help," I snapped.

Waters looked at me, trying to figure out if there was anything in it for him.

"Can you help me with my case that I'm in here on?" he asked hopefully.

"No. I can only take on clients when the court assigns me to them. I'm sorry there's nothing in it for you, but I won't lie and say I'm going to help you when I'm not. That wouldn't do either one of us any good."

I refused to look away. We sat there in silence, with me staring at the top of Waters's head while he looked down, thinking. I expected him to feed me some line about how I didn't understand how it was on the inside and end our conversation.

But to my surprise, he looked up and said, "Okay, I'm in."

I wrote out the essential facts, he signed the bottom of the statement after swearing to its truth, and Roy notarized it. Roy could come back another day to get a more formal, typed version signed. But at least I was not going away empty-handed. I knew that once Waters was not being held against his will, I would have a hard time finding him. He was not exactly a motivated witness.

Roy and I returned to his car for the drive back to Lower Manhattan.

"I hope you don't mind, but I gave our boy some money to put on his books there," Roy said nonchalantly.

"What are you talking about?" I asked, frantic. "Are you telling me that you just bribed our witness? Is that what you're saying?"

"Jesus, calm down. It was ten bucks. I don't think anybody would consider that a bribe. The guy wanted to buy some smokes. I won't do it again," Roy muttered.

"I'm sorry. I didn't mean to snap at you. But in the future, please don't feed the animals. I have enough problems. The witnesses are all felons. Waters gave a statement to Corrections blaming Eastman for the attack the day after it occurred. This is not the stuff reversals are made of."

"Okay. I get it. It won't happen again," Roy promised.

When I got back to the office, I slapped the signed statement down on Rich's desk.

"I got it. You asked for it, and I got it," I practically shouted.

Rich eyed the statement. "Okay, so now what?"

"The note. I want to prove that Johnson wrote the note that Eastman told the court about at sentencing. The one in which Johnson said he was really in love with Brad. But I'm going to need money to hire a handwriting expert."

"See if you can convince one to do it cheap," Rich replied.

Money to hire experts—many of whom charge hundreds of dollars for a single hour of their time—is always limited. As a result, I spend more time haggling over fees than actually consulting experts. To find an expert in handwriting analysis, I went to the *New York Law Journal's* advertising section. There was one, Owen Peterson, listed in New Jersey. His office space was undoubtedly less expensive than that of the Manhattan experts.

I dialed the number and asked for Peterson. A few minutes later, a cigarette-roughened voice announced, "Owen Peterson here."

I introduced myself and explained the situation, how I needed to have a handwritten note examined to verify who had written it, but that I did not have a lot of funds available to pay for testing. Peterson didn't want to talk money, only handwriting. He was from a different time, when a man did not measure the value of his labor simply by the money he could earn from it.

"First things first. Do you have a known writing sample from the suspected author of the note?" he asked hopefully.

"Yes, I do. I have three pages of a handwritten statement the alleged victim gave to the Department of Corrections immediately after he reported the incident, and I know the note I want verified was written around that same time."

"That should do it," Peterson replied enthusiastically. "If you bring the documents out here to my office in New Jersey, I won't charge you anything unless I can come to a pretty definite conclusion for you. If you need a report, I'll charge you half our usual cost, the same as we charge the district attorneys who use us."

The following morning, I drove out to Peterson's office, which was conveniently located across the street from a famous New Jersey diner, recently made more famous by the discovery of the body of a mob boss in the trunk of a car left in its parking lot. When I walked into the small office, the first thing that struck me was the smell of cigarette smoke.

Peterson was there to greet me at the door, eager to see the documents. He looked like a character out of a pulp fiction novel: thick white hair greased back with hair gel, hard blue eyes, yellow-stained nails, smoldering cigarette in hand. And like any hard-boiled character, he did not flinch when I relayed the background of the Eastman case and what I was trying to prove.

"That's fascinating," he observed in his gravelly voice. "I'll call you as soon as I know anything."

The phone on my desk rang early the following morning. It was Peterson, anxious to tell me what he had discovered.

"Johnson definitely wrote the note. He has many distinctive handwriting characteristics shared by both the written statement he gave to the corrections officers and the note you provided. I can say with almost 100 percent certainty that he was the author of that note," Peterson explained.

"That's great news! Thanks for doing the examination so quickly. I'll let you know if I need a formal report."

"There's something else," Peterson said, his voice filled with excitement. "The note has indentations on it. Apparently, the paper was taken from a pad and so whatever Johnson wrote before he wrote this note, on the sheet of paper above the one used for the note, left its indentations on the note that you have. There's this test called an ESDA, or electrostatic detection apparatus, that can retrieve the indentations and tell you what Johnson was writing before he wrote your note."

"How much is that going to cost?" I asked.

"I'll do it for free. I sort of want to know what it will show myself," Peterson said. "Come by tomorrow and we'll go over the results."

I hung up thinking the gods of justice were finally smiling down upon me and Eric Eastman. Only a week before, I had been filled with despair. Now I had an expert doing tests for free because he wanted the answers himself.

I was back in New Jersey the next morning to review the results of the ESDA test. It had not retrieved all the indentations, but it did reveal that Johnson had written to Brad Waters to complain about the course of their romance before he had written to Eastman and blamed him for his romantic woes.

In his note to Waters, Johnson wrote, "Brad, I don't understand. First of all our business is not your homeboys. Since it's between us." The remainder of the words were too blurry to read.

Over the next several weeks, I would carry the ESDA results and review them every night on the train ride home. One night, as I was staring down at the faint words, willing them into clarity, the man sitting next to me asked what I was doing.

"You don't really want to know, believe me," I told him.

"It's just that you are looking so intensely, as if you are expecting to see the face of Christ or something on the page," he joked.

"I am sort of looking to be saved," I explained, and returned to examining the document. There was not much more to be gleaned from its blurred images.

# FOR LOVE OR MONEY?

Maybe it was my belief that some benign force was guiding my investigation that prevented me from questioning the ease with which my request to visit the cell block on Rikers had been granted. I wanted to see for myself if Johnson's story was even physically possible.

It struck me as odd that a prisoner would be allowed to keep his cell door propped open with a bucket, as Johnson had claimed Eastman was doing immediately before the attack. Prison gates are electronically monitored, and when they become jammed, it seemed to me, there should be some alarm that would sound somewhere.

The day after my April 23, 2001, thwarted attempt to view the cell block, I called Rhoda Levine at the Department of Corrections Legal Department. I explained who I was and how I had been instructed to call her about my request to view the scene.

"We already went to the scene," Levine told me.

"Why are lawyers from Corrections viewing the scene now, years after the criminal trial?" I asked.

"This has nothing to do with the criminal trial. Johnson has filed a multimillion-dollar lawsuit against the Department of Corrections and the City. The corporation counsel's office is taking the lead. You really want to speak to Rachel James. She's the lead attorney for the City."

My heart had started racing in my chest.

"When exactly did Johnson file the suit?"

"Hold on. I'll check my computer." I heard the sound of a keyboard clicking. "It says here January 31, 2000."

I calculated quickly. Johnson had filed just weeks after my client's sentencing, obviously intending to sue all along. So much for his having no reason to lie.

"Yeah, the criminal case is a problem for us. Johnson's using it to argue that he has proven beyond a reasonable doubt that the attack took place," Levine explained.

"I think I can help you with that. I've got some evidence you might be interested in," I offered.

"You'll have to speak with Rachel James; like I said, the City is taking the lead on this one."

Levine gave me James's number, which I immediately dialed. Her secretary told me she was out of the office, coincidentally taking David Johnson's deposition for the civil suit up at Sing Sing.

I gave the secretary my contact information and immediately dialed the superintendent's office at the prison.

"There's a deposition going on right now in a civil rights action. The complainant, David Johnson, is being deposed by an attorney named Rachel James. I need to speak with her immediately about the case," I told the receptionist, making no attempt to sound calm or collected, and she promised to relay the message.

Around lunchtime, James returned my call.

"This is Rachel James. I heard you've been trying to reach me? What's up?"

The voice was young and slightly brash, more Queens than Manhattan. There was also an open, upbeat quality to it, suggesting that James enjoyed her work.

"I'm representing Eric Eastman on his criminal appeal. I was told you're deposing David Johnson today and I've got some information you might want to ask him about," I explained.

I went through my conversations with Brad Waters, how Johnson had told him that they could both get rich if Waters would just back him up. I also told James about the note Johnson had written to my client describing his love for Brad and how I had been able to verify its authenticity. James was grateful for the information.

"This Johnson guy is such a piece of work. He lies as easily as you and I breathe. I'll focus more on his relationship with Waters and see if I can get him to lie some more about it on the record. Thanks for your help. I'll call you tomorrow and we can get together and share," James promised.

Hanging up the phone, after wishing James luck, I knew that my discovery of the lawsuit would be the turning point in the case. I later learned that our computer searches of the courts' data banks had turned up nothing because in the civil complaint Johnson had spelled his name Jonson. That one omitted letter, whether purposeful or not, had prevented us from discovering the suit.

The following week, Rachel James, Rhoda Levine, and I were sitting around the large dark wood veneer table in my office's conference room. Rachel James looked exactly as I had pictured her—highlighted blond hair, freckles, raspy voice, and eyes that seemed on the verge of laughter, even when she was speaking seriously. Rhoda Levine was older, darker, heavyset, more serious.

I had asked a more senior attorney from my office, Zach Murphy, to sit in on the meeting. Zach had been my sounding board throughout the Eastman case. He had a quiet, low-key but powerful intelligence that forced me to voice my ideas in a rational way, reigning in my tendency to spew hyperbole. I hoped his presence would prevent me from ranting throughout the meeting.

After thanking everybody for coming, I explained that my client insisted that nothing had ever happened to Johnson and that I believed my client. I handed out copies of the note that Johnson wrote to Eastman expressing his love for Brad Waters, a copy of the document examiner's report reflecting that Johnson was the true author of the note, and the signed, notarized statement from Waters saying the attack had never happened.

Rachel James did not have to review the documents to share my opinion that

Johnson was a liar. Having spent an entire day with Johnson the previous week questioning him at the deposition, she was already convinced his story about the alleged rape had been concocted.

"You would not believe Johnson," she declared. "He's your typical con man, totally convincing until you scrape the surface. Then when you catch him in a lie, he changes his story so fast he makes you feel like you're the one who got it wrong in the first place. We have plenty that's going to help you," she promised.

Rachel reached into her litigation bag and pulled out a stack of papers over a foot tall. It contained the civil complaint, which set forth that Johnson was seeking to recover $4 million from the City of New York for his alleged ordeal.

Glancing at the complaint, the prosecutor's trial summation—insisting that Johnson had no reason to lie about the rape—swam through my head: *He wasn't trying to scam the City, doesn't have a lawsuit filed. He's not one of those guys trying to make a dime on the citizens of New York.* Well, technically it was true that Johnson wasn't trying to make a dime. He was trying to make forty million of them.

I looked down at the name of the attorney who had filed the complaint, Joe Goldberg. I had never heard of him.

"What do we know about this Joe Goldberg guy?" I asked Rachel.

"Joe? Good guy. You should talk to him. Try to convince him that his client is a fucking liar. Maybe you can prevent him from throwing good money after bad."

"I assume he's working on contingency?"

"Yeah, if Johnson doesn't recover, Joe is out of luck, which would almost be too bad. That's how much I like Joe. Really, you should talk to him," Rachel prodded.

"Why would he speak to me?"

"Because he'll want to know what your client is going to say if he's called at the civil trial."

"He'll say Johnson is a fucking liar. What else could he say?"

"Joe will want to know your impression of Eastman. How he'll come off to a jury. Believe me, he'll want to talk to you," Rachel assured me.

"I'm willing to speak with anybody if there's a possibility it could help us clear up this mess."

As Rachel and I spoke, I skimmed the pile of papers she had given me.

Depositions of a number of corrections officers were there. All swore under oath that Johnson had not reported the attack that evening and that they had seen nothing unusual on their tours.

Wendy Ross, the female officer who Johnson claimed had seen him crying in his cell after the alleged attack, testified at her deposition that Johnson "made a joke about" being caught in his cell with Waters and then walked toward the pantry area to talk to another prisoner. When Ross followed him to see what Johnson was doing, Johnson said to her, "Ms. Ross. You so nosy. It's girl talk." Again Johnson laughed. Ross did not learn of the allegation of sexual abuse until days later, when she was asked by her supervisor to issue a report; she was certain that "nothing unusual" had occurred on the cell block that evening.

The reports of the other corrections officers—John Alder and Jason Bridges—all reflected the same thing. Nothing happened. Johnson never complained about the assault until the next morning.

Of course, these statements denying that anything had gone wrong on the watch of the individual corrections officers were all self-serving. They were facing a civil lawsuit in which their respective responses or lack thereof would be a central issue.

But there was another report from an entirely neutral party, an inmate named Patrick Simpson. I had never heard his name before, although I had reviewed all the inmate statements that had been turned over to the defense before my client's trial.

"Who's this Patrick Simpson guy?" I asked Rachel.

"Simpson? Oh yeah, he's great," Rachel practically snorted with amusement. "He reported the day after the alleged incident that Johnson had told him he was going to make up a sex scandal to get off the block."

I read Simpson's statement in its entirety:

David Johnson told Simpson at approximately 8:20 p.m., on the night of the alleged sexual assault, that Johnson was upset about him and his partner being found together inside a cell and was complaining about the other inmates on his block getting involved in his business and that inmate Johnson told Simpson that he [Johnson] was going to get a transfer for him and his partner by implicating several inmates in a sex scandal.

As far as I had come in the investigation, this latest revelation stunned me.

"How is it possible that Simpson reported that Johnson said he was going to manufacture the whole thing, and my client still gets prosecuted and sentenced to life in prison for this fiction?"

Rachel paused to access the proper response. Then she answered with brutal honesty.

"The truth is nobody gave a shit. From the City's perspective, Rikers is a self-cleaning oven. Just close the door and let the heat take care of the grime. Nobody really cares what goes on out there until there's money on the table. Then all of a sudden it matters," Rachel explained.

Her answer left me speechless. I was not about to launch into a tirade about how the crud and grime she was referring to were actually human beings. There was no point in getting up on a soap box. Rachel James did not have to sympathize with my client or feel the justness of my cause to help me win Eric Eastman's case. *The enemy of my enemy is my friend*, I reminded myself, as I laughed cavalierly at her remark.

But my forced laughter left a bad taste in my mouth. I was anxious for the meeting to end. I thanked my guests for their time, collected the piles of paper they had provided, and promised to keep them apprised of my investigation.

As soon as I got back to my desk, I dialed Joe Goldberg's number, which was listed at the bottom of Johnson's civil complaint. He answered his own phone.

After introducing myself and explaining whom I represented, I told Goldberg that I had just gotten out of a meeting with the City's lawyers.

"I can't say that I have any information that would be helpful to you. But I do have lots of stuff you want to be prepared for when they throw it at you," I explained, seeing no downside to playing both sides of the civil suit.

"Sounds intriguing," Goldberg responded.

By the time I left to catch my afternoon train, I had a 10:00 appointment to meet Goldberg the next morning. It was clear to me what I needed to get from him. The existence of the multimillion-dollar lawsuit that Johnson was obviously intending to file against the City gave him a strong motive to fabricate the attack.

The legal issue was whether the prosecutor knew about the looming suit when he made all those summation remarks urging Eastman's jury to accept

Johnson's account because Johnson was not the type of guy trying to scam the City out of a dime. If I could prove that the prosecutor knew of the potential suit, my motion to vacate would be strong. It would also be terribly embarrassing for the district attorney's office if I could show that the trial prosecutor had purposefully misled the jury into believing that Johnson had no financial motive to fabricate his claims.

I arrived early at Joe Goldberg's office the following morning and was surprised by the upscale neighborhood and tasteful decor. There were leather chairs, a decent view of the river, and a nicely dressed receptionist behind a solid, dark-cherry desk. I began to tell her that I was early and that I would wait, but before I finished my explanation, Joe Goldberg himself came out to greet me.

"No reason for you to wait, if you don't mind watching me drink my coffee," Goldberg said, extending his hand and taking mine with a less-than-firm grip. He was roughly my age, with thick brown hair combed neatly to the side, a style a seventh grader would be forced by his mother to wear on picture day at school. There was something slightly asymmetrical about his face, a lopsidedness to his grin.

Walking into his office, I was struck by its total emptiness. No diplomas adorned the walls. No family pictures cluttered the desk. As Goldberg sat down, I sensed that the emptiness was not merely his attempt to segregate his professional and personal lives. Rather, it was a symptom of a determination not to forge relationships close enough to encroach upon his professional life.

The office I shared with Zoe was so cluttered with our children's pictures and artwork that we had declared it our manifest destiny to annex an adjoining office to acquire more space for our stuff. Just that week, I had added a new piece to our collection, a paper flower Jessie had made in preschool. In the center of the flower, the teacher had written "My Mom Is" and Jessie had selected petals describing me. "Smart, Caring, Helpful, and Funny" were the adjectives Jessie chose. I hung the gift on the wall directly in front of my office chair and felt pride bloom in my chest whenever I looked up from my work. I wondered how Joe Goldberg weathered life's gale forces without a single paper flower on which to lean. But such questions were not the type I had come to explore with him.

"I hear you're a really decent person," I said, smiling. "Which is strange to hear from the adversary of a personal injury attorney. Sort of an oxymoron."

"I'll take that as a compliment, I think, especially coming from a criminal defense attorney," Goldberg smiled back as he regarded me.

There was something sad behind the smile, something that went deep. In my college days, that grin would have been a mystery I would have found hard to resist. I would have spent hours over coffee and alcohol tracing its source. But by the time I met Joe Goldberg, I was not free to explore such things. *Be careful,* I thought to myself.

Goldberg had no reason to want to help me. He was attempting to recover millions from the City and the Department of Corrections by alleging that those institutions had not adequately protected his client from mine.

I sat back in my chair, took my hands out of my lap, and rested them at my sides, attempting to broadcast that I was going to approach our interactions with total honesty. I tried not to rush the conversation, wanting to gauge the impact of my words.

"I understand we don't share the same interests here. I think your client is a liar, and you think my client is an animal. We'll probably never agree about that. But there's something that I would like to know from you that has nothing to do with whether your client is lying."

Goldberg listened carefully, his face betraying nothing.

"What I want to know is if you spoke to the prosecutor before the criminal trial at any time? If you can tell me that, it would help me a lot."

Joe Goldberg looked squarely at me and grinned again. "I don't see why I shouldn't tell you that. Yeah, I spoke to the prosecutor. The trial assistant actually called me when Dave failed to show up for a trial preparation meeting. It must have been a few days before the trial started."

Bull's-eye.

"Did he know who you were? Did you tell him that you were contemplating filing a lawsuit?" I asked hopefully.

Goldberg smiled again. "I don't know that I said that I was 'contemplating filing a lawsuit,' but Ron Rivera knew the deal. He knew I was Dave's civil attorney and that we were waiting for the outcome of the criminal trial to file the civil complaint," Goldberg explained, looking even more amused.

"Too bad Rivera forgot to mention those conversations to the defense, especially since failing to do so is reversible error," I said.

"I'm sure technically Rivera should have told the defense, but honestly I don't think it would have made a difference. You've never seen my client. He comes off as the most sincere person you could ever hope to meet. There's just no way he's lying about what happened to him," Goldberg said softly, with palpable sincerity. "There's no way somebody could make that stuff up or fake the emotional damage he's suffered from it."

"Did he come clean to you about his love affair with Brad Waters, his great savior during the attack? Did he give you all those dirty details? Because at the criminal trial, he swore under oath that there was nothing between them. And I have proof that your sincere client perjured himself on that front," I announced, a little more snidely than I had intended.

I handed Goldberg a copy of Johnson's notes and the forensic document report.

"Also you should know that Brad Waters now says the whole thing never happened and that your client told him he was going to make up the rape so that the two of them could get rich and live happily ever after," I continued.

Goldberg did not rattle easily. His face betrayed no surprise. His pleasant tone did not change a bit.

"Unfortunately for you, Waters gave a written statement backing Dave up immediately after the incident. Did you ever stop to think that your client's reach is long and that those on the inside might want to stay on his good side?" Goldberg countered.

"Well, it would have to be some reach. Long enough to touch inmates who gave written statements right after the incident saying your guy admitted he was going to make up a sex scandal."

I was trying to sound confident, but Goldberg's remarks had thrown me. If my client truly was a monster, capable of orchestrating a vicious attack on Johnson, maybe Waters was recanting his initial accusations out of fear. Maybe Waters had regarded my visits as a veiled threat. I pushed the thought out of my mind and focused on Goldberg.

"Why don't we just agree to disagree on this one," I said. "You're going to want to ask your client about those notes so he can come up with an explanation for them. And I'm going to need you to sign a statement saying you spoke to the prosecutor before the trial."

For the first time in our interactions Goldberg seemed tense. I could sense that he felt conflicted, that he wanted to do the right thing, to help me, but not my client. Goldberg didn't refuse my request outright.

"I'm going to have to think about that one. I don't think I should be signing anything that could lead to the reversal of your client's conviction. I'll sign something that says I spoke to you, and that because of my ongoing representation of David Johnson, I don't feel free to disclose the contents of our discussion in a sworn statement. I will *not* testify about our conversation, so you're going to have to call ADA Rivera himself to get that information on the record. That's about as far as I'm willing to go for you," Goldberg smiled that mournful, lopsided grin again.

"If that's all you can do, that's all you can do. A lot of attorneys would never have agreed to speak with me at all, so I guess I can agree that you really are a good guy, for an ambulance chaser, anyway."

"That coming from a hired gun. A lot of people would debate which one of us is lower on the food chain," Goldberg observed.

"I hate to disappoint you, but I'm assigned counsel. Unlike you, I do it for the luvvv, baby, not the money," I joked, trying to sound like Barry White.

"Well, I hope your client loves you. Not too many people would be trying to move this mountain for him," Goldberg said seriously.

"You'd have to ask Mr. Eastman about that. I don't think he's loving anything right now. He's pretty pissed."

"I bet," Goldberg replied, in a tone that reflected his intense dislike for Eric Eastman. It was the same tone I used when I talked about David Johnson.

I changed the subject to small talk, asking how long he had been in his office space and learned that he had been there for two years—long enough for even the busiest trial attorney to unpack some pictures. The emptiness was not the result of a recent relocation.

I did not shake Goldberg's hand when I left. There was something about the encounter that made handshaking seem out of place. Although I had only been in his office for an hour, I felt like we were old friends. The fraternity of the bottom-feeders.

As my investigation proceeded, whenever I learned something new and inter-esting, I would feel the urge to call Goldberg. Sometimes I would succumb and call to tell him about whatever I had discovered. I wanted to convince him that my client was innocent and his a liar, but I never did.

Even years later, long after I had closed the Eastman file, the urge to call Goldberg would arise, like a weird craving to smoke a cigarette or drink full-sugared instead of diet cola. I wanted to visit his office to see if there were any pictures on his desk. The few times I did reach out to him, Goldberg would be slow to return my calls; sometimes he wouldn't return them at all. I stopped trying after a while and allowed the unsolved mystery surrounding him to slip away.

# ROAD-TRIPPING

For weeks after meeting Goldberg, his comments about my client's reach bothered me. I knew that Goldberg had presented the argument that the prosecution would raise to discredit Waters's statement exonerating Eastman, along with any other statement given by the still-imprisoned witnesses. They were just trying to stay on the good side of a very bad guy, the prosecution would claim.

I had to determine for myself how strong an influence Eastman was exerting. The answer to that question meant visiting the man himself. *I wouldn't recommend your going to see him without a bodyguard.* Uninvited, the words spoken months earlier by Bruce Pucci, Eastman's trial attorney, rang in my head. Adding to my dread was the eight-hour distance between Manhattan and Southport Correctional Facility, the ultra-max prison where my client was being held, in Pine City, New York.

Charlie and I had planned to spend the Fourth of July weekend that year up in the Adirondacks with my in-laws at their lake house an hour outside of Albany. I figured I could go up with Jessie and Lila a couple of days early, drop them with their grandparents, and then make the additional five-hour journey to Southport. I had never left both girls for any length of time with my in-laws, but Lila was nineteen months old and Jessie was an unnaturally mature four-year-old. I figured the grandparents could handle the assignment for the day.

I packed the kids into the car on a Thursday and headed north. From the minute the car pulled out of the driveway, the trip was hellish. It was raining, hard, the water pounding the windshield, obscuring my visibility. I had never driven any distance alone with the two girls, and I felt tense and nervous, the precious weight of the cargo I was carrying weighing heavily on my shoulders. The girls picked up on my tension. Lila started crying about fifteen minutes after we left, when the Cheerios she had been eating fell to the car floor. She didn't stop for over three hours.

When we arrived at my in-laws' house, they had friends visiting from Manhattan. The skies had cleared. Four adults were sitting on the deck overlooking the lake, drinking chilled white wine. Classical music played softly in the background. Walking through the door, loaded down with a weekend's worth of children's paraphernalia, an exhausted toddler grasping my leg, I felt like a bedraggled refugee from another land.

The next morning, I was out the door by 7:00 a.m. After the trip up to the lake house the day before, the car's empty back seat felt like a blessing. I was learning that there were two ways to travel: easily or with children.

I pulled into a gas station and bought a full carton of cigarettes for twenty-two dollars, thinking that Eric Eastman would be able to trade the smokes for whatever he needed in prison. I had watched plenty of prison movies where cigarettes served as the currency of trade.

Any trip to visit an upstate prison presents a bracing mixture of freedom and confinement. Because New York State's prisons are located in such isolated areas, the trip up is inevitably marked by portions of open thruway where the sixty-five-mile-an-hour speed limit seems to be more a suggestion than the law. There are mountains and pastures, with red barns straight off the pages of a child's story book dotting the rolling hills. There are vistas, blue skies, cumulus clouds, ten different shades of green around every corner. There is singing at the top of your lungs to bad pop songs to stay awake and eating junk food while throwing the wrappers on the car floor. A road trip by any other name is still a road trip.

And then there is the arrival at the prison gate, which announces in certain terms that your freedom is about to come to an end. For the next few hours, you will submit to body searches, metal detectors, electronic gates, and invisible fluorescent stamps on your hands.

And you will wait. Wait for the guard to find the gate pass, to process you through, to determine that it is your underwire bra that is causing the metal detector to go crazy. Wait for the guards to produce your client, who will inevitably be stuck somewhere within the prison walls while an administrative count is being performed by officers who are in no hurry to record the tally.

While you wait, you will be surrounded by the gray of institutional furnishings and cinder blocks painted the light green color of Crest toothpaste, which some researcher must have determined long ago soothes the savage breast. You will watch the visitors come and go, the women in tight clothing carrying babies, pushing up against the prison regulations about appropriate visiting attire, the sad white-haired parents, the pastors out to save a few souls with scripture.

Only after waiting a good long time will you be allowed to see your client. The meeting itself usually lasts less than an hour. There is just not that much to talk about in the context of appellate representation. It is not as if trial strategy needs to be planned, witnesses uncovered, testimony prepared. That has already happened long before, the decisions frozen in the record, like prehistoric insects trapped in amber.

I did not know what to expect in July 2001 when I went to visit Southport Correctional, one of only a few super-maximum-security prisons in New York State. It is home to those prisoners deemed the most difficult in the system, those who need to be isolated from the general prison population at all times. The prisoners are locked inside their cells except for a single hour of outdoor recreation when they are allowed to go outside, one at a time, to an enclosed pen. While the conditions sound torturous, strangely, few of my clients have complained about spending time at Southport. Apart from the food, which they tell me is particularly awful even by prison standards, the solitary conditions are the focus of little griping.

Upon arriving in Pine City, I had difficulty locating the prison. I was expecting to come upon an imposing structure like Sing Sing, Auburn, or Eastern. Those older correctional facilities announce their purpose from miles away. They are made of stone quarried from the local countryside. Many were built by the prisoners themselves at a time when forced manual labor under arduous conditions was deemed a proper part of any prison sentence, no matter what the prisoner's crime. The older prisons groan with the history of their walls.

In contrast, Southport looked like a commercial office park, with unimpressive, low-lying buildings. But for some razor wire here and there, it could have passed for a Cosco storage facility.

After turning into the parking lot, I walked from my car, cigarette carton in hand, entered the empty visitors' reception center, and announced that I was an attorney from Manhattan who had come to visit a client. The guard looked at me from across the counter, focusing on the cigarettes.

"You can't bring those in here, Counselor. This is a nonsmoking facility. You'll have to return those to your car," he explained.

I glanced back toward the parking lot. It looked pretty far away—a long and uncomfortable walk in the July heat.

"Can't I just store them in the locker with my purse?" I asked.

"That would be against regulations. No contraband can be stored in visitor lockers at any time," the guard announced, sounding like a recorded message.

I returned to my car, threw the cigarettes into the back seat, and walked back to the processing center. The prison movies I had been watching apparently were out of date.

When I walked through the metal detector, it beeped angrily even after I had emptied my pockets of change, removed all my jewelry and my shoes. "It's my bra," I explained apologetically.

"You'll have to take it off," the guard said in the same tone he had used to tell me to get rid of the cigarettes.

"You've got to be kidding me—I'm an attorney. I've been to prisons all over the state. I have never been asked to remove my bra before," I protested.

"Have you ever been to Southport before, counselor?" the guard asked. "Our security classification forbids your carrying any metal on your body into our facility," he said, using the same monotone.

I went into the ladies' room, took off my bra, stuffed it into my pocketbook, and returned to the guard's station. "Can I store the bra in the locker, or is that considered contraband too?" I asked, pushing out my unrestrained breasts as far as I could before stepping through the metal detector again. The guard was legitimately unimpressed with my display.

"No, the bra can go in the locker. That doesn't qualify as contraband," he explained.

I entered the first locked gate and was escorted down a fluorescent-lighted hallway, painted bright white, into a large glass room. Southport had a gleaming new gloss throughout that made it feel all the more oppressive. I missed the gray and toothpaste tones to which I had grown accustomed.

Within minutes of sitting down, I heard a number of people out in the hallway. I turned to see the door open. There were three corrections officers escorting a large African American man into the room. I could not see my client clearly because he was surrounded by the guards. But when they set him down in the chair positioned across the table from where I was seated, the first thing I noticed was that he was shackled from head to toe. Eric Eastman sat before me in handcuffs, which clipped to a restraining belt around his waist. His legs were also shackled.

I looked at the guards, who were making no efforts to leave.

"This is a legal visit," I announced, summoning a tone of authority. "I am this man's attorney. I've driven nine hours to visit him and I have no intention of conducting this visit under conditions that will compromise the attorney-client privilege."

The guards got up to leave. Before doing so, they shackled Eric Eastman to a metal ring protruding from the bolted-down table.

"I need his hands uncuffed," I announced to the backs of the retreating officers.

"No way," the most senior one responded. "He stays cuffed."

"No way," I said right back. "I need him to review a pile of legal documents, and he can't do it with his hands cuffed. If I have to speak to the warden or put in a call to Legal in Albany, I'll do it. But there is no way I'm speaking with my client bolted to the table by both his hands and his feet. I'm willing to compromise on the feet because I don't plan on dancing, but I need his hands free," I insisted.

The senior guard looked uncertain. Time to try a different tack.

"Officer, can you please uncuff him? Please? I'll take full responsibility for my own safety and for Mr. Eastman's behavior. You have my word that this visit will be conducted entirely professionally. There will be nothing but appropriate behavior from me and Mr. Eastman, I promise you that." My voice brimmed with sincerity.

To my great surprise, the guard came over and freed my client's hands. Eric Eastman would later tell me that nothing I did for him, not all the miles I logged during the investigation nor all the hours of research and writing, meant as much to him as my simple insistence that his hands be uncuffed during our visit. To him, it meant that I trusted him. Nobody had trusted him in quite a while.

When the guards left the room, I fully looked at my client for the first time. He did not appear threatening to me. He did not even seem that large, and Eric Eastman looked older than his forty-six years. His grizzled hair was too long, as were his fingernails. His dark black skin had an unhealthy ashen quality to it, as I guess anybody's would if forced to spend almost every moment inside. And his eyes were unnaturally bloodshot. He seemed like a deep-sea diver raised too quickly to the surface who was suffering the ill effects of too much oxygen coursing through his system.

I spent the next two hours reviewing with my client every statement and legal form that I had uncovered. I showed Eastman the statement I had gotten from Waters denying that he had seen any attack on Johnson, the complaint Johnson had filed seeking to recover millions of dollars, Goldberg's statement that he had spoken to the trial prosecutor before the trial began, the depositions of the corrections officers reflecting that nothing unusual had happened on their respective watches, the forensic document reports relating to the analysis of Johnson's note, and Patrick Simpson's original statement reflecting Johnson's announcement of his intent to fabricate the sex scandal. As I went over the materials, I could see the relief washing over Eric Eastman's entire being.

"I sort of remember that Simpson guy," Eastman recalled. "He and Johnson were always talking through the gates."

I asked my client to draw the layout of the cell block, since I was pretty sure I would never get inside to see it myself. I wanted to know if the gates through which Eastman had regularly seen Johnson and Simpson speaking were the same ones the corrections officer Wendy Ross had described in her deposition when she testified about seeing Johnson speaking with another prisoner after being found in his cell with Brad Waters on the night of the incident. "*Ms. Ross. You so nosy. It's girl talk,*" Ross had recalled Johnson joking at the time. Johnson must have been talking to Simpson.

"Did you know Pat Simpson?" I asked casually, as Eastman sketched, trying to get a sense of my client's reach.

"Not really. He was on the other side of the cell block. Johnson knew him from before he got transferred to C-74. Have you found Simpson yet?"

"That's the next thing on my to-do list. I have my investigator looking for him now. So far we haven't found him. But I have faith we will. It's just a matter of time," I explained.

"And then what?" Eastman asked, his face tense, but his fatigue still obvious.

I outlined my plans to weave all the new information together to argue that he had been denied due process by the prosecution's failure to disclose some of the information, and that the rest of it qualified as newly discovered evidence, entitling him to a new trial. I predicted that once I found Simpson, I could draft a strong motion in a few weeks and then file it back in the trial court, asking for the judgment to be vacated. Such motions, alleging new facts that are not part of the appellate record because they were previously unknown, need to be filed before the judge who presided over the trial.

Throughout my explanation, I tried to balance optimism against the always-present danger of instilling false hope. Eastman did not look very hopeful when I stopped talking.

"The truth is that if the system really worked, I never would have been convicted based on nothing but lies. If the system can be so wrong, what makes you think it'll get it right this time around?"

"I can't promise it will. All I can promise is that I'll work as hard as I can to see that it does. I'll fight it as long and as hard as I have to. If you can't have faith in the system, try to just have faith in me, okay?" I looked into his red eyes.

"You're the only thing that's kept me going all these months. I truly believe you were sent as some sort of angel from heaven."

"I'm too much of a pain in the ass to be an angel," I said, trying to lighten the moment. The intensity of Eastman's admiration was making me uncomfortable. I was already craving the trip home; a visceral longing for Charlie and the girls, the bad pop songs, and junk food filled my entire body.

I told my client that I needed to go. But before I left, I held his eyes and made him promise me not to contact anybody connected to the case, explaining that it would only cause problems down the road.

"I won't do anything to cause any problems. I promise you that," Eastman said solemnly, looking me straight in the eyes.

"Okay then, I'll be in touch. You hang in." I banged loudly on the door, signaling to the guards the end of the meeting.

"You be careful," Eastman said. "I worry about you going to visit all these fools."

I didn't even bother to put my bra back on before I left Southport. Back in the car, I broke open the carton of cigarettes and smoked them one by one for the next five hours. I hadn't smoked since law school, and by the time I got back to the lake house, I felt wired and nauseated. The girls had been asleep for hours when I pulled up into the long winding driveway, its gravel crunching loudly. I took the carton of cigarettes down to the water and sat near the dock. Looking up at the sky with tears streaming down my face, I smoked yet another cigarette.

"Please, please, let this one come out right. I won't ask for another one if you just give me this one," I prayed, attempting to broker a binding bargain with the fickle gods of justice. Apart from my whispered pleas, the only sound was the lake water lapping against the shore, broken by the occasional croak of a yearning bullfrog. I crushed the cigarette on a rock, took it back inside the house, and snuck upstairs to get rid of it.

I was showered and fresh, no trace of cigarette smoke on me, before the girls awoke early the following morning. I banished Eric Eastman from my mind and concentrated hard on splashing and canoeing, feasting on the lake's natural beauty, the sound of the girls' laughter, the meals we cooked outside, the simple pleasures of freedom that most people take for granted every day of their lives.

# ANSWERING THE HARD QUESTIONS

We returned home to tragedy, arriving late at night to discover that our air-conditioning had broken while we were away. The weathered bricks of our old house had trapped all the summer's heat inside. It felt as if we were walking into a tandoor. Jessie's pet frog, Froggy (ours is not a home of creative pet naming), had succumbed and was floating belly up in his small tank.

The girls, who had fallen asleep in the car, were transferred smoothly to their beds by Charlie. I immediately picked up the phone and dialed my parents' number looking for my father. Throughout my life, no tragedy has been too large or small for me to seek his advice. I pick up the phone and call him without thinking.

When my father answered the phone, I told him about the frog and solicited his guidance about breaking the news to Jessie.

"You've got a couple of options," he advised. "You can sneak out tomorrow morning, get a new frog, and flush the old one. Hope that Jessie won't notice."

"I'm pretty sure she would. It's hard to sneak that stuff by Jessie."

"When your pet frogs died, I used to preserve them in formaldehyde, remember?"

Visions of mason jars stored on the basement shelves of my childhood home, filled with floating horned toads, lizards, and frogs, flashed before me: my father's solution to the problem of mortality.

"Yeah, Dad, I remember. Only now do I appreciate how weird you were, how truly warped my childhood."

My father laughed until he coughed. He laughs like nobody else, with his entire being. The more snide my remarks, the harder he laughs.

"I think we'll give Froggy a good Christian burial behind the garage. You want to come out and give the eulogy?" I asked.

"We're going to the ballet tomorrow, otherwise I would," he demurred. "Let me know how Jessie takes it. I'll call you tomorrow night."

Hanging up the phone, I felt better, as I always do after speaking with my father. I might not always take his advice, but I always feel better for hearing it.

When Jessie woke up the following morning, her hair wild with rumpled curls and face flushed from the still-overheated house, I told her about the loss, explaining that Froggy was no longer "with us." I informed her of the impending funeral rites. She accepted my explanation unblinkingly.

"But where did Froggy go? Why can't we just keep him in his bowl?"

"Well, honey, if we did that, Froggy would start to smell bad, and he wouldn't look like himself after a while," I explained.

"But what will happen to him after we bury him?"

Detailing further the process of decomposition didn't feel like the appropriate option. So I decided to sugarcoat it.

"He'll go to a place where frogs go after they die. A nice place where they have everything they need, food and fresh water and other frogs to play with," I said, as seriously as I could manage.

Jessie wasn't one to buy into sugarcoating.

"How do you know? That sounds like something people make up to make themselves feel better," she said seriously, thinking out loud.

I was stunned into silence by my four-year-old's skepticism. My father's granddaughter. After a moment, I tried again.

"Well, actually I don't know for sure. I was never a frog as far as I know, and I've never died. People believe different things about what happens when things die," I said.

"What do you believe, Mommy?" Jessie asked, her tone suggesting that she would believe it, too.

"I believe that after people or animals die, they live on through the people that remember them and the good things they did during their lives. Froggy was a great pet, and we'll always remember him fondly and think about him, so he'll stay with us forever that way."

I was explaining the Jewish concept of remembrance—remembrance of a frog, whom I had been too lazy to name and whom I fervently wished had not died, because I would have preferred to focus my full attention on finding an air-conditioning repairman over the Fourth of July weekend.

Jessie considered my explanation, her eyes focused on my face, gauging whether I was being honest about my beliefs.

"That makes sense. Can I dig the hole myself to bury him?" she asked.

"Of course you can. That would be a mitzvah, a good deed," I replied.

We held the funeral behind the garage, with Jessie digging the grave. She never cried over the loss. The concept of death's permanence does not immediately resonate with children. But Jessie was quieter than usual for the rest of the weekend, and she asked me to stay with her when she went to sleep. In her white poster bed with her pink and purple princess sheets, she pressed her face against my neck and looped her leg over mine so that I could not easily extricate myself. I knew that on some level my oldest daughter now understood that if frogs could die, then so could mommies. I didn't have an easy answer to that one either.

..................................

Upon my return to the office, there was a message on my answering machine from Roy Swain, saying that he had found Pat Simpson, the inmate who had reported Johnson's plans to concoct a sex scandal. Simpson had been rearrested and was awaiting trial on new charges out on Rikers.

I called Roy back to plan yet another trip out to the Island.

"I guess they all come home eventually," I joked. "When can we go?"

An hour later, we were inching our way once more through security. The smells were particularly strong in the July heat.

"Ahhh. Rikers in the summer, just smell that air. Who needs the Hamptons?" I said to Roy.

"No place I'd rather be," he responded merrily.

By the time we got back into the public visiting area of Pat Simpson's housing unit, it was early in the afternoon, the hottest part of the day. I could actually see the heat bouncing off the water. I was sweating beneath my blouse. Roy wasn't looking too crisp either.

But Pat Simpson sauntered in looking fresh as a daisy. His light brown skin had a matte finish, as if it had been recently dusted with powder. His hair was neat and closely cropped. There was a peacefulness that hung around him.

I introduced myself and told him why I wanted to speak with him. I asked if anybody had contacted him yet about the Johnson case and showed him a copy of the statement he had given immediately after the alleged incident.

"No ma'am. I haven't spoken about that night since I told them about what Davie was gonna do," Simpson explained.

"Can you tell me about the whole thing from the beginning, starting with your relationship with Johnson? How did you know him? Did you have anything against him?"

"Oh no ma'am, not at all. Me and Davie was close. He's gay like me, and it's none too easy being gay out here. So we all tend to stick together, watch each other's backs. Sometimes, it felt like Davie was the only person who I could talk to about my problems. Even though we weren't on the same block, we could talk near the pantry area, through the gates," Simpson explained.

I remembered that Corrections Officer Wendy Ross had testified during her deposition that Johnson had been speaking through the gates in the pantry area to another inmate after being found in his cell with Waters. Johnson must have been speaking to Simpson, I figured.

"Tell me what happened that led you to give this," I said, pointing again to the statement Simpson had given immediately after Johnson first made his allegations.

"Well, that night Davie was really upset. He was angry because other inmates were constantly getting into his business. That's what he said, anyway. Then he says that he's going to make up a sex scandal to get him and his boyfriend out of there, transferred off the block. He didn't tell me his boyfriend's name," Simpson continued.

Simpson might not have known the identity of Johnson's lover, but of course I did. It was Brad Waters, the first witness I had interviewed months earlier.

"So why did you rat out Johnson? What was in it for you?" I asked too sharply, always skeptical of people's motives.

A hurt look passed briefly over Simpson's face. But his voice remained soft and kind.

"There was nothing in it for me. I just thought that what Davie was doing was horrible. We really do get attacked a lot out here, beaten, abused. For him to be making up stories, crying wolf for no reason, I just thought that was wrong. I told the officers because it was the right thing to do," Simpson explained.

Looking at Simpson, I knew that he was a rare find indeed—an honest man. Hard to find under any circumstances, I never expected to discover one out on Rikers Island. Simpson was a disinterested witness who had never changed his story and had no motive to lie. I had found the key to Eric Eastman's prison cell.

"Will you sign a statement reflecting what we have discussed here?" I asked, and held my breath for his response.

"Yes, ma'am, of course I will," Simpson agreed without hesitation.

· · · · · · · · · · · · · · · · · · · · · · · · · · · · · ·

From that point on, I imagined that the case would be easy. I drafted a motion setting forth all that I had discovered, arguing that Eastman's conviction should be reversed on newly discovered evidence grounds and because of the prosecution's suppression of Simpson's statements and their knowledge of the civil lawsuit. The compiled exhibits accompanying the motion formed a stack of papers almost two feet tall: depositions, statements from all the prisoners who had been present near Eastman's cell at the time of the alleged attack, the civil complaint, the forensic document report authenticating Johnson's note declaring his love for Brad Waters, and the results of the ESDA test, all bound together to tell the tale of Eric Eastman's innocence.

When I was getting ready to file it, I heard from the attorney representing Brian Michaels, my client's co-defendant at trial. I returned from picking up lunch to find a message waiting on my answering machine.

"Hey, my name is Nick Robleski, and I've just been assigned to handle the appeal of a guy, Brian Michaels, who tells me that you have Eric Eastman and are way ahead of me. Give me a call. Thanks."

I did not know Nick back then, didn't know if he was the type of attorney who would insist on reinventing the wheel so that he could impress his client with how hard he was working. My main concern was that he might slow down the progress of my client's case. Usually in cases involving co-defendants, courts prefer to consider both sets of motions at the same time. I called Nick back immediately. When he asked me what was going on with the case, the task of recounting all I had learned seemed impossible.

"From my perspective what's going on is that you're way behind here. I've been investigating this case for months. I've spoken to everybody who needs to be spoken to. I'm going to send you everything. My motion, my exhibits, my legal memorandum. And then you're going to do nothing but say 'me too.' How's that sound?"

To my relief, Nick laughed. "That sounds great to me. Send me what you have and I'll see if there's anything more I think I need to do for my client."

"You'll have it by tomorrow," I promised. "But I'm filing next week, with or without you."

I heard back from Nick the next afternoon.

"Holy shit! I've never seen anything like this, never. And I've been practicing a long time. Longer than you. This stuff is incredible. I don't know how you got it all," Nick said, clearly amazed.

"It's been a long slog. We've gotten some incredible breaks. Are you going to join?" I asked.

"Yeah, I'm going to join. If that's okay with you?" he said.

"It's fine. All I care about is getting the case heard."

"Have you thought about just giving it to the DA and seeing if they'd agree to just concede?" Nick asked.

"What are the chances of that?" I responded, all world-weary cynicism. It was the Eastman case that would lead to my adopting my present approach of always giving the prosecution a chance to make things right voluntarily.

"Not good usually. But like I said, I've never seen anything like this. It might be worth a try," Nick offered.

I promised to think about his suggestion and let Nick know what we decided. After I hung up, I went into Rich's office to tell him about Nick's reaction to the motion.

"I have a pretty good friend over at the Bronx DA's office, he's pretty high up. I can give it to him," Rich offered.

"Yeah. Let's give it a try. But we can't hold off filing forever. There are limits, remember?"

Rich laughed. "Yeah, limits, I understand, limits," he said, echoing my promise from months earlier when I had refused to file the appellate brief until I had spoken with Brad Waters.

We sent off a copy of the motion to the Bronx district attorney's office in August 2001. A week later, we heard back. They agreed to reopen their investigation of the case. It was a good sign, but I was concerned it might just be a delaying tactic.

"Remember to tell them we won't hold off forever," I told Rich.

"You can talk to the prosecutor assigned to the case yourself. His name is Douglas Stern. Here's his direct line." Rich ripped off a piece of paper from his pad on which he had written Stern's number.

I spoke to Stern later that afternoon. After giving him the contact information I had for each witness, I agreed to wait until the end of September to file the motion. A month was plenty of time, we agreed, for the prosecution to figure out whether they would voluntarily vacate the conviction on the grounds I had alleged.

Then September 11 happened. Our carefully negotiated time schedule crumbled to dust. For months after the attacks, I felt afraid. Afraid of going out. Afraid of the sound of planes flying over my house. Afraid of thunder and loud noises. A few weeks after the attacks, I was walking on the Upper West Side one day when a car backfired and I found myself flat on the ground, my face pressed against the sidewalk's pavement, not quite understanding how I had gotten there.

I wrote to Eric Eastman to tell him that I had survived. It was not until weeks later that I received a bundle of frantic letters, written in all capital letters, each one beginning "WHERE ARE YOU? ARE YOU ALIVE? I'VE BEEN PRAYING FOR YOUR SAFETY SINCE I HEARD THE NEWS."

Around that same time, I started lighting candles on Friday nights and celebrating Shabbat. In all my life, I had never done that; praying in the home would have been more than my father could bear.

But in the days following September 11, I reached for any talisman I could to help me manage my fears. Charlie arrived home one Friday night after work to find the table set with a white linen tablecloth, candles waiting to be lit in their brass holders, fresh-baked challah in the center of the table with a bottle of wine sitting next to it.

Although Charlie looked surprised, he did not say anything. Silently he put his arms around me, while trying to figure out if he had somehow walked into the wrong house. I was all business.

"We're celebrating Shabbat. Go get changed. We'll be starting in ten minutes," I announced.

"Okay," Charlie responded unquestioningly, avoiding eye contact with me, as he'd do with any obviously insane person. I think if I had told him I needed to start handling venomous snakes or to be baptized in the Delaware River, his response would have been the same.

But by November 2001, it felt as if we'd always been "doing Shabbat"—the term Jessie coined for our observance. By then my office had temporarily reconstituted itself in rented space in Chelsea. There weren't enough desks for all the attorneys, so we took turns going into the Chelsea office. I was happy not to go in. I signed up for an art course with Lila and spent a lot of my mornings making collages with lima beans. It was Mommy and Me and art therapy for post-traumatic-stress sufferers all rolled into one. I would arrange my lima beans into calming circular patterns. It seemed as useful an activity as any at the time.

One morning toward the end of November, when I was actually in the Chelsea office, Douglas Stern called to say that he was almost ready to voluntarily vacate Eric Eastman's conviction. But he wanted to speak with my client first. I knew that Stern wanted a chance to size up Eastman for himself, just as I had, to get a sense of his reach, to determine if he had pressured any of the witnesses.

But I was hesitant to allow Stern to speak with my client, even with me there. I was afraid that Eastman would be angry and difficult. I had no concerns that he would tell Stern anything that could substantively hurt his case. His story had never changed, not from his first letter to my office.

I went to speak with Zach Murphy about the prosecution's offer.

"What do we have to lose?" he asked.

"I'm just worried my client will come off badly. He's a smart guy, but I think he has an emotional side," I said.

"If we don't agree, they'll think we're hiding something, and then we might have to fight this thing for years," Zach observed.

In the end, we agreed to the interview as long as I could be present. Zach and I went up to the Bronx. The two of us gathered around a circular table with prosecutor Stern and my client. One side of the small room was mirrored. I figured there were other prosecutors or investigators outside, watching and listening.

To my surprise, it started out very well. Stern was respectful to my client, and Eric Eastman responded in kind.

Then Stern started to ask about the deal Eastman had arranged with Johnson to smuggle drugs onto Rikers, and the role Eastman's wife had agreed to play in the scheme. Suddenly the atmosphere in the room changed, the air tightened.

I had never discussed Eastman's wife with him. She never contacted me, and he never asked me to contact her; I assumed they had become estranged, not an uncommon occurrence when a spouse is hit with a life term. I never probed the issue.

When Stern asked about his wife, my client turned to stone. He just stopped talking, put his head in his hands, and refused to continue with the interview. I felt panic welling up inside me.

"I need a moment alone with my client," I told Stern. He agreed and left the room. Zach remained but got up from the table to stretch his legs.

I pulled my chair over to Eric Eastman and put my hand on his knee. I sat there in silence for a minute, just breathing. Then I started to speak, using the same calm tone I would use years later when Jessie needed to get her severed fingertip repaired.

"Listen to me. I know this is hard. You're doing great. You and I have run a marathon together, and I see the finish line. It's right there. I can see it. But you have to help me. You have to keep it together."

Eastman looked up at me with those too-red eyes. "It's just that I've lost everything because of this case. Everything. And I can't get it back. Not the time, not my wife, none of it," he explained.

"It's all right," I continued in the same tone I used to hush Lila when she was crying. "But now's not the time to think about that. Now's the time to look for that finish line. To stay steady. To breathe deeply and know that there is an end to this one. We can talk about the other stuff later. But now it's time to work, okay? Can you do that for me?"

Eastman looked into my face. "Yeah, I can do that," he agreed.

"Okay then, I'm gonna call Stern back in here and we're going to finish this strong. Let's keep going."

And Eric Eastman did. He answered every question the prosecutor threw at him without flinching.

A week later, I was in the office in Chelsea when I received a phone call from Stern. "We're going to voluntarily vacate your client's conviction," he said.

"Okay" was all I could manage to say before hanging up the phone and screaming as loudly as I could.

Almost two years to the day after Eric Eastman had been originally sentenced in December 1999, we were back in court as Judge Davis accepted the prosecution's concession without any apology or emotion.

I hugged Eastman in the pens afterward. He was not free to walk out the door. He had been out on Rikers awaiting trial on a low-level robbery charge when Johnson had accused him of the rape. After receiving his life sentence in the Johnson case, he had pleaded guilty to the robbery. He still had a couple of years to go until he could get out. I knew that we would keep in touch.

"You behave yourself," I told him before leaving the pens.

"I will. I won't disappoint you, I promise," he said. "You saved my life."

Walking back to the subway, I had never felt so good about my work. I had saved two men from spending years in prison for something I knew had never happened.

Judaism teaches that if you save one life, it is as if you have saved the world, and that's how I felt as I walked down the hill from the Bronx courthouse to the subway, past the storefronts with their throngs of people busy buying sneakers and fast food. A tremendous sense of relief and gratitude came over me.

"Thank you," I whispered, to nobody in particular.

On Friday nights, I still gather my children around the dinner table to celebrate Shabbat. We light the candles, say the prayers, and in that way I am assured that we eat at least one dinner together during the week.

Lila is presently in a stage where she likes to complain about having to pray on Fridays. I explain that when she gets older and has a family of her own, she will not have to celebrate Shabbat. But as long as she lives with me, she will have to wait a bit to eat one night a week. Jessie, who is now in Hebrew school, can recite the prayers herself and knows their meanings. Maya, still too young to know the words, hums along merrily.

I do not teach my children that God does not exist, as I was taught by my father. I do not pretend to know the answer to that question. I do know that there are times when I need to believe in something, when I cannot accept that the universe is completely random. If others view that as a sign of intellectual weakness, so be it.

But I must admit there are also days when belief in anything seems foolish, akin to a child's hope that the monsters beneath the bed can be banished with the proper nightlight and stuffed animals. I accept that there will always be cases that test my faith in the system to which I devote my professional existence. There will be times that test my faith in my daughters' respective abilities to make wise decisions—just as my poor in-laws still wonder how their brilliant, sensible son chose such an odd wife, a woman who would rather consort with murderers and rapists than devote herself completely to raising their beautiful grandchildren. And when those challenges present themselves—when I find myself in those foxholes of my future—I will sit quietly in the dark and pray, to the gods of justice or the God of my grandfather. You never know who might be willing to help.

# part 4

# Dust

When my second daughter, Lila, turned ten months old, she started to walk. I, of course, was at work when she took her first steps, as I had been when Jessie took hers. Marie, our incredible nanny, was thoughtful enough to videotape both girls for me so that I could at least watch the instant replay of their milestones when I arrived home. I was luckier with my youngest. Maya took her first steps on a Friday, my regular day off.

Lila was not simply an early walker. Once she was up, she refused to slow down. Unlike my oldest daughter, Jessie, who has always been a cautious person, Lila is physical in a way that makes her a danger to herself and others. She will flip down the staircase or off the couch onto where the dog is sleeping, somehow slipping a foot into Charlie's groin on the way down. I will hear a loud crash, followed by Lila's breathless "I'm okay!" or her crying. Thankfully, more often it's the former. She has started to say "I'm okay" before she lands, knowing that I am waiting to hear it. I ignore the dog's whimpering and Charlie's grunts, taking for granted that they'll recover.

Once when she was eighteen months old, I turned around from the pasta I was boiling to see Lila standing on the kitchen table, literally swinging from the low-hanging, faux-antique chandelier we had chosen to illuminate our meals. I caught her as she flew over the tabletop.

When Charlie came home that night, I announced that we had to get the basement finished, preferably with padded walls, so that I would have a safe place to store Lila while I cooked dinner. He accepted the decree with surprisingly little fight, considering the enormity of the renovation job. Our house was built circa 1930, and during the seventy-plus years of its existence, the basement had remained in its original state, like some sealed Egyptian crypt. When we moved in, we had hired somebody to remove the asbestos lining the ancient heating pipes, and that was it.

In its day, the basement must have been quite a swinging watering hole. Dark oak paneled the walls. In one corner there was a wet bar with mirrors behind the wine racks, and in another an art deco–style bathroom with green and black tiles. The floor bore a snazzy checkerboard pattern formed with more interesting tiles, which we were later to learn also contained asbestos. Each of the basement's several rooms was guarded by a thick wooden door with elaborate, decorative stained glass windows.

But by the time we moved into the house, the basement was simply scary. There was some weird stuff hanging down from the ceiling, which I imagined was more asbestos, just in case we hadn't developed mesothelioma from the pipe insulation or the floor tiles. The walls' oak paneling was warped and moldy. The snazzy floor had started to chip and crumble. I was actually surprised when the town issued a certificate of occupancy for our house without compelling us to either fix up or board up the basement.

I never allowed the girls to go downstairs for any reason, and I tried to limit my own time down there as much as possible. But it was not only Lila's swinging from the chandelier that made me crave a finished basement.

The girls' toys had started to encroach on every room. Barbie playhouses, stuffed animals, plastic tricycles, and bouncy seats were strewn throughout the dining and living rooms. As I would pick them up and pile them into our small family room, only to find that they had somehow multiplied and returned to the living room moments later, I dreamed of banishing the plastic to the basement, putting a full flight of stairs between the land of the children and that of the adults, between chaos and order. I was finding the lure of a living room without Cabbage Patch dolls too great to resist.

Charlie and I agreed that he would take on the basement renovation project, even though our marriage had barely survived our first phase of home remodeling a few years earlier. From that first renovation, after much fighting and marriage counseling, I had learned that any large home improvement project cannot have two people fully invested in it. Somebody must take primary responsibility, while the other exercises a carefully circumscribed veto power. At such challenging times, clearly defined spheres of influence are necessary to prevent your marriage from dissolving amidst endless battles over marble versus tile countertops. With two small children, I was not about to risk that scenario again.

And so I did not complain when Charlie hired Russ LNU (Last Name Unknown, as the police say) to renovate the entire basement on his own for some undisclosed (to me anyway) sum of cash. But from the moment Russ walked in the door, I didn't like him.

Anybody who has attempted to renovate an old home on the cheap knows that contractors can be a dysfunctional lot. During the first phase of our home renovation, I had planned to host my father's sixty-fifth birthday based on the assurance of Tony, the painting contractor, that the job would be completed by September. The party was scheduled for the end of October, so I figured the house would be painted by then. But by the end of September, Tony had not shown up in two weeks and my dining room furniture remained piled high in my foyer, like some warped postmodern sculpture commemorating an ugly battle of a long-ago lost war.

When I called to complain and reminded Tony that he had promised to have the job done by the end of September, and that I was planning on hosting thirty people based on that promise, he explained that I was not paying him enough to have him forgo his outside painting jobs, which the unexpectedly nice fall weather had allowed him to take on. No matter how much I screamed and threatened, Tony remained unmoved. Finally, toward the middle of October, I asked our kitchen contractor, Scott, to call Tony and try to reason with him, thinking maybe there was some secret contractor language I didn't speak fluently. Scott conveyed to me that Tony had shown little interest in completing my painting job, but he had asked Scott to join his wife-swapping club.

At the end of October 1998, I hosted my father's birthday, in my still-unpainted house. I had relatives bring up crabs from Maryland, and we didn't have to worry about messing up the pristine paint job as we cracked them on rented tables and toasted my dad with beer instead of champagne. It was a great party. Tony never did finish the job. I had to cancel the last check and hire another, more expensive painter.

So maybe it was a holdover from my experiences with Tony that initially left me negatively disposed toward Russ. But as the summer progressed and the basement project lagged, Russ definitely made his own personal contributions to my dark feelings.

He had this habit of not closing the door entirely when he would come upstairs to use the bathroom located right off our kitchen. He pissed louder than any man I had ever heard. Probably, I surmised from his ruddy complexion and late arrival time, because he was out doing some very hard drinking most every night.

The loud pissing seemed like both an invitation and a challenge. As if Russ were simultaneously asking, "You want some of this?" and, if not, "What are you going to do about it?" I had recently helped a colleague with a case in which a woman had been beaten senseless by a contractor after she had refused to kiss him good-bye on the final day of the job. Russ's refusing to close the bathroom door, combined with the gory details of that case, set me on edge.

On my Fridays at home, I would shuttle the girls out the door before Russ's arrival and return only when it was time to cook dinner. Russ was usually still there and would come upstairs to comment on what we were having. If I were cooking steak, he would announce that the liver smelled good. Everything about the man irked me.

I started to complain to Charlie.

"Are you sure he knows what he's doing?" I would ask. "There's dust everywhere. Do you know if he's dealing with all the hazardous materials properly?"

"I know he's doing the job for what we agreed to pay him," Charlie would respond in a flat tone intended to remind me of my promise to keep out of it.

"Great, we can use the savings to pay for my chemotherapy," I'd grumble.

But I had agreed that the basement would be Charlie's project, and I was determined to abide by that agreement. And while Russ was busy blanketing our entire house in dust, a new situation had arisen at work that required delicate negotiation.

..................................

Around the time we started the basement renovation, there was whispering around the office that we were about to receive the very, very large record in a very, very notorious case. I had heard that *Dateline* had already called seeking verification of our assignment to represent Karen Shanes. The Shanes case had been one of those trials that had provided endless fodder for the New York tabloids throughout 1998. It involved the irresistible New York combination of mystery, family, and real estate.

Karen Shanes had been convicted of murdering an elderly Upper East Side socialite, Edith Goldblum, in order to steal Goldblum's multimillion-dollar Upper East Side townhouse. That was the real estate piece. The family piece was that Karen Shanes was accused of acting in concert with her son, Stuart. There were tabloid reports that Karen and Stuart, at the time of their arrest, had been found in bed together and that they had left a trail of bodies in their wake as they crossed the country. The mystery piece was that Edith Goldblum's body had never been found, despite a massive police search.

A murder prosecution without a body is always troublesome. There are reported cases from England of defendants convicted and hung for murder, only to have the alleged victim show up years later, in perfect health. By that point the accused was well beyond the point where he could benefit from any appeal.

The phenomenon wasn't limited to England. In 1932, Edwin M. Borchard, a Yale law professor, in his book *Convicting the Innocent*, compiled a group of cases in which innocent people had been convicted of notorious crimes. Included in the compilation was a case involving two Vermont brothers convicted of murdering their brother-in-law.

It was well known that the two brothers had little use for their sister's feebleminded husband, who had a habit of regularly disappearing. When the brother-in-law went missing in 1812, nobody paid too much attention at first. But when he failed to return, rumors began to fly. A witness came forward to say he had seen the brothers arguing with their sister's husband shortly before his disappearance. When a barn burned down on the brothers' farm, more rumors ignited. According to the town gossip, the fire had been intentionally set to conceal evidence of the brother-in-law's murder. A short time later, a dog dug up bones on the property, and an examiner pronounced them to be of human origin. The brothers found themselves imprisoned while a grand jury was convened to investigate the killing. Then a fellow prisoner came forward claiming that one of the brothers had confessed to the murder.

The two brothers were convicted in 1820 and sentenced to hang. Only when an advertisement was taken out announcing the brothers' impending fate and asking for help from anyone who might have seen their brother-in-law was the "victim" located, alive and well and living in New Jersey. The brother-in-law had just been attempting to leave his wife when he disappeared.

Without a body, there is always room for some doubt about whether the alleged victim is even dead. The essential element of murder is the killing, the most obvious evidence of which is the dead body and the medical examiner's testimony about the cause of death: The victim was shot by a .38-caliber gun that was recovered from the accused; the victim was stabbed twenty times, and her blood was recovered on the shoes of the accused; the victim was strangled and, during the struggle, scraped her attacker, and the skin under her fingernails was traced through DNA analysis to the accused. . . . In a murder prosecution, the body is the prosecution's big-ticket item. Proving a murder case without a body is like trying to feed a football team at a backyard barbecue without any meat. It can be done, but it is going to take a lot of effort.

Without a body, the prosecution must attempt to prove death in some other way—by painstakingly recounting the victim's routines and practices, the last time she was seen, her final conversations, the state of her health, her stated intentions to remain nearby and not slip off undetected to some foreign land. In the Shanes case, not only had Edith Goldblum's body never been recovered, but there were no eyewitnesses to the killing, and Goldblum had lived alone, with only servants to attend to her and a cadre of close friends who visited regularly.

It was the prosecution's theory that in the summer of 1998, Stuart Shanes had rented a room in Goldblum's townhouse weeks before the murder and, with the aid of his mother, had studied Goldblum's routines. He learned when the servants would have time off and when Goldblum's friends could be expected to visit. The prosecution claimed that over the long Fourth of July weekend, with the servants off and the friends departed to cooler climes, Stuart and Karen had somehow killed Goldblum, wrapped up her body, and disposed of it in parts unknown without leaving any forensic evidence—no fingerprints, no murder weapon, nothing.

The prosecution's case was entirely circumstantial, based on Stuart's proximity to Goldblum prior to her death and a forged deed purporting to transfer the title of Goldblum's Upper East Side townhouse to a shell corporation linked to the Shaneses. The story was certainly interesting when splashed across the front pages of the tabloids, but from an appellate perspective, it threatened to be a hopeless morass for a variety of reasons.

First, there was the sheer length of the transcript generated by the prosecution's attempts to fill in the huge gaps created by the failure to find the body, unearth an eyewitness, or recover any forensic evidence. The transcript was bigger than any our office had previously handled, running over thirteen thousand pages in length.

Second, although Karen Shanes had been convicted of murdering Goldblum and sentenced to what amounted to life in prison, the New York conviction was far from Shanes's biggest problem, because while Karen Shanes was serving her life sentence in New York, the state of California was proceeding with capital murder charges against her for the first-degree murder of a man. The New York appeal would have to be coordinated with the California prosecution. While Karen was imprisoned in New York, she would have to return to California for her trial. By the time my office had been assigned to the case, the California authorities were attempting to extradite Shanes, and she was fighting the extradition with the help of an assigned attorney working out of the Westchester County Legal Aid office. Shanes was being held, at Bedford Hills Correctional Facility, in Westchester County.

There was also the media angle, with reporters remaining intrigued by the case long after the conviction, each angling to be the one to learn where the body was buried. It is unusual for the media to continue to follow a case during the appeal. The conviction, and the announcement of an inevitably lengthy sentence, usually offers itself up as the natural ending to any story. But there was something about the Shanes case that held the media's attention and promised to present additional challenges to our representation. With reporters asking to interview our client, there was always the danger that she could say something that might hurt her case or prejudice her in the California case.

So when Rich called me into his office shortly after we received the Shanes record, I had serious reservations about taking it on. I was still working a reduced schedule and I was plenty busy. But Rich was making me an offer that I couldn't refuse. For whatever reason, if there was going to be a high-profile case that demanded our office to present a public face, Rich wanted that face to be mine.

"It's too much," I complained. "I can't do it on three or even four days a week, and I don't want to come back full-time."

"There are plenty of people who have already come in here asking for the case," Rich said, attempting to appeal to my vanity and my ambition simultaneously.

But Rich was mistaking me for a different lawyer—one who had left the Legal Aid Society because it offered her no immediate or clear path to advancement.

"Look, I'm ambitious, and I want to work at a place where that's not considered a bad thing," the twenty-eight–year-old me had told Rich when explaining why I was leaving the public sector to join a private law firm.

Rich, in his initial sales pitch on the Shanes case, seemed to have temporarily forgotten that I was no longer twenty-eight and looking to make a name for myself. Now I cared only about making the 5:03 train home.

"How about if you agree to take a piece of the case?" Rich asked, trying a different approach.

"How would that work? I'll take pages 1 through 5,000 and somebody else can take the rest?"

"No. I'll give you a team of worker bees. You can be the queen bee. What you say goes. But you'll have a group of workers so that you can still meet your professional and personal obligations. How's that sound?" Rich seemed delighted to have come up with such a creative solution to the problem of having too many volunteers on one hand, coupled with too much reluctance on the other.

"In theory it sounds okay, I guess, depending on who my worker bees will be, I suppose." Despite the surface appeal of Rich's offer, from its inception I had my reservations. Ours was not an office of team endeavors. What I valued most about my job was my autonomy, the ability to make my own decisions in my own cases without too much interference from anybody else.

"Well, both Kevin and Paul have expressed interest in the case," Rich explained.

This revelation was far from surprising. Both volunteers were single men, without any obvious encumbrances outside of work on their time. I disliked them both for different reasons.

Kevin Drumm and I had been hired around the same time, but I had joined the office several months later because of Jessie's birth. As a result, Kevin had never quite realized that I was two years senior to him, that I had been defending clients when he was still in law school. Kevin was also a true believer, who had never sullied his public defender image by stooping to work for a law firm, even as a summer associate. Instead he had clerked for a federal judge and then went on to clerk for the New Jersey Supreme Court. At the time Rich offered him up as a worker bee, if I had been asked to describe Kevin in one word, I would have selected "arrogant."

Paul Alexander I disliked for entirely different reasons. Paul had followed an unorthodox path to the Office of the Appellate Advocate. He had been a JAG (Judge Advocate General) officer in the United States Marines. In that capacity, he had prosecuted cases where defendants had been eligible for the death penalty, which Paul personally supported as an acceptable punishment for the criminal justice system to mete out. I found that stance hard to swallow in a criminal defense attorney.

Both Kevin and Paul were hardworking and intelligent attorneys. If I had given myself any opportunity to actually get to know either one, I probably would not have disliked them. But getting to know my colleagues, making small talk, and listening to their complaints or stories was not a luxury that I afforded myself once I became a working mother. I was always at my desk, focused on a case, with my eyes seeking the clock only in the afternoon when the time to rush for the train approached.

Against my better judgment, I agreed to head up the Shanes team. Although I often complain about the size of my caseload, I have a hard time turning down assignments, especially when Rich personally asks me to take something on.

My resistance overcome, Rich immediately called Kevin and Paul into his office for our first team meeting. He thanked them for their interest in the case and let them know that they would both have a chance to work on it. But Rich made it clear from the outset that if there were disagreements about tactical decisions, my word was final.

Sitting in that first meeting, I felt nothing but embarrassed. Both Kevin and Paul knew how few hours I actually spent in the office each week. We all had to sign in and out like steelworkers punching the clock. Both Kevin and Paul would be in at 8:00 a.m. and not leave until late into the evening, while I was lucky if I made it in by 9:00 a.m. and lasted until 4:00 p.m. without having to dash home for a sick baby or a broken water heater. I knew both men thought that Rich put me in charge of the case simply because he liked me, not because I was the most qualified attorney for the job.

Recently I was talking to Kevin—who is now one of my closest friends in the office—about a problem I was having with a judge who refused to grant a request I believed to be reasonable.

"It must be hard now that you're getting older and you can't bat your eyelashes and get whatever you want whenever you want it," Kevin chided. "Welcome to the world where the rest of us live."

Kevin's remark stung because I knew that he truly believed I had won assignments, including the Shanes case, based on attributes other than my professional competence. But at the time of our initial Shanes meeting, I understood that if I was to have any success at all in leading the team, I had to tamp down my self-doubt and act as if I believed I was the obvious choice as lead counsel.

From the first day, Karen Shanes's case demanded special attention. With the extradition proceedings in full swing and our client about to be sent against her will to California to face capital charges, we did not have the luxury of waiting months to familiarize ourselves with the case before our first visit.

Within days of our team meeting, we had arranged a trip to Bedford Hills to meet Karen Shanes. I had no reservations about the trip, because I had been to Bedford before and never had any problems with the prison administration. But I had never before represented a client of Karen Shanes's notoriety.

Upon our arrival, an extra security detail of corrections officers was there to greet us at the gate. Days earlier there had been reports that Karen's devoted son, Stuart, had held a Court TV reporter hostage, threatening to slit her throat with a pen unless certain demands were met—including that his mother not be sent to California to face the death penalty. Of course, even if the New York State prison officials had wanted with all their hearts to grant Stuart's wish list, they had no authority to deny the extradition request of a sovereign sister state. The crisis ended without anybody getting hurt except for Stuart, who earned himself a serious time-out in the prison's special housing unit.

For us, just clearing Bedford's front gate took a half hour and included a personal visit from a deputy superintendent who outlined the special security pre-cautions that would be in place throughout our visit. We were then escorted to the visiting area, where I usually would meet with my clients at a table or in a private room without any guards nearby.

Not so with Karen Shanes. We were led into a room with a small Plexiglas window cut out of the concrete wall. Our client was brought into the adjacent concrete room. I could barely see her face. There were holes punched out of the Plexiglas to allow us to speak through it, but we were strictly forbidden from passing any objects to our client or having her pass anything to us. Guards remained stationed outside the door to each room. If we needed to exchange legal documents, it was explained, they would be given to our client after being fully vetted by the guards.

Never in all my years of practice had I experienced such heightened security measures. The fact that the client sitting in the adjacent room, visible through the Plexiglas window, was a gray-haired grandmother made the situation all the more surreal.

I looked at Kevin and Paul. If I'd been alone, I would have tried to sweet talk my way around. But I felt self-conscious taking that approach with them as witnesses. I turned to Kevin and suggested that he speak directly with the superintendent. He agreed and left to try and find someone with the authority to loosen the security measures. I turned my attention back to Karen Shanes, leaned toward the Plexiglas, and told her we would wait to see what Kevin could work out, but he returned a few minutes later with the news that the prison officials would not budge.

"I guess we're going to have to meet like this for now," I said, arranging three orange, plastic chairs in a semicircle far enough from the Plexiglas so that our client could see all of our faces clearly for the first time. Karen Shanes looked directly at me. For a woman who had the reputation of being a great manipulator of men, she was really very ordinary looking, with short grayish brown hair and large glasses covering brown eyes that appeared myopic. Her skin had a sallow, tight quality.

In fairness, she was wearing a wholly unflattering prison uniform and not a speck of makeup. As I knew all too well, by the time most women turn forty, makeup has become a prerequisite for looking decent. I know this because I myself reached that milestone years ago, well before I actually hit forty. I don't want to imagine what cosmetic assistance I will need by the time I turn sixty.

"You're very pretty," Karen Shanes offered, her voice warm and sincere. The compliment worked: I actually felt prettier for her having said it. Only later did I realize that Shanes had pegged me as a person whose vanity could be exploited, who would be vulnerable to flattery.

There was something vaguely familiar to me about my client, and it wasn't only that I had read newspaper clippings containing several pictures of her at different stages of her life. There was something else, something I could not quite place at first.

We discussed the status of her extradition proceedings, the likely date of her hearing and departure to California were she to lose her opposition motion, which was almost inevitable. The government has to prove very little at an extradition proceeding, mainly that the accused is the person named in the warrant issued by the requesting state. I explained that we were only beginning to review her murder case, but that we anticipated being able to file a brief on her behalf within the year, given that our office had three attorneys, instead of just one, devoted to the matter.

Kevin, Paul, and I also sought to impress upon Karen that we wanted to try to lower the profile of her case by avoiding any additional press coverage. We explained that the more her case remained in the public consciousness, the greater its notoriety, the more pressure the courts would feel not to grant her any relief on appeal. She was skeptical of this approach. She wanted us to use the press to try to locate the alleged victim, who Shanes insisted could very well still be alive.

"Let's just try to lay off the press for a while," I suggested, not wanting to pick a fight with a new client during our first meeting. Karen Shanes also seemed eager to get along.

"Okay," she agreed in her breathy, low voice. "I'll do whatever you say. I'm just so grateful to have such wonderful, bright, young people working on my behalf."

*Wonderful, bright, young people.* Then I realized what was familiar about Karen Shanes. She was a mother and a grandmother. Even though she was a convicted murderer serving a life sentence who was about to be extradited to face additional capital murder charges, she radiated an unmistakable maternal quality. She could have sidled up to the Thanksgiving table at my parents' house and passed for some long-lost great-aunt.

Months later, Shanes was present (only in the conversation) around our Thanksgiving table, when my in-laws asked me how the case was going.

"What's she like?" my father-in-law asked.

I had never been reticent about discussing my cases before. I would describe my clients, what they had been convicted of doing, and which issues I was exploring, without censoring my thoughts. But for some reason, I felt strangely reserved when it came to Karen Shanes.

"It's not really dinner table conversation," I had responded. My father-in-law had appeared disappointed by my response, as if my refusal to discuss the case was somehow a personal rejection of him.

My reticence was born from the intensity of people's interest in the case, the sheer fatigue of repeating the story. Upon learning that I was representing Shanes, nobody responded, "That's nice" or "Sounds great."

At friends' dinner parties, someone would inevitably mention that I was working on the case, and all eyes would be on me. "Oh my God, what's she like?" I would be asked over and over again. "She's your typical mother-in-law" became my stock reply, designed to deflect the question. It always got a laugh.

At a friend's fortieth birthday party (a Hawaiian luau), a few weeks after my initial visit with my new client, Charlie and I were seated around a table covered with fake grass mats, sipping cloyingly sweet frozen drinks with paper umbrellas in them, when somehow the Shanes case was mentioned.

Charlie remarked nonchalantly that I was representing Karen Shanes. My friend's cousin was sitting next to me. He was one of those thick-necked Wall Street trader types, good-looking in a fraternity-boy way. I often saw his wife around town with her son, who was a few weeks older than Lila. She always looked miserable, as if her whole life had devolved into one prolonged episode of postpartum depression. There was a shadow of gloominess that never left her face, even when she smiled.

"How can you defend a monster like that?" the trader demanded, his voice heavy with disgust. Instantly I could sense Charlie bracing for a fight.

"It keeps me off the streets," I responded, attempting to cast off his contempt with a joke.

There was a time when his remark would have sent me into a tirade about the importance of the adversarial system our Constitution guarantees, how the cost of liberty is eternal vigilance, and the value of my work. But by the time of the Shanes case, I had learned that there are certain people who would never understand the value of the right to counsel until they were staring down the barrel of a criminal prosecution themselves. Then those Wall Street types would cry in their defense attorneys' offices, because they never expected to be caught insider-trading or addicted to painkillers or patronizing a prostitute.

When I was in private practice, it was the affluent clients, barely facing any prison time, who would cry the hardest about their fates. Understandably, they feared losing their jobs, their spouses, their homes, all vestiges of respectability.

And while I sympathized with them, their blubbering had made me crave my indigent defense work, where even those clients serving life sentences did not feel entitled to whine incessantly.

But this Wall Street trader was not willing to back down without an admission from me that Karen Shanes did not deserve a defense.

"How would you feel if you got her off on a technicality and she got out and killed someone else?" he asked, self-righteous indignation dripping off him like sweat in the summer evening humidity.

"Honestly, I'd feel surprised, considering that she's not only serving a life sentence in New York but is facing multiple life sentences on murder charges in California as well," I responded, still unwilling to engage.

I get so few people convicted of violent crimes "off on technicalities" that I have had little opportunity to worry that one will get out and hurt someone else. Still, every once in a while, when a particularly nasty crime is splashed across the morning papers, I find myself hoping it has not been perpetrated by one of my former clients. To date, it never has been.

The trader still refused to let it go.

"I just don't understand how you can represent someone like that. How can you live with yourself?"

It must have been all the strong, sweet drinks, because nothing the guy said could rile me. But Charlie had heard enough.

"Look, asshole, her job is to make sure people aren't fucked over just for being poor. What she does in one day is more important than anything you'll accomplish your entire life. You don't know shit."

The party went silent. "On that note, I think it's time for us to say good night," I said, extricating myself from the bamboo mats that entangled my legs and reaching for Charlie's hand. "Our babysitter can't stay too late tonight."

Walking back home, I made Charlie promise not to mention my role in the Shanes case again during cocktail party chatter. I just did not want to deal with the prurient interest or strong passions the case seemed to arouse.

Along with the continuing interest of friends, neighbors, and the press corps, the police too had been keeping their eyes on the Shanes case, despite the conviction. The week after we got back from our initial visit to Bedford, I received a frantic message from Karen Shanes telling me that a group of detectives had paid her a visit. They'd wanted to know where the victim's body was and told her they were not leaving until she told them. When she responded that her appeals attorneys had told her not to speak with anybody about the case, the detectives laughed.

"What are they gonna do about it?" the lead detective scoffed, refusing to leave.

*What* are *we going to do about it?* I wondered. Usually when the police overstep during an interrogation by failing to honor a defendant's right to counsel, the remedy is for the court to suppress any statements improperly obtained, meaning the prosecution can't introduce them as evidence against the accused at trial. But in this instance, the police were not trying to obtain a confession for the trial. Our client had already been convicted and sentenced. The police just wanted to locate Goldblum's body so they could finally close the file on the case.

I walked down to Kevin's office, told him about the message, and asked him what he thought we should do about it. We decided that he would call the trial prosecutors, who had likely worked with the detectives. Later that day, Kevin reported that he had gotten in touch with the lead prosecutor, who in turn had promised to reach out to the detectives and advise them that speaking with a represented defendant whose case was pending on appeal probably was not the best idea.

But two days later, there was a similar desperate message on my answering machine. The detectives had come back, asking the same questions over and over again, telling Karen that they would be there again every day until they learned where the body was buried.

"Fuck," I muttered to myself, simultaneously feeling angry and nervous.

I knew that the detectives were violating my client's rights to remain silent and to have an attorney present during her questioning; I just didn't know how to make them stop doing it. Lofty constitutional principles are one thing, enforcing them quite another.

After spending the morning researching the issue, I decided that the most likely way to dissuade the detectives from continuing their visits to Bedford was to file a lawsuit in federal court alleging that the NYPD was violating Karen Shanes' civil rights. The problem was, I really did not want to spend my time litigating in federal court over an issue that would in no way help me get the brief filed in the Shanes appeal.

I walked into Rich's office to tell him what my research had uncovered.

"You really want to drag us into federal court on this?" Rich asked, his tone suggesting that he did not believe the battle worth fighting.

"What else can we do? Let them keep harassing our client and not fight back?"

"You can make them stop," Rich said.

"I already had Kevin speak to the lead prosecutor and it didn't help."

"I didn't say you should have Kevin speak to the prosecutor. *You* make it stop."

"Okay then. I'll wave my magic wand and make it stop," I said sarcastically.

"You'll figure it out," Rich said with certainty.

Back in my office, I considered the problem some more. Rich was right. Asking the prosecution to look into the police misconduct had not worked. It was time to play hardball.

I picked up the phone and dialed David Morgan, the highest ranking prosecutor in the district attorney's office who might consider taking my call. When Morgan picked up the phone, I told him that I was having some problems with the detectives running the Shanes investigation, that they refused to stop visiting my client despite her repeated invocations of her rights to remain silent and to counsel.

"You need to tell the detectives that unless they stop harassing my client they can each expect a civil rights complaint against them personally, not just against the police department," I warned, trying to sound tougher than I felt. "We'll be seeking money damages. It's gotta stop now. I'm done playing games with them. One more episode and the complaint is being filed."

As I spoke, I prayed nobody would call my bluff. If they did, I would have to follow through, despite Rich's displeasure.

"You shouldn't have to file a federal lawsuit to get them to obey the law," Morgan observed. "That shouldn't be happening. It'll end today."

And he was right. The detectives never again went back to Bedford to see my client. Now, thankfully, I could go back to devoting my time to the appeal, reviewing thousands of pages of transcript in a search for relevant issues. Kevin was turning out to be the best worker anybody could hope for, even offering to boil down the thousands of pages of text into its bare essentials for my review. But while I knew that we would need a condensed version of the transcript when we started writing, there was no way I was not going to read every word of the record myself.

Throughout the summer of our basement renovation project, I would drag home a volume of the Shanes case every night and read it at the dining room table after the girls went to sleep. Every volume was huge and heavy, numbering over 600 pages. In the morning, there would be a faint coat of dust covering the transcript's plastic cover, evidence of Russ's ongoing handiwork, a reminder that it was impossible to keep the forces of chaos from creeping into the realm of order.

I was grateful when September finally came (the month in which Russ had promised to complete the basement project). There is something comforting about September in the suburbs around New York. When you wake in the morning, you can just begin to feel a hint of chill in the air, but it lacks any real threat. There is still a balmy coating surrounding it, assuring that you'll be overheated by the end of the day, when you disembark from the train wearing the autumn outfit that seemed perfect just that morning. Then one day in October, the morning chill does not dissipate and summer is gone—the smell of mowed grass replaced with wood smoke, the lawns of quaint colonials suddenly decked out in pumpkins and scarecrows.

Personally, I am never sorry when summer ends. By September I have grown tired of summer's unstructured ease, the way the heat zaps my desire to perform even the lightest task, the weight of my hair on the back of my neck in the humidity. I crave the resurgence of energy that the cooler days bring, the discipline of school schedules, the resumption of regular court hours when work can actually get done.

I felt compelled to finish reviewing the Shanes transcript that September, to provide myself with some small measure of progress. In addition to poring over the volumes at night, I also began to forgo the morning newspaper. Instead I dragged the transcripts on the morning commute, always careful to keep the title of the case hidden, lest it attract unwanted attention. Many mornings, when the train pulled into the station, I wouldn't even put the transcript away as I walked to catch the PATH, the underground railway that shuttles New Jersey commuters into Manhattan. I would cram in fifteen more minutes of transcript reading and often be the last passenger off at the final stop, the World Trade Center, because I was so eager to finish a witness's account or to absorb a particularly interesting detail of the proceedings.

On the way to work one morning, I was reviewing the testimony of the police witnesses, explaining how they had recovered a cache of incriminating evidence from the luggage storage room of the Plaza Hotel by following a private investigator who had been hired by the Shanes defense team to recover it. The bag was ultimately revealed to contain several diaries the prosecution claimed were Karen's that outlined the plot to kill Goldblum, as well as a couple of Halloween masks of the type worn by the killer in the movie *Scream*, and some cash.

*Are the police allowed to follow a defense investigator, or is that some infringement on the attorney-client privilege?* I wondered as I stepped off the PATH train. I didn't get much further in the thought. There was a strange smell in the station, gasoline or fuel of some sort. Nobody else seemed to notice it as they wandered around, buying their morning papers, lingering to look at magazines on the newsstand racks, or buying smoothies at the juice stand.

There is a vigilance that comes with my job, an awareness of how thin the line is between the ordinary and the tragic. Every homicide that my work has acquainted me with over the years seems to have been carried out on what started as a normal day for the victim. Those victims did not awaken on the morning of their deaths knowing that the date of the incident—or DOI, as the police call it—would be their last day on earth. There is also a vigilance that comes with motherhood, an ability to recognize nascent dangers and negotiate them on a subconscious level with some primordial part of the brain.

When I walked out of the PATH station that September morning of 2001, I knew right away there was something seriously wrong. *This whole place is going to blow,* I thought to myself as I started running up the steep escalator leading to the street-level mall, while others stood still, passively enjoying the ride.

The World Trade Center mall was like a little piece of suburbia in Lower Manhattan. It was there whenever I needed to buy a box of Godiva chocolates to cheer up Charlie, or a new suit at Barami on the way to court because I felt too frumpy in the one I was wearing, or a pair of jeans at the Gap to replace ones that had suddenly become too tight.

Up at the mall that morning, you didn't need any finely tuned instincts to sense the danger. There was a stronger smell on the street level, an acrid burning mixed with the metallic smell of panic, an unexpected insult, like biting into a custard doughnut but catching your tongue and tasting blood instead of sugar.

And instead of buying coffee or perusing the magazine racks for the morning paper, people were running. I immediately joined them.

"What's going on?!" I called to a woman racing alongside me toward the Liberty Street exit. I could see the Barami store to my right, the perfume store to my left. It was the exact same route I had walked every weekday for almost four years—a laboratory rat programmed never to veer from the quickest route through the maze, the surest path to the reward pellet, even when it required walking through a ring of fire.

"I don't know," the woman responded, struggling in her high-heeled pumps to keep up with me. I was wearing black canvas rubber-heeled flats. A lucky choice.

"But that guy back there looked pretty bad," she continued, turning her head slightly back toward the Gap.

When I glanced in that direction, all I could see was a stumbling figure wearing a black hooded sweatshirt. There was smoke rising from his body, and people were gathering around, trying to figure out what was going on, what had happened to him. It didn't occur to me until much later that he had not been wearing a black sweatshirt; his entire body had been burned, apparently by a fireball that had raced down an elevator shaft and engulfed him.

There was another crowd of people stopped cold at the exit door opening on to Liberty Street. The smell of gasoline was stronger now. Out on the street, things were falling out of the perfect, blue sky, as if somebody had decided to throw an impromptu ticker-tape parade but had forgotten to shred the paper. Whole sheets of paper and debris billowed and crashed to the ground.

I thought of how my oldest brother, Nate, had once told me that if you threw a penny from the observation deck of the Empire State Building and it landed on somebody's head, it was certain to kill him. The objects falling to the ground were larger than pennies. And the World Trade Center was taller than the Empire State Building.

The first of many critical calculations had to be made at that moment, the most essential being which path would most likely result in survival. Running through the falling objects presented a very real risk of being struck in the head and dying instantly. But staying at the mall, with the acrid smell of fuel burning my lungs and an imminent explosion likely, did not seem to hold out any greater promise of survival either.

For the entire time I had been running through the mall, I had been carrying the Shanes transcript in my hands. Its weight had slowed me down, but now it was the decisive factor in my choice to flee, rather than stay put. I plopped the transcript onto my head, as if I had been caught without an umbrella in an unexpectedly heavy downpour, and sprinted the two blocks to the lobby of my office building.

"What's going on? Should I go upstairs?" I asked the doorman. Sirens had started blaring as the first 911 calls sent from the towers were bringing unprecedented numbers of police cars and fire trucks in response.

"Upstairs is probably the safest place to be," he advised.

So I pushed the elevator button and went up to my office. When I got there, Rich was already at his desk, working away, oblivious.

"Something's going on at the Trade Center," I told him. "It's like a Godzilla movie out there."

Rich looked up at me. "Yeah? I heard something that sounded like thunder a couple of minutes ago," he observed, still totally unconcerned.

"Thunder? Rich, have you looked outside? There isn't a cloud in the sky. It's not thunder." I was annoyed at his failure to pick up on the panic in my voice, to comprehend what I had just dodged, although I had no inkling yet as to the gravity of the danger.

Nonetheless, I felt an overpowering urge to speak to my husband. I went to my office and dialed Charlie's office number. When he picked up, I told him that he was going to be hearing a lot of news reports about the Trade Center, but that I was fine and that he didn't need to worry.

"Okay," he said steadily, immediately sensing that something was seriously wrong. "But I want you to get out of there now."

"It's really a question of which is worse right now. Staying inside seems pretty safe. Out on the street, things are falling. Honestly, I think I'm better off staying put for the moment," I explained.

I promised to call back as soon as the situation cleared up to let him know if I was going to leave. Before I hung up, I made sure to tell Charlie that I loved him.

I walked to the other side of the office, the one closest to the North Tower, to see if anybody knew what was going on. I found a group of people clustered there looking out. There was black smoke billowing out from the North Tower. My colleague Kevin was standing there too, looking up at the smoke.

"There must be thousands of people trapped up there," he said gravely.

People were speculating about what possibly could have caused such massive damage. There had been radio reports that a private plane had crashed into the building. The scene outside the window seemed unreal to me. At first all I felt watching it was an overwhelming sense of relief that I'd gotten away, a joy approaching mania. Somehow my brain was as yet unable to otherwise process the disaster unfolding before me. I walked back toward my office without speaking to anyone.

Rich was still seated at his desk, typing at his computer. He was e-mailing Zoe, my closest colleague, who was at the capital defender's office in Midtown that morning on a temporary assignment. "Something's going on at the Trade Center," he typed. The message was sent at 9:02 a.m. There would be no others sent from that location for over three months.

As I stood in the doorway of Rich's office, the second plane hit the South Tower. It was the loudest noise I have ever heard. We all felt the reverberation of the plane's impact. Our office rocked, its windows rattled, lights flickered on and off.

"What's happening?!" I screamed.

"They're bombing us!" Rich screamed back.

Having already convinced myself that I had survived my brush with death when I initially fled the towers, this second assault was more than my psyche could now bear. I started screaming incoherently. "I've gotta get out of here! I've gotta get home to my kids," over and over.

The next thing I remember was Rich yelling at me as loud as he could.

"You're not going anywhere. Go take a Valium or whatever else you need to do, calm down, and get control of yourself," he screamed.

I had never heard him yell before, and it sobered me up but pissed me off at the same time. I walked back into my own office. It was darker now; the lights and computer screen were no longer working. The burning smell from the towers had infiltrated the office air.

My phone was ringing. I picked it up and heard my friend Jen, who worked in Brooklyn at the federal courthouse.

"Listen to me. You've got to get out of there. It's an attack!"

"I've got nowhere to go," I cried. "The streets outside are chaos. Things are falling everywhere. I don't know where to go."

"Run away from the towers, toward the water. Just leave and run in the opposite direction as fast as you can," she ordered.

But I didn't listen. I stayed. Too frightened to leave the office, I curled beneath my desk.

Fifty-six minutes passed between the time the second plane hit and the time the first tower fell. Those minutes are lost to me. I don't remember whom I spoke with or what I did. I remember at some point finding myself in an empty office across the hall from mine and looking out the window, contemplating my own death.

*What are my regrets?* I asked myself. *What would I have done differently?* I couldn't think of a thing. I remember feeling grateful that I had known true love in my life and that I had found work that had felt meaningful.

A horrible sadness came over me when I thought of my daughters, as I imagined their future without a mother. Jessie was only four and Lila not yet two. They would never understand what had happened to me. Why I had simply failed to come home one night. I trusted that Charlie would do everything right, would teach them well. But I knew that without me, both my daughters would carry a vast emptiness for the rest of their lives.

Charlie might remarry, but no matter how wonderful his new wife, the best the girls could hope for was that she would be "like" a mother to them. No one but me would sense when they woke up in the middle of the night before they cried out. No one would know the exact sequence in which to sing their lullabies or how to comfort them in the same way. No one but me would know and love every freckle, every hair, every finger and toe.

*I just want more time*, I thought. But I did not pray or ask to be spared. For me there was no God there that day. The absence of anything holy was palpable. Although I was surrounded by people with whom I had worked for years, I felt totally alone.

At 9:59 a.m. there was a loud cracking sound. I remember watching the first tower fall. Its crumbling demise looked different from how it would later appear on television. Before it fell straight down, as if through some planned demolition, the tower swayed slightly toward my office, then away from it. When it swayed toward the office, I held my breath and waited for it to topple onto all of us.

Then there was total darkness and dust. Dust everywhere. It was gray and light, like the embers left over after the coals in the barbecue have long finished burning. It blanketed my hair, my eyelashes, the red blouse I was wearing, and my shoes. Once the dust came, staying in the office was no longer an option, because it was becoming harder and harder to breathe. I made my way out to near the elevators, where people were gathering. I didn't wait to hear what they were doing before opening the door to the emergency staircase and fleeing down into the darkness.

When I reached the bottom, I realized I was in the building's basement. The building's day-care center was located there, and children of every age were huddled before me on the floor. The sight of babies and toddlers covered in dust, struggling to breathe the foul air, was one of the images that would come back to haunt me, over and over again in the weeks to come. There were desperate parents already arriving to find their children. Part of me felt that I should stay to help with the children whose parents were not yet there, but my overriding feeling was that I wanted to be with my own children. To be sure they were safe. Nobody yet knew the scope of the attacks. My daughter Jessie's preschool was housed in a synagogue, and although it was in New Jersey, synagogues are always a tempting target. I wanted her home. As far as I knew, Lila was safely there already, but I had been unable to reach Charlie after our initial phone conversation.

I looked across the room and saw Alan Brewster. Alan worked in the office next to mine and lived on the Upper West Side.

"Are you leaving?" I asked him.

He nodded his head. I signaled that I would join him. Before we left, I found a sink and soaked my shirt with water. I used it to wipe the dust from my face and around my mouth, hoping that by breathing intermittently through my wet shirt I could avoid inhaling at least some of the bigger particles.

I followed Alan up a flight of stairs into the lobby, which was utterly unrecognizable. There was a foot of dust covering the reception desk. I could barely see my hand in front of my face or make out the outline of the doors. The empty street outside was eerily silent, as if snow had blanketed the city or we were in some post-nuclear winter. Alan and I clung to the building line to avoid anything that might still be falling from the sky, and together we headed toward the water.

I could smell the water before I could see it. The dust started clearing as we made our way to the South Street Seaport. There were hundreds of people on the exodus out of Lower Manhattan. All were covered in the same dust.

As we walked, reports and rumors about the scope of the attacks swirled around us. "The Pentagon's been hit," someone reported. "The Capitol's on fire," someone else announced. "They're saying there was anthrax on the planes," another man chimed in. "I'm heading for the mountains, I'm not stopping until I get there," a voice declared from behind me.

I asked to borrow Alan's cell phone and dialed Charlie's number. The connection was bad, but I reached his secretary.

"Donna, I need to speak to Charlie."

"Where are you? Are you okay?" Donna's voice, which usually conveyed nothing but cool professionalism, was beyond frightened.

"Yes, but I need to speak to Charlie."

"He left after the second plane hit to go pick up Jessie," Donna explained.

Exactly what I was calling to tell him to do.

"Donna, you need to call and tell him I'm okay. I'm walking out of downtown right now. I'll call him when I figure out where I'm going."

I handed the phone back to Alan, and we continued to walk from Lower Manhattan to the Upper West Side. Along the way, I asked every police officer I encountered if there was any way off the island of Manhattan. Repeatedly I was told there was none. I would be sleeping in New York that night, either on Alan's floor or my oldest brother's. His apartment building was close to Alan's.

As we walked and walked, what struck me was how well behaved everybody was, how courteous and caring. People lent out their cell phones to strangers, until cell phone service was lost completely some time after the second tower fell. Others were giving out water. There was a warmth, a camaraderie, a feeling of shared resolve, that made me feel strangely proud. New York City can be hellish on a routine day, the traffic, the rudeness, the frenetic pace. But on September 11, 2001, New Yorkers really did come together. I am glad I lived to see that.

By the time we reached midtown, the air appeared clear, the beautiful September day unbroken once again. It was hard to reconcile the relative normalcy with the havoc we had just escaped. Alan and I quickened our pace as we passed the United Nations building, worried that a bomb might be waiting there to detonate once all the police and fire trucks were downtown.

I reached my brother Nate's apartment at around noon. His doorman told me that he wasn't there. A friend who was visiting him let me in. It turned out that my brother, upon hearing the news, had jumped into his car and sped toward Lower Manhattan to rescue me.

I called my mother to tell her that I was fine and had made it to Nate's apartment. She sounded calmer than I would have expected. I later learned that Charlie, unable to deal with her anxiety on top of his own, had called my mother after the second plane hit to falsely assure her that I had left immediately after the first plane and was already out of Lower Manhattan. Then he prayed there would be no reason to explain the lie later.

An hour after I'd gotten to my brother's apartment, there was a knock at the door. When I answered, it was my father standing there. He was wearing a khaki green suit, and the cast of his skin matched his jacket. He looked like a man who had been tossed at sea for hours and was suffering seasickness of the severest form. My mother had been unable to reach him in his Manhattan office to tell him that I was alive.

When my father's mind registered that it was me answering the door, some color returned to his face. "I'll never ask for anything again," he said, his eyes involuntarily looking upward. Knowing that my ultra-atheist father had been reduced to praying for my safety made me realize just how dire my situation had been. I went to hug him and burst into tears.

"It was so bad, so, so bad. There was death everywhere," I sobbed. My brother arrived at that moment and put his arms around me.

"I've been looking everywhere for you," he said. "I must have gotten a thousand dollars' worth of tickets running checkpoints."

Despite the police officers' assurances that there was no way off Manhattan, my father managed to drive me to my parents' home in Westchester that afternoon. Once there, I took a shower. With the dust removed, I could see that I had cuts all over my feet, because I had walked in my open shoes through broken glass. There were also small cuts on my face and neck. I have no idea how I got those. My lungs were burned, but there was nothing to be done for that injury. They would just have to heal on their own.

After I had showered and changed, my father drove me over the Tappan Zee Bridge to my house in New Jersey. As we crossed the bridge, I held my breath and prepared to swim out the car's window if a bomb caused the bridge to collapse. But there was nothing but the blue sky over the Hudson, and the trees along its banks still lush and green with no hint yet of autumn color.

The beauty of the landscape contrasted with the radio reports we listened to in silence. There were predictions that 10,000 people had been killed at the trade center. That grossly inflated estimate did not include those on the planes or at the Pentagon. The magnitude of the loss, the change in the world, was just beginning to be calibrated.

"It's the end of the world as we know it," my father predicted.

I could not focus on the full meaning of the day's events. I was just so happy to be alive. That was all I felt. An overwhelming joy to be breathing, to be heading home, to be able to sleep next to my husband and have the chance to see my children.

But by the time we arrived at my house, I was numb. I hugged Charlie and the girls, but my earlier mania had already subsided to make way for what would be weeks of wretched sorrow. Charlie was totally stoic. He never cried or broke down; he treated my arrival home almost as he would have on any other night. Later I learned that throughout the day, he had somehow convinced himself that my office was located in the Legal Aid building where I had worked years earlier. That office had been several blocks away from the towers, not directly in their shadow.

A few minutes after I came home, Russ, the ever-present contractor, came upstairs from the basement to use the bathroom. He looked me over, took in my cut feet, my red eyes, my undoubtedly dazed expression.

"You're lucky to still be vertical," he remarked, in the same flat tone he used to tell me the liver smelled good.

"I am," I replied.

I walked into the family room, where the girls were watching a Disney movie. I didn't notice if Russ closed the door entirely when he used the bathroom. I didn't hear him. I was too busy watching the girls, huddled next to each other in their pajamas on the faded flowered couch, Technicolor images of mermaids and princes reflecting in their eyes. "I know I am," I repeated softly.

.......................................

My office never filed a brief in the Shanes appeal. Sometime after the dust had settled, Karen Shanes became disenchanted with our efforts on her behalf and asked for new counsel. She wanted a complete reinvestigation of the entire case, an enormous task I could not agree to undertake. After new counsel was appointed, Shanes was sent out to California to stand trial and was convicted of first-degree murder based in part on the testimony of her son. Her California murder conviction and life sentence were upheld on appeal months before the New York courts heard and rejected all her appellate claims. In California they had the body. Goldblum's has never been found.

Although I felt bad about all the wasted time and effort our office had devoted to the case, I was not sorry when the court granted Shanes's request for new counsel. In the aftermath of September 11, I was mainly relieved not to be dealing with such a demanding assignment.

I sometimes wonder, if I hadn't been working on the Shanes case, if I hadn't had that massive transcript to shield my head as I fled the towers, if I would have been tempted to stay, too afraid to move. I probably would have left at some point anyway. I'd been able to run mainly due to my lucky choice of practical shoes that morning, not because I was carrying the transcript.

I still commute every day through the pit where the towers used to stand, to "ground zero," as the tourists now call it. The first day the PATH trains reopened and I had to get off in almost the same spot as I had on September 11, I found it hard to breathe. There still are days, traveling under the river, when fear overtakes me and I close my eyes and count backward from one thousand until it subsides.

It has been said that you should live every day as if it is your last, because someday you will be right. But of course that is impossible to do. If I knew that tomorrow would be my last day on earth, I would not leave my house. I would gather all my family around me and spend time with each person I love individually. I would eat whatever I wanted and split with Charlie the best bottle of wine I could get my hands on. If I did that every day, I would be unemployed, fat, and heading toward alcoholism within a month.

So I don't try to live every day as if it were my last. But I do wake to consider each a bonus; so many people did not get the chance to go home that day or to see their children grow. When I leave my daughters in the morning, I never forget to look into each girl's sleepy, vibrant, or cranky face and be thankful: for the moment, for the day, for my life. And I remember to wear comfortable shoes.

*part 5*

# Guilty as Sin

Any doubts I had about my sanity and judgment were confirmed in September 2002 when I found myself standing in the hallway of a decrepit Bronx apartment building at 7:00 on a Tuesday morning, knocking over and over again on the door to apartment 2D. My investigator, Roy Swain, was standing next to me, his back pressed against the wall, his hand resting lightly on the gun holstered at his waist, just in case the sleeping people inside the apartment woke up and started shooting. Roy's training as a police officer still governed his actions, almost subconsciously, even though he had left the force over a decade earlier.

He ordered me away from the door and started pounding on it, with more authority than I could have summoned. Roy didn't announce himself as a police officer, but something about the knock and the tone of his voice created the very definite impression that if the apartment door did not open soon, it was going to be busted down.

"C'mon, Mario," Roy ordered, his deep voice loud and commanding. "We're not goin' nowhere 'til we talk to you."

There was a shuffling noise inside the apartment, followed by the sound of several locks sliding. The man who opened the door was not entirely awake, and his eyes squinted at the harsh light cast by the hallway's exposed fluorescent bulbs. He was naked except for a brown bath towel slung too low around his waist; a thin trail of black hair ran from his navel down to where his hand was holding the towel.

"What ya want, man?" Mario Gonzalez asked, his voice clearly conveying that he just wanted nothing more than to go back to bed. He probably had not been up this early since high school, if then.

"We want to talk to you," Roy answered, politely, but in that same cop tone.

Mario looked at Roy, then noticed me for the first time. He smiled, exposing crooked but perfectly white teeth, the smile of a man who had learned that women find him attractive when he smiles. "Come on in," he said and opened the door all the way to let us go by. My hand scraped the towel at his waist as I passed him.

The inside of the apartment was small and dark. There was an opened convertible sofa in the living room with rumpled sheets and a yellow, tattered blanket balled up on top of them. The sound of footsteps, soft and padded, emanated from the rear bedroom. Somebody else was in the apartment. My throat went dry.

"Who else is here?" Roy demanded, loudly.

"Relax man, it's just me and my grandma," Mario assured us.

The bedroom door opened and a small, older woman stepped out long enough for me to register a flowing white nightgown cut in two by a long black braid. Mario said something fast and low in Spanish and the woman wordlessly retreated into the bedroom.

Mario turned his gaze back toward me. "Why are you here?" he asked, raising one eyebrow and smiling again, but this time not quite so fully. Another dazzling smile would have required more energy than he could mount this early in the morning.

"I think you know why I'm here," I said.

I had not planned what I would say when I actually confronted Mario Gonzalez, a multiple felon who I believed had gotten away with attempting to murder a college student during a senseless attack, a crime for which my client was wrongly serving fifteen years in prison while Mario slept in and enjoyed his grandma's home cooking. I had hoped the right words to rectify that situation would come when I needed them.

"I think you've been expecting me since you let Corrie Angelo go to jail for something you did. I think you've been waiting to tell me the truth."

My speech energized Mario to the point of laughter.

"You're kidding, right? I told the truth when I testified at trial. That's all I know. I don't got no more to say to you or nobody else."

"Do you got anything to tell Corrie Angelo's mother? She's crying herself to sleep every night. You got anything to say to her?" I asked, mimicking his tone.

"I feel bad for his *madre*, I do, but there's nothing I can do about it."

Mario and I stood silently, staring at each other. After a minute, I asked to use the bathroom, hoping that in my absence Roy could find some other way to break Mario down.

Like the rest of the apartment, the bathroom was small and dark but relatively clean, though the white tile floor was cracked and yellowing. I flipped down the toilet's lid and sat down, trying to get accustomed to the dim lighting. A hairbrush, flat and square, sat by the sink next to a bottle of Pepto-Bismol, its contents the same bubble-gum pink as the antibiotics I had been spooning into my two-year-old daughter Lila's mouth to treat yet another ear infection.

The idea of stealing some of Mario's hair from the brush to obtain a DNA sample passed through my mind before I remembered that there was no evidence that I could test that would exonerate my client. I had been watching too many cop shows lately.

I closed my eyes and pressed my fingers against my temples, suddenly embarrassed that I had allowed myself to be dragged into this fool's errand, attempting to get a street-hardened drug dealer to confess to a stabbing for which others were already serving time. But on some level I just couldn't believe that Mario, who I truly believed had done the crime, did not feel crushing guilt. When I opened my eyes again, the flash of neon pink emanating from the Pepto-Bismol bottle reminded me that I had to make a follow-up doctor's appointment for Lila. Guiltily, I wondered if her tiny ears were hurting. Sure, she had seemed fine when I had left hours earlier, but she could have gotten worse by now.

I felt a moment of flickering admiration for Mario, for his ability not to let guilt shake him, not to entertain even for a second the possibility of confessing and cleansing his soul. I longed for a small portion of his psychopathology to rub off on me, to alleviate the working-mother guilt that seemed to linger about me, like low-lying clouds that would never quite burn off.

I opened the bathroom door and walked back to the living room. Roy stood up, met my gaze, and shook his head slightly, conveying that he had gotten nowhere. As we left the apartment, Roy gave Mario his card and told him to call if he ever wanted to talk about the case. I knew it would be a cold day in hell before Mario reached for the phone.

...................................

My mother worked from the day she left her childhood home at age seventeen to make it big in New York City, until the day she gave birth to my oldest brother, well over a decade later. When her singing voice failed to pay the bills, she sold retail apparel. Standing barely five feet one, with green eyes and jet-black hair, my mother could sell anything to anyone.

She spent her summers in Vermont working as a music counselor at an all-girls camp I would later attend. When she grew tired of working retail during the winter, she went to work as a hospital administrator and climbed her way up until she was overseeing an entire unit at Mount Sinai. Then she taught music throughout Westchester until she was seventy-eight. She still has ten times my energy.

After my oldest brother's birth, my father worried about my mother giving up her career, though not because of the money. Back then they certainly needed the second income, but he worried that my mother's energy reserves would barely be tapped by caring for a single infant.

"What will you do with yourself?" my father asked apprehensively.

"I'll figure it out," was the only response my mother would give.

For the next fifteen years, until she returned to the workforce when I was nine, she devoted herself to raising my brothers and me, taking cooking classes and tennis lessons, volunteering as class mother, singing in the choir at our synagogue. Never once did I hear her complain that raising children was hard, that she found the laundry or the cleaning overwhelming, that she needed more time to herself.

Never once did my mother express any guilt about her parenting decisions. If she slapped my wrist when I darted into the grocery store parking lot or because I was bugging her incessantly as she tried to talk on the phone, she never came to beg forgiveness while I sobbed in my room. If I packed my bags and pretended to run away from home, she didn't follow, urging me to come back. When I threw a tantrum and told her I hated her, she never once sought to engage me in deep discussions about my feelings. "But I love you," she would say softly and close the door until I regained control of myself.

Not until I had my first child did I appreciate the genius of my mother's guilt-free parenting. Like baking a perfect piecrust, mothering is a skill whose difficulty cannot be appreciated until your sleeves are rolled up to your armpits with the effort. For me that effort has always involved wrestling with guilt, second-guessing my parenting decisions, and perpetually wondering if I am getting it right.

My maternal guilt came on early, even before Jessie was born. At twenty weeks, a full four months before my due date, I started having contractions. My doctor put me on bed rest for a week until I called to say that I was going crazy. She then let me return to work only after I promised to drastically cut back my hours. I spent the next several months worried that my refusal to remain in bed would somehow harm the baby.

Then when Jessie was born, a day before her due date, she gained weight incredibly slowly, and I had to decide whether supplementing her diet with formula would be preferable to watching her struggle to gain weight on just breast milk.

"Just give her the bottle," my mother urged. "Formula never hurt you."

But back then I was not taking anyone's advice. By the time I was finished researching the issue, reading every article, talking to my pediatrician, getting a second opinion from another pediatrician, and consulting a lactation support group, Jessie refused to take formula with any regularity. I felt guilty every time I took her to the doctor, convinced that her low weight reflected some failure on my part.

When I would call my mother following each doctor's visit to report on Jessie's unimpressive gains, she would advise me not to worry, that Jessie would one day be in Weight Watchers, like the rest of us. But my mother's efforts at reassurance never convinced me that I was getting it right.

Sometimes I wonder if guilt is a job hazard, if on some level I know that there is no true balance between work and home, that the act of trying ends up compromising the well-being of both my children and my clients. Conventional wisdom holds that you can't please all of the people all of the time. But as a working mother, it sometimes seems that despite all your efforts, you can displease all of the people all of the time.

I frequently arrive at the office with two-year-old Maya's screams of "No more work for Mommy!" still ringing in my ears (my older daughters long ago recognized that such edicts were futile), only to find a client's angry letter waiting on my chair, berating me for not doing more to address his plight. Such mornings used to send me into spirals of self-doubt. Now I am better at pushing Maya's screams from my mind and dashing off a reply to that angry client specifying exactly what I intend to do and *not* to do on his behalf.

Sometimes nothing is good enough, and Maya is still cranky that night when I get home and the client remains angry despite my best efforts to appease him. But by this point, I know when it is time to accept that I am not the sole determinant of Maya's happiness or the client's displeasure, to let go of the vain notion that every decision I make is of critical importance. There is freedom in accepting that reality. But then again, accepting reality has never been one of my strengths. If it were, I would have never gotten involved in Corrie Angelo's case at all.

## BORROWING TROUBLE

In the spring of 2002, I was feeling vaguely restless at work. During the preceding months, I had won the motion to vacate Stephen DeLuca's conviction. I had gotten the case against Eric Eastman dismissed. I had survived September 11 and its aftermath. I felt strangely invincible, as if I had discovered some secret method of sensing the rot that lay just beneath the carefully polished floorboards of every case I was handling.

With Lila weaned months earlier, sleeping regularly through the night and out of diapers, I found myself with renewed energy. It was the first time in years I was not trying to get pregnant, was not actually pregnant, was not recovering from being pregnant. It was as if I'd surfaced from a deep, dark lake and was finally able to take a breath.

At the beginning of May 2002, Rich mentioned during a team meeting a case that had him stymied. Once a week our office breaks into small assigned groups to discuss our cases in depth and to strategize. It was unusual at such meetings for Rich to seem in need of help—he had started representing clients when I had started fifth grade. But a case that had appeared to be routine when it had been assigned to our office by the court was rapidly becoming a far more complex undertaking, due to the repeated requests of the client's family for a complete reinvestigation of the crime. Rich didn't know where to begin.

Rich's client, Corrie Angelo, along with his little brother, had been accused of attempting to murder a college student during a gang assault. The victim and four undercover police officers explained in detail how the unprovoked and vicious attack had occurred. Four police eyewitnesses and the victim—five witnesses in all—testified that Rich's client had done the stabbing while his cohorts had pounded on the victim with their fists and various weapons, including a garlic press. Ordinarily, producing five eyewitnesses would be considered overwhelming evidence of guilt, so overwhelming that few errors would be expected to impact the verdict.

But the defense had presented several witnesses of its own to contradict the prosecution's. One woman who lived in the neighborhood and had been watching the melee from her apartment window insisted that Rich's client had not been the stabber, that in fact a neighborhood drug dealer, Mario Gonzalez, had done the stabbing. Other witnesses came forward to testify that Mario had actually admitted stabbing the victim and escaping during the chaos that erupted after the cops had arrived on the scene.

As I listened to Rich, I heard myself asking to review the transcripts. I didn't know what I was hoping to prove. I had plenty of my own cases needing my attention, but there was something about the facts that I found intriguing. *How could there be so many witnesses on both sides telling such different stories?* I wondered.

In my arrogance, I thought that just by reviewing the record I (unlike Rich) would be able to tell who was lying and who was telling the truth. I assured Rich that I would look over the case on my own time and still meet all my obligations to my own clients. My offer was too good to refuse. Within a few hours, a complete copy of the record, all 1,500 pages of it, was sitting on my desk.

I opened the first volume and started reading about events that had taken place almost exactly two years earlier. On May 15, 1999, Ramon Jiminez had just returned home from his freshman year at Boston University to spend the summer at his family's home in the Hunts Point section of the Bronx. Despite his humble beginnings, Jiminez was one of those inner-city kids who was clearly going places. Before going to college, he had been a scholarship student at a prestigious private school in Riverdale. He did not tend to hang out much in Hunts Point. His crowd hailed from Manhattan's Upper West Side—the sons and daughters of doctors and lawyers.

On that warm spring evening, he would have been looking forward to catching up with his high-school buddies in Manhattan. Jiminez must have forgotten about the dangers of his old neighborhood, because he took the subway home at a very late hour, around 2:00 a.m. He emerged from the Hunts Point subway station and walked toward his parents' house. A group of men were hanging out at the street corner.

As Jiminez crossed the street, he heard the men screaming "Ay, yo!" but he paid no attention. The men continued to summon him. "Ay, yo, you with the red shirt!" they cried. Only then did Jiminez look down at his own red shirt and realize that the men were attempting to get his attention.

When he turned around to see what the group wanted, there was a lone man, identified at trial as our client, Corrie Angelo, asking what Jiminez was doing wearing a red shirt; the man ordered him to take it off. Jiminez might have run with a more elite crowd than the group hanging out on the corner, but he still understood that when you are confronted in the wee hours of the morning by the locals asking about your choice to wear the color favored by members of the Bloods gang, it has nothing to do with offending anybody's fashion sense. Jiminez assured the man that his red shirt was not gang related. The man pulled out a knife. Jiminez took off the shirt.

Jiminez's compliance did nothing to appease. The man now ordered him to turn over his money as well. Having just spent the evening in Manhattan, Jiminez had little money left to cough up. He reached into his back pocket and pulled out a bunch of singles. Four other men had now joined the man with the knife, including

Corrie Angelo's brother, Robert. At trial, Jiminez identified two other men from pictures, Juan Peres and Peter Richardson.

Once Jiminez had surrendered his money, the men demanded his watch and everything else he had. While Jiminez unlatched his watch, he was struck by one of the men. The others soon joined in. Jiminez hunched over, covering his head and face while the gang went at him. Within seconds, he felt a stab wound to his side. He looked up and saw the man who had originally approached him pulling the knife away.

Luckily for Jiminez, four undercover Bronx Gang Unit police officers were on routine patrol in the area. Sergeant Dillon Malone was responsible for supervising police officers Kyle Marks, Richard Ponce, and Dennis Chang. While stopped at a traffic light in their unmarked car, the officers saw a group of youths acting rowdy and putting on red bandannas, a typical accessory of Bloods gang members (and suburban mothers having bad hair days).

Rather than blowing through the red light at 2:00 a.m. to follow the boisterous pack, Sergeant Malone waited dutifully for the light to change. Only when they had cleared the light could the police see the group attacking Jiminez.

It was party time. The gang unit officers jumped out of their car without activating their police lights, putting on their siren, or calling for backup. While they claimed that they identified themselves as police officers, Jiminez testified that he did not hear anyone screaming "Police!" All Jiminez knew was that there was a big struggle between his assailants and some other people who were trying to help him. Jiminez did not wait to see which group emerged victorious. He dragged himself home, his chest rapidly filling with blood from his stab wound, and collapsed on the floor.

Malone testified that upon arriving at the scene he ordered Corrie Angelo to drop the knife. Our client complied and started to walk away. When Malone tried to subdue Corrie, our client allegedly started punching. According to Officer Marks, Corrie, in addition to punching Malone, had attempted to reach for Marks's gun. As a result, our client ended up with his head cracked open by Marks's flashlight and his eyes sprayed with Mace before he was successfully cuffed.

Malone then followed the drops of Jiminez's blood down the street, like the bread crumbs in "Hansel and Gretel," until he arrived in Jiminez's living room. While

EMS workers readied Jiminez for transport to the hospital, where he would remain for a week with a collapsed lung, Malone assured him that all his attackers had been caught.

Back at the scene, the other team members were collecting physical evidence, none of which would tie Corrie Angelo to the stabbing. The knife used during the stabbing was recovered from the ground, as were Jiminez's watch, credit cards, and a garlic press. All were dusted for fingerprints, though no fingerprints were recovered.

The police collected the suspects' clothing as evidence of their gang affiliation. From Peter Richardson they recovered a red bandanna; on Juan Peres they found a red skullcap and green beads, another favored fashion accessory of the Bloods. From the third assailant, Martin Gray, they retrieved red beads, a red bandanna, and his bloodstained underwear.

But unlike Richardson, Peres, and Gray, who were decked out in the Bloods' signature items, our client had not been wearing any red that night; nor had his brother, who was dressed in a multicolored designer sweater and blue jeans. There was blood, however, on Robert Angelo's pants, spattered high above the knee, up toward his waist.

The origin of the blood on Gray's underwear and Robert Angelo's pants was never determined. Even though the police had escorted Jiminez to a doctor to have his blood drawn in the weeks immediately preceding the trial—presumably to test it against the blood recovered from the clothing of those accused in the attack—the results of those tests were never introduced into evidence.

In addition to escorting Jiminez for blood tests, the police officers spoke with him on a number of occasions about the case. They reassured him about testifying and told him what they had done to rescue him. Jiminez wrote a letter to the NYPD commending the four officers for saving his life. That gesture earned him another personal visit from Officer Chang, who dropped in to thank him.

Sometime after the incident, the officers also brought Jiminez to the station house and displayed Mario Gonzalez to him through a two-way mirror. Jiminez testified at trial that he had seen Gonzalez around the neighborhood but did not think he had been involved in the attack.

After reading the prosecution's case, I did not consider the evidence of Corrie Angelo's guilt overwhelming. The police testimony sounded all too familiar to me.

Half a decade earlier, I'd spent a year defending police officers against civil rights complaints while simultaneously pursuing similar complaints against other officers whose departments had not retained my law firm. I'd learned a lot in that year about police policy and practices, more from defending my police clients than from representing civil rights plaintiffs.

Much has been written about the blue wall of silence, the reticence of police officers to rat out their brothers, even if those brothers had behaved badly. But not much has been said about the blue wall of stupidity, which causes some cops to lie even when telling the truth would be quicker and easier.

I remember cases involving young police officer clients where it was apparent to me from the record that they had done everything by the book, done nothing wrong, yet asked me which "version" of the truth I wanted to hear and recounted for me what brother officers were going to say when they were interviewed by Internal Affairs. When I would tell them that there were no "versions" of the truth, that truth is a singular noun, they would look at me in disbelief, wondering why they were not being represented by a real lawyer, someone who understood how the game was played.

Just looking at them, I remember being confident that they had done everything right, or even if they had made mistakes, we could deal with them. But if they lied in their official reports or if the other officers lied to try to make it all seem picture perfect, there was a greater chance that things would end badly for them.

In those cases, Internal Affairs ultimately deemed my clients' actions entirely proper. But they had been so filled with worry and doubt, so willing to listen to the veterans on the force who wanted to give them a prepared script, that my clients were ready to lie themselves out of their jobs. In one case I actually sat at the typewriter in the police precinct, my pregnant belly making it difficult to reach the keyboard, and typed up my client's reports for him. I was worried that if I failed to babysit, somebody else would convince him to change his story.

The police testimony from the Corrie Angelo trial had that prefabricated, scripted quality to it. It was some "version" of the truth, a story the officers had cobbled together after they had busted open some heads.

There was also something about the way the incident unfolded that made me suspect that the Bronx gang unit officers were cowboys who made up their own rules as they roamed through the darkened streets. They had failed to identify themselves, to place a bubble light on top of their car, to call for backup, and they'd used a flashlight as a club. None of these were in the NYPD manual of standard operating procedures.

As for Ramon Jiminez, he was so grateful to the officers for saving his life, so ready to accept that they had caught all those responsible for harming him, that his account did not seem particularly reliable either. He'd observed his attackers on a dark street; they were strangers to him, and the whole incident unfolded in a matter of seconds, during which he was hunched over with his face covered.

But Jiminez was a most sympathetic victim. I still remember how he described having difficulty fishing out his spare singles to surrender because his hands were shaking so badly. That fact never made it into anybody's brief, but it has remained with me over the years. Thinking about that small detail, the image it evokes, still makes my chest hurt. When my daughter Lila is tired or frightened, her hands tend to quiver. Maybe that's why the image has stayed with me over the years.

......................................

When I finished reading the testimony of the prosecution's witnesses, I temporarily closed the transcript to search the file for the pre-sentencing report. This report, prepared by the Department of Probation to aid the court in imposing a proper sentence, outlines the defendant's criminal history and inevitably makes for some interesting reading. But the criminal history section of Corrie Angelo's report was entirely blank. *That's weird,* I thought.

We all have our petty offenses of choice. If I walk into the living room and there is a pile of dirty clothes on the floor, I know Lila is the culprit. When I suddenly find my socks soggy and look down to see a puddle at my feet, I know that

Maya has been experimenting once again with the impact of gravity on the $H_2O$ molecule. A hairbrush left on the kitchen counter with long hairs waiting to waft into our food means Jessie has been styling again, while the food-encrusted dishes piled next to the sink were undoubtedly left by my husband—remnants of a late-night snack. Cotton balls carelessly discarded in the toilet, challenging our temperamental plumbing and thus threatening the foundation of our family unit . . . I'll take the Fifth on that one.

I have reached a stage in my career where few of the cases that cross my desk involve petty offenses. Having risen to Senior Appellate Counsel—a title that makes me feel as if my invitation to join the AARP will arrive any day in the mail— I know that most of my clients are not virgins to the criminal justice system.

And that is why if I had doubts about Corrie Angelo's guilt after reading the prosecution's case, the testimony of the defense witnesses only added to them. The most convincing witness was Corrie Angelo himself. At twenty-six, he had never been convicted of a crime. At the time of the incident, he was still living at home with his mother and little brother, Robert. He had just quit his job at the Hunts Point market.

Corrie testified that on the night of his arrest, he had gone to a birthday party for his friend Ronnie Torres in the basement of an apartment building located on Bryant Avenue. Like a lot of men in Hunts Point, Ronnie had a criminal record. He had just finished an upstate bid for selling drugs.

The party was hot and crowded, with lots of people from the neighborhood hanging out eating and drinking. There was a big birthday cake served at around midnight, and the revelers sang "Happy Birthday" to the guest of honor. By 2:00 a.m., the party was still going, but it was winding down. Corrie and Robert left and walked to a nearby store on Hunts Point Avenue. Robert bought some cigarettes while Corrie spoke to some people hanging around outside.

Suddenly, a "melee" broke out across the street, and a crowd of people, including Robert, rushed to check it out. Corrie Angelo followed his little brother, undoubtedly worried that Robert might get himself into trouble. When Corrie walked over to the crowd, the police arrived and ordered him to the ground. Corrie turned to explain that he had done nothing wrong. The explanation was greeted with the butt of Officer Marks's gun bashing into Corrie's head, splitting it open. Corrie fell to the pavement hard, and the officers continued to hit him. The defense introduced pictures of Corrie shirtless in the hospital with bruises on his chest, shoulders, and face. Corrie insisted that his clothes had been splashed with his own blood from a gash on his head, which required numerous staples to close.

Robert, who was nineteen at the time of the 1999 incident, testified that when he crossed the street toward the gathering crowd, he saw two or three guys beating up another guy. The police pushed Robert to the ground, causing him to cut his knee, which bled. Following his arrest, the police took his pants because of the bloodstains on them.

Another witness for the defense, Cara Reilly, lived in a first-floor apartment overlooking the crime scene. In May 1999, Reilly had a friend staying at her apartment who had just had a baby. On the night of the stabbing, the baby woke up for a feeding, and Reilly heard a ruckus outside her living-room window. Peering out the window, she saw Mario Gonzalez stab another boy while a crowd looked on. When the police arrived, Gonzalez ran away.

The defense also called one of Mario's girlfriends, who testified that during a quiet, intimate moment Mario had admitted to her that he had stabbed the victim. Some men play soft music or buy flowers to set the mood. Mario apparently confessed to gang assaults.

By the time I finished reading the defense case, I was leaning toward crediting it over the prosecution's. It seemed plausible that Corrie and Robert had gone to a party, seen a skirmish, gone over to investigate, and been beaten by the cops, who in the ensuing melee let the true perpetrator, Mario Gonzalez, escape. But the prosecution was not about to let the defense have the last word.

To rebut the testimony of the defense witnesses, the prosecution called the EMS worker who had tended to Corrie Angelo to refute any claim that Corrie could have been the source of the blood on his brother's pants. According to the EMS worker, there was no blood on Corrie's clothes, and a cut on his head was not actively bleeding.

Then the prosecution called Mario Gonzalez himself. In May 1999, Mario had been on parole for selling drugs. He first got arrested when he was fourteen years old and had spent most of the late 1990s in and out of prison. Two weeks before the assault on Ramon Jiminez, Mario had been arrested again, at the corner of Bryant and Seneca avenues. This time he was accused of selling drugs with Juan Peres.

Mario admitted that he too had been at Ronnie's party. There he had seen Corrie and Robert, both of whom he knew from the neighborhood, as well as Peres, Richardson, and Martin Gray. But Mario claimed he was at the party with his baby's mother, Janet Avery, and their infant son.

At first Mario testified that he had left the party around 11:00 p.m. and that by 2:00 a.m. he was staying with Janet at her grandmother's house. Mario was on parole at the time, and being out after 11:00 would have been a violation that could have resulted in his returning to prison. But Mario then admitted that he "probably" was outside at 2:00 a.m., because he remembered seeing a commotion involving "mad cops," but Mario claimed he had just kept walking.

Almost immediately after the People announced they had no further evidence to offer and the defense too had rested, the defense attorneys moved to reopen their case. They had recently learned that Sergeant Malone, the commanding officer of the undercover unit, had a lengthy history of complaints being lodged against him with the Civilian Complaint Review Board (CCRB), the City agency responsible for vetting citizens' complaints against police officers. The defense had subpoenaed the CCRB records before the trial began, but the records had only been turned over after the defense had rested. The attorneys had served the subpoena and then in the heat of trial forgot to follow up—some very sloppy lawyering.

Turns out, Malone had a total of twenty-two charges lodged against him arising from thirteen separate incidents, all accusing him of abusing his authority in some way: illegally detaining suspects, illegally stopping and searching their cars. Four of the complaints had been "substantiated"—the CCRB's jargon for determined to be true. In three of the substantiated cases, Malone's partner in crime had been none other than police officer Kyle Marks.

But the judge had run out of patience. Although little time had passed since both sides had rested their respective cases, Justice Albert refused to allow the defense to reopen in order to question Malone about his sordid past. The application was untimely, the information about Malone's misdeeds was irrelevant, and a delay of the trial for further cross-examination would be most "inappropriate," Justice Albert concluded.

Corrie Angelo's case would be among the last that Justice Albert would preside over. He'd retired a few months later and at the time of the case had obviously been looking forward to leaving behind the drama of Bronx Supreme Court. He'd been cranky and impatient throughout the Angelo proceedings.

On summation, the prosecutor, Yasmin Krane, focused on Ramon Jiminez's account. Jiminez had no reason to lie about who had attacked him, Krane argued over and over again. The defense's claims that Mario Gonzalez had done the stabbing were ridiculous, she insisted. Mario himself had testified that he had been with Janet Avery and his son that evening, not stabbing anybody. All the defense witnesses were persuaded to lie by the defendants' mother, the prosecutor suggested.

The blood evidence also played big in the prosecution's arguments. "How would Robert Angelo have gotten blood on his pants, near his waist, if he had never gone near Ramon Jiminez?" the prosecutor asked rhetorically. The blood on Robert's jeans was not near the knee, where it would have been if it belonged to Robert himself.

The blood could not have come from Corrie Angelo's head wound, the prosecutor insisted, recounting that Corrie didn't have blood on his own clothing. This serological evidence was "so important" because it proved that Robert, and by implication Corrie, had been in close contact with Ramon Jiminez and not, as they claimed at trial, late-arriving innocent bystanders.

Almost immediately after beginning their deliberations, the jurors asked to have the minutes of Ramon Jiminez's testimony read to them. It would be the only witness account they asked to hear. But they did not reach a verdict that first day and were sequestered for the evening.

The next morning the defense again asked to reopen its case. Janet Avery, the mother of Mario's baby, had come forward to admit that she had lied to the police and the prosecution when she said that Mario had been with her on the night of the incident. She had actually been homeless and staying at a women's shelter with her baby; Mario had admitted to her that he had done the stabbing and had forced her to provide him with a false alibi. But Justice Albert had denied the application to reopen the case as untimely, and thus, Janet Avery was not allowed to testify.

Janet was still seated in the courtroom when the jury returned its verdict convicting Corrie and Robert of attempting to murder Ramon Jiminez. Corrie Angelo screamed at Justice Albert, asking why the judge had not allowed Janet's testimony. "She's right there!!" Corrie yelled.

The judge was not interested in hearing a convicted felon question his rulings. Corrie and Robert were swiftly removed from the courtroom, before the jurors were polled—individually asked if they agreed with the verdict.

At the sentencing four months later in November 2000, Corrie Angelo's defense attorney, Paul DePaulo, himself a former Bronx prosecutor, announced that a "tragic mistake" had been made. Corrie personally stood to tell the judge that he was innocent. Justice Albert declared that the prosecution had introduced overwhelming evidence of both brothers' guilt. "If you guys aren't guilty, then Santa Claus exists," the judge said, before sentencing both Corrie and Robert to fifteen years in prison.

I closed the transcript and smiled slightly. *Yes, Virginia, there is a Santa Claus*, I thought to myself. I turned on my computer and started furiously typing a memo to Rich, outlining my plans to reinvestigate the case.

# THE SINS OF THE FATHERS

If I counted all the fathers of my various clients whom I have actually met over the years, using the fingers on my right hand as my daughter Lila does when confronted with even the simplest addition problem, I would still have one finger left over to point at all the other fathers who failed to materialize. They failed to show up in my office, I imagine, as they failed to show up at every critical juncture in their children's lives.

Anybody who doubts the importance of having two parents fully invested in a child's well-being should come sift through the pre-sentencing reports in my files: "Defendant was raised by a single mother. He did not know his father." "Defendant's father went to prison when defendant was a young boy and thereafter failed to play any role in his son's life." Over and over again, these phrases appear—probably a macro by now programmed on some bureaucrat's computer.

Talking to sobbing or stoic women, mothers, girlfriends, sisters, and wives is part of my daily routine. Their stories are heartbreaking, their emotions raw. I never hurry them out of my office or glance down at my watch as they speak. I consider listening to them to be an important part of my service, a way of helping my clients who cannot be there themselves to offer any comfort. However, as much as I might sympathize with these women, their tears run together in my mind—tributaries into a river of undifferentiated pain. But I remember in vivid detail each father I have met.

There was Stephen DeLuca's father, Gerald, he of the homegrown lilacs. Gerry would call to say he was coming to see me, inevitably get lost in the maze of Lower Manhattan, and leave me waiting hours for his arrival. He was a sweet man, boyish, well-meaning, genuinely concerned for his son. He died a few years back. I miss hearing from him, knowing that he is out there supporting Stephen, even if he rarely made it up to visit him. In the spring, I miss the lilacs he used to bring me when we did manage to meet.

There was Timothy Grant's dad, who, with his wife, had raised eight children in the St. Nicholas housing projects. He'd hobbled into my office that first time, hunched over a cane, insisting that his son could not possibly have murdered anyone. Mr. Grant's other seven children had all gone on to better things. A daughter had become a nurse, a son a police officer. But I could tell that my troubled client held a special place in his father's heart.

The third father I met was Michael Rinaldo. He had raised all of his children as a single parent. Like his mother, my client, Ben Rinaldo, had been diagnosed with mental illness. He had the IQ of an eight- or nine-year-old child, and the thought of "Benny" spending eighteen years in prison clearly broke his father's heart.

And then there was Carlos Angelo. He was the most impressive of all. The only father who not only came on time to every meeting but arrived wearing a suit and carrying a leather briefcase from which he would remove a yellow legal pad in order to take notes of our conversations. I liked Carlos Angelo immensely. He was smart and charming, concerned about his sons, invested in their cases, but never rude or overbearing.

I met Carlos and the boys' mother, Renee, soon after I started working on their case. Renee's presence had hung heavily over the Angelo trial. According to the prosecution, she had persuaded every defense witness to lie for her sons. She had done so not through bribes or threats, but simply through her mournful pleas and tears. Renee was a weeper. Unlike Carlos, who remained clear-eyed at all times, Renee's mascara had often streamed down her face by the time she left my office.

The way the trial had been conducted infuriated the elder Angelos. The jury had not heard important information about Sergeant Malone's background or Janet Avery's admission that she had lied to the police to protect Mario. I explained that those errors could be challenged on appeal, but that my goal was to find new evidence that had not yet been uncovered.

At our first meeting, I laid out for the Angelos what I had outlined in the memo I prepared for Rich right after reading the record. I wanted to speak to Juan Peres, who had pled guilty to assaulting Jiminez and was still serving his sentence in an upstate prison. Peres had sold drugs with Mario two weeks before the attack, and I figured he would have some insights into Mario's past criminal behavior that might prove interesting. I also wanted to delve deeper into the complaints that had been lodged against Sergeant Malone and Officer Marks.

The prosecution's failure to test the blood found on Robert's pants also troubled me. The possibility of the prosecution's testing the blood had first been mentioned immediately before the trial began, well after such tests should have been ordered. Then all discussions of testing vanished from the record. Both sides seemed content to go forward without any definite results. The prosecution had argued that the blood belonged to Jiminez. The defense countered that the prosecution had not conclusively proven its source. But if the blood belonged to somebody else other than Jiminez, it might tend to exonerate Corrie and Robert by supporting their claims that they had never come into close contact with the victim.

Carlos suggested that I visit both Corrie and Robert to discuss my investigation strategy with them. But Robert, who had not yet been assigned his own attorney by the appellate court, was not my client. I would plan my strategy with Corrie alone. He was being held at Coxsackie Correctional Facility, over two hours upstate, and was likely to be transferred to an even more remote prison in the near future.

My office had two law student interns working with me that summer, Alexandra Davis and Sophie Travetski. They were both enthusiastic and bright, unbelievably young, with a lot of pierced body parts. Alex had around seven holes in one earlobe alone. Sophie had her belly button pierced along with her ears. I knew about the belly button because she wore low-slung pants to work with skimpy shirts. Whenever I looked at them, I felt incredibly old and nervous that by the time my girls entered adolescence, even more outrageous ways to mutilate the female body would be in fashion.

I sat both women down the day before our first trip to visit Corrie Angelo and explained that they could not wear their various hoops and studs. They would set off the prison's metal detectors. On the day of our trip, I was pleased to see both interns dressed in dark suits that actually covered their bellies and hips and lacking their usual metal accoutrements.

We made it through security quickly and sat in a small private counsel room, waiting for Corrie Angelo. When he walked in, I could feel the interns' excitement at their first face-to-face visit with a real client.

Corrie Angelo's face was angelic. He had curly dark brown hair, evenly tanned skin, good cheekbones. His brown eyes were round and bright, with thick dark lashes framing them, the kind of eyelashes any mother would bemoan on a male infant because no daughter would ever be lucky enough to be graced with them. I observed that Corrie smiled easily, but without real joy. There was a self-consciousness about him, as if after adjusting to prison life surrounded only by men, being in a room with three women embarrassed him.

I introduced myself and explained that Alex and Sophie would be helping me with his case over the summer. Corrie had been expecting me to be alone. His parents had told him of my impending visit when they came to bring his daughter to visit. When I asked his daughter's name, Corrie responded, "Lila, she's five."

Hearing my own daughter's name being spoken by a client in prison momentarily startled me. When I regained my composure, I told Corrie that I had a two-year-old Lila. His face lit up with his first real smile.

"That's weird," he said. "It's not that common a name."

"It is weird," I agreed, as sadness for my client's daughter made my voice catch for an instant in my throat. I thought of how instead of having her father to tuck her into bed every night, she was being dragged up to prison once a week to see him in a crowded cafeteria, surrounded by other inmates and their families. If Corrie were transferred further upstate, even those weekly visits would stop, I imagined. He would fade further and further from his daughter's life. I pushed this familiar, sad scenario from my mind and turned my full attention back to the interview.

"So what can you tell me about Mario Gonzalez?" I asked, looking for any leads that might prove Mario to be the true culprit.

"Not much. I mean, I knew him from around the neighborhood. Everyone knew he was trouble. He was always getting drunk, fighting. My brother knew him better. I heard after the incident Mario was talking to people, trying to get them to say me and Robert did the stabbing. Some people said it was like he was trying to record them, like he was wearing a wire or something. Nobody from the neighborhood ever said they saw me or Robert stab anybody."

"Did you ever talk to him after you were arrested?"

"No. I know my sister spoke with him. He told her that he felt bad for us, but there was nothing he could do, because he was on parole and would go back to jail forever if he went down for this. You three should go talk to him, see what he has to say now," Corrie suggested, smiling.

"You really think he would admit anything to us?" I asked, not telling Corrie that I would never let the interns go near Mario Gonzalez. If I did and their law-school placement offices learned about the visit, they would be the last two interns to work at my office. I would go alone with Roy Swain after the interns had returned safely to school.

"Three pretty ladies come to his door, you never know," Corrie responded. Alex and Sophie smiled warmly.

"I'll have to think about that one," I said. "Tell me about Juan Peres."

"Don't know too much about him either. I didn't hang out much with that crowd. They're all younger than me. I was working. I would see Juan and Mario hanging around the neighborhood. But like I said, I was pretty busy. I didn't pay too much attention."

After meeting with Corrie for an hour, I ended the interview. I wasn't learning anything that I hadn't already read about in the transcript. Either Corrie Angelo really didn't have any more information to disclose, or he wasn't willing to tell me what he knew. I had no way of knowing. Ordinarily, when I meet with clients I find it easy to impress upon them the importance of their being entirely candid with me. But with two young interns present, I had been thrown off my rhythm. I have learned that when I really need to press a client about sensitive information, it is better to visit alone, without providing another set of eyes for him to seek in order to escape my gaze.

When I arrived home later that afternoon, after dropping off Alex and Sophie at the train station, my daughter Lila was sitting at the kitchen table eating sardines like a sea otter, bones and all. She asked me where I had been, being clearly confused by my midafternoon homecoming. I told her that I had been visiting someone who also had a little girl named Lila, just like me. Lila was instantly delighted to learn that there was another little girl somewhere who shared her name. "When can I meet the other Lila?" she asked. I explained that the other Lila lived too far away for us to visit.

Over the years, Lila remained fascinated by Corrie Angelo's case. Whenever I would dress up for court or to visit a client, Lila would ask if I was going to see the other Lila's daddy. Her interest always made me feel guilty for mentioning the case to her at all.

Once Lila becomes fixated on something, there is no shaking it from her brain. Even the most innocuous facts can brew into a troubling potion. Recently we were watching a nature program discussing evolution and the shrinking human Y chromosome. The narrator mentioned that in a million years the Y chromosome could shrink to such a degree that there will be no more male human beings. It was the sort of dry scientific speculation that escaped from my mind immediately. But two hours later, Lila burst into tears, explaining through her sobs that she was worried that in a million years there would be no daddies left. I stifled my laughter and told her that nobody knew for sure what would happen tomorrow, never mind a million years from now. I didn't dare tell Lila that fathers tended to disappear for reasons that had little to do with the size of their chromosomes.

# 911

If you were going to commit a crime with someone, a serious offense for which you could go to prison for years, whom would you choose as your partner? You would probably pick your cohort with care from among the people you know well, which is why I was willing to travel six hours to Auburn Correctional Facility in upstate New York to speak to Juan Peres in person. Peres, who had pleaded guilty to participating in the attack on Jiminez, had been arrested for selling drugs with Mario Gonzalez two weeks before the attack. I wagered that Peres would have deeper insights into Mario than just about anybody else.

One Sunday evening toward the end of July, I picked up my interns at the train station nearest to my house, piled them and their bags into the back of my small, black Volvo wagon, and headed north. Sophie and Alex had saved me the time and effort of planning the trip's logistics, finding hotel accommodations near the prison, mapping the quickest routes, arranging gate passes with the proper authorities. After all that work, I figured they deserved to come along for the ride. I also wanted to get their impressions of Juan Peres.

A six-hour road trip with two single twenty-four-year-olds chattering about their latest loves, music, movies was like crossing into a different universe. Alex had recently fallen in love with another woman and waxed poetic about the joys of lesbian sex, its different pace, the benefits of not having to wait for a man to reboot. On the other hand, Sophie was having the usual problems with men, their inscrutability, their stupidity, their refusal to commit. Having been married for close to nine years, I had little to add to the conversation. But I found their eagerness to discuss their experiences with me strangely endearing.

When they were not talking about sex, they wanted to listen to their own bad pop music of the Britney Spears variety. I had never heard a Britney Spears song before that trip, although back in 2002 she was quite popular and had not yet become a punch line in nearly every late-night comedian's opening monologue. Still, I sat in the front disbelieving that anybody would spend money to hear Spears croon about being a slave for you or doing it again. But by the time we reached the hotel located right outside the prison gate, Spears's voice was trapped in my head, so bad it was almost, but not quite, good.

It was close to midnight when we finally got to the city of Auburn and checked into our rooms at the Holiday Inn. I immediately realized that I was starving. I had forgotten to eat before I left the house. The pressure to reach our destination before I fell asleep behind the wheel had prevented me from stopping for anything other than a bag of chips on the road. I called the hotel restaurant and got no answer. Nobody picked up at the local Pizza Hut. Same story when I called the front desk.

It was strange to feel hungry. I had gotten used to constantly carrying food with me just in case Jessie or Lila needed a snack. I rarely had the opportunity to experience hunger myself, because in the process of constantly feeding them, I was perpetually scarfing down their leftovers. Finding myself without raisins or animal crackers made more than my stomach feel empty. Aching for the girls, I curled up by myself to catch a few hours of sleep.

The morning broke bright and beautiful, the sunlight streaming through the plastic vertical blinds I had forgotten to close the night before. I showered and dressed in my conservative black suit. It felt slightly liberating to get dressed without being interrupted by my daughters' demands, their pleas to read a book, to help them find a towel or the toothbrush they had misplaced. I had forgotten how easy it could be to simply get showered and dressed. I raced down to the hotel restaurant's breakfast buffet. By the time Alex and Sophie strolled in, I had already been finished eating my breakfast for an hour. To be sociable, I ate a second one with them.

The Auburn Correctional Facility is located directly behind the Holiday Inn, the prison gate visible from outside the rooms' windows. There is nothing updated or modern about Auburn, the first prison built in New York State. It is a hulking structure constructed of roughly hewn stone mined from the local hillsides. Auburn looks as if little mortar was used during its construction, the rocks sloppily thrown together into an impressively massive heap. Staring at it from across the hotel parking lot, I could tell there would be no air-conditioning inside.

Unfortunately, we had quite a wait in that heavy, unconditioned air. Apparently Juan Peres had not been behaving himself in prison. He had recently received time in SHU, the prison's special housing unit, and had been cut off from the prison's general population. When he finally arrived at our meeting, close to two hours after we had cleared security, the first thing I noticed was his hair, which was black and thick and stood straight up, defying all the laws of gravity. The second thing was the blue-black ink etched into his arms, elaborate prison tattoos of dragons shedding tears or daggers dripping blood; I couldn't exactly tell. Then I surveyed the scars Peres had intentionally branded into his skin, three perfectly round raised dots in the shape of a triangle placed just beneath his shoulder.

Despite his classic prison gang member appearance, Juan Peres was a friendly kid. He was clearly pleased to have escaped from SHU, even if our visit would grant him only a temporary reprieve from his solitary confinement.

After introducing ourselves to Peres, I explained that we were representing Corrie Angelo and that I was interested in learning everything he could tell me about Mario Gonzalez. Any camaraderie Peres and Mario might have shared in the past had been burned away by the Auburn heat. At the mention of Mario, Peres's expression changed, as if an unpleasant taste had entered his mouth.

"Fuckin' Mario," Peres spat. "That guy gets away with more shit than you would believe."

"Like what?" I asked.

Peres launched into a long elaborate tale. Turns out he and Mario had been part of a large-scale drug operation, not merely pitching dime bags on the corner. It was a scheme that controlled the flow of heroin throughout a large swath of Hunts Point surrounding Bryant and Seneca avenues. Right after Mario and Peres were arrested, a joint task force of DEA agents and Bronx narcotics officers had busted a whole bunch of the organization's leaders. Those men were being prosecuted on federal drug charges in the Southern District of New York, facing a whole lot more time than Mario or Peres himself had ever served.

"What brand were you selling?" I asked, not that it mattered—I just wanted to keep the conversation flowing.

Drug dealing is a business, and dealers, like any other businessmen, try to build brand loyalty with their clientele. Drug users develop their own preferences for particular brand names. Just as I remember Ballet Slippers, the name of the pale pink nail polish I select on the rare occasions I treat myself to a manicure, a heroin user will remember her experience with a particular type of heroin.

Peres and Mario had been selling heroin branded 911. Their sales took place before the September 11 attacks; the name merely referred to the emergency number. After the attacks, dealers started naming their heroin WTC and Osama. Unlike cosmetics marketers who name nail polish colors with happy-sounding gibberish, heroin dealers invariably invoke deadly images to move product.

"Did you ever hear any rumors that Mario was snitching on anybody in the organization?" I asked.

When law enforcement authorities are trying to infiltrate a large-scale drug organization, they frequently do so by using informants. During our first interview, Corrie had mentioned that Mario had been going around the neighborhood in a van asking questions about the stabbing. That seemed snitchlike to me. If I could prove that Mario was a police informant, it could provide a motive for the police to fail to aggressively investigate Mario's role in Jiminez's stabbing. The authorities would not want Mario sent away for some small-time stabbing incident, if they were using him to infiltrate a major drug organization.

"Nah. I didn't hear that," Peres remarked. "But it wouldn't surprise me if the fucker was a snitch. He was always getting off easy. He would be in and out, and I would be sitting on Rikers waiting for my court dates, even though we was arrested at the same time for the same sale. Then the night of Ronnie's party, he stabs the kid and everybody else gets arrested but Mario," Peres complained.

"Did he ever mention getting special treatment or having connections with the police?"

"No. But there's no way anybody would say that. Good way to get yourself killed," Peres explained, obviously feeling the need to educate me on the ways of the street.

From Peres I obtained a list of people who had been arrested in the Bryant Avenue organization investigation. I would spend the next several months visiting them, trolling the federal court files, trying to get their defense attorneys to speak with me about the case. Mario's name never made it into any documents. But there were plenty of references to the use of anonymous informants throughout the investigation.

Mario had all the qualifications necessary to be a good police informant. He was deeply embedded in the Bryant Avenue organization. He had a tendency to get himself into trouble. And he was willing to sell out other people when doing so served his self-interest. Put it together and what do you have? A snitch. I was sure of it. Proving it—now that would be a different matter.

Upon returning from Auburn, I had Alex draft a formal request under the Freedom of Information Act to the New York City police department, asking it to disclose all the reports in its file relating to Mario's involvement in the Bryant Avenue organization. The department refused to provide the requested information, not because it did not exist but because access to the records "would endanger the life or safety of witnesses," a statutorily recognized exception to the duty to disclose.

Eventually, I became so frustrated at not being able to uncover any direct evidence of Mario's informant status that, following our early-morning meeting in his apartment, I phoned to pose the question directly to him. I sensed that on some level Mario felt guilty about Corrie Angelo's predicament. He didn't feel guilty enough to risk going back to jail by admitting the stabbing himself, but I hoped Mario might be willing to admit that he had been aiding the police in other investigations at the time of the Jiminez stabbing. Once again my approach seemed to amuse him.

"Man, I'd rather tell you I stabbed the dude. I'd only go to jail. If I admitted being a snitch, I'd be dead tomorrow," Mario explained, almost laughing out loud before hanging up on me.

*Fuckin' Mario*, I thought, Juan Peres's bitter tone echoing in my head.

......................................

Mario Gonzalez was not the only witness whose past deeds interested me. I was equally sure that Sergeant Dillon Malone's history would prove intriguing, if only I could find someone with insights willing to share. Unfortunately, I could not count on any of Malone's brother officers ratting out their sergeant to a defense attorney.

But sometimes numbers tell their own stories about police misconduct. Forty-one, the number of bullets fired at Amadou Diallo, the unarmed man killed by four Bronx Street Crimes Unit undercover officers in February 1999, left little doubt that excessive force had been used. Twenty-two, the number of civilian complaints maintained in Sergeant Malone's file, left me with little doubt that he was a rogue. That four of those complaints had been "substantiated," or deemed true, was also stunning. I had never come across an officer with so many substantiated complaints in his file.

I was hoping that one of the citizens who had filed a complaint against Malone with the Civilian Complaint Review Board had gone on to pursue a civil rights lawsuit against him in state or federal court. The CCRB does not award money; it is merely an administrative oversight agency that investigates citizens' complaints against the police. To recover damages, a lawsuit would need to be filed alleging that the police misconduct deprived the plaintiff of his civil rights. The plaintiff in such a suit would be entitled to discover details of Malone's disciplinary record. But Malone's misconduct, illegally stopping and searching people and their cars, was not the type of case likely to result in a quick profit for a plaintiff's lawyer. Fortunately, one of the people whose car Malone and Marks had illegally stopped and searched under false pretenses hadn't needed a lawyer. He was one himself.

On March 26, 1999, two months before the Ramon Jiminez stabbing, Edward

Childs, an African American attorney working for the Legal Aid Society in the Bronx, had just dropped off his girlfriend at a subway stop when Sergeant Malone, Officer Marks, and another officer drove up alongside Childs's new red Acura Legend. Apparently, a young black man driving an expensive car was all the probable cause Malone and company needed. They got out of their undercover car, ordered Childs out of the Acura, and started searching for drugs.

When Childs, a criminal defense attorney, demanded to know the reasonable suspicion the police officers had to stop him and search his car, Malone falsely accused Childs of failing to wear his seat belt. Childs became irate and wound up being arrested for disorderly conduct. Back at the precinct, Malone realized his mistake when Childs's Legal Aid Society identification card fell from his wallet. Malone picked it up, saw where the arrest was headed, and got Childs out of there as quickly as possible.

Childs was probably detained illegally for five hours. But with the help of a civil rights attorney friend, he vigilantly pursued his complaint with the CCRB and then a civil rights complaint against Malone and Marks on principle, not for money. The CCRB investigation determined that Malone and Marks had indeed stopped and searched Childs's car under false pretenses. The board also concluded that both Malone and Marks lied to cover up their misbehavior. Ultimately, Childs agreed to accept a $12,500 cash settlement and an apology from Malone to dispose of the civil rights lawsuit. The settlement terms required Malone to pay part of the money personally, from his salary, rather than from the city's coffers.

I decided to call Ed Childs to get his impressions of Malone, which Childs was more than willing to share. I could tell that even though more than three years had passed, he was still smarting from the contempt Malone had shown for him. A degree from an elite law school offered little protection for a young African American man driving a fancy red car in the Bronx. Such knowledge, once acquired, must be hard to forget.

"Do you think Malone would actually lie and get the other officers to lie about what happened in an attempted murder case?" I asked. "We're not talking about traffic violations here."

"All I can tell you is that when we were settling my case, Malone told me that he was the only one who was guilty, that the other officers were just following his lead. I don't see why it would be different, no matter how serious the case. That's how Malone operates," Childs explained.

Ed Childs's experiences with Malone and Marks convinced me that all four officers had lied at Corrie Angelo's trial. But from a legal perspective, the evidence Childs could offer would be of little use. The CCRB complaints were already part of the trial record, even though the jury had never learned of them. They could not be considered newly discovered. Malone's lying to cover up his wrongful arrest of Childs did not conclusively prove that he or any other police officer had lied at the Angelo trial. That Malone was a sinner did not convert Corrie Angelo into a saint.

# BLOODLUST

I was tired of walking down dangerous winding roads that led nowhere. Every time I felt that I had discovered a lead in Corrie Angelo's case that would become the turning point in my investigation, an impenetrable brick wall seemed to emerge.

Mario had been part of a large-scale drug operation, yet he'd seemed to avoid apprehension and serious punishment over and over again. Still, I could not find any evidence that conclusively established his identity as an informant. One day I went to interview yet another witness who claimed to know Mario well. The interview proved of little use, and days later I read in the newspaper of a drive-by shooting on the same block that killed an innocent bystander in broad daylight. *That could have been me,* I thought to myself as I closed the newspaper. I vowed to be more careful, to not let my frustration override my common sense.

Malone and Marks were dirty cops with a history of lying to cover up their misdeeds. But I could not conclusively prove that any officer had lied during the trial.

I craved hard evidence, the accuracy of which would be beyond dispute. Over and over again, my mind returned to the blood on Robert Angelo's pants, the blood the prosecution had insisted belonged to Ramon Jiminez, but which had inexplicably never been subjected to DNA testing. The police had gone through the trouble of escorting the victim to a doctor to have his blood drawn weeks before the trial began. *What happened to those tests?* I wondered.

In the autumn of 2002, six months after I first reviewed the case, I contacted the attorney assigned to represent Corrie's brother, Robert. Jennifer Stein worked in the same office as Nick Robleski and had been out of law school for two years. Robert Angelo's case was one of the first cases she had ever handled. During our first conversation, Jennifer's voice ranged from sweet to sweeter, perky to perkier. In all the time we worked together on the Angelo brothers' cases, well over a year, I never heard her once sound tired, frustrated, or cynical.

In fact, her constant good cheer made me wonder whether my personality had been negatively altered by the years of sleep deprivation. It occurred to me that perhaps parenting had changed my cells on the molecular level, irreversibly accelerating the aging process, a thought that seemed more likely whenever I spoke with Jennifer. Even though my youngest, Lila, was now sleeping through the night, the damage had been done. I had fallen into a state of permanent crotchetiness.

I shared with Jennifer what I had discovered over the summer, including the scale of Mario Gonzalez's drug dealing; my suspicions that he had been acting as an informant for the joint Bronx/DEA investigation into the Bryant Avenue cartel; and Malone's tendency to violate citizens' rights first, ask questions later, and lie about it after that. Jennifer and I also discussed the blood on Robert's pants and decided that she should take the lead on getting that evidence tested. Jennifer would contact the New York City Office of the Chief Medical Examiner, determine if the blood evidence was still in that office's possession, and learn how to get DNA tests conducted to resolve who was the source of the blood.

Less than a month after our original phone call, Jennifer Stein called me back with the answers to all those questions. Finding them had been surprisingly easy, because the blood tests had been completed years earlier, months *before* Corrie and Robert had each been sentenced to fifteen years in prison. In other words, as Corrie and Robert stood to protest their innocence before the sentencing judge, the prosecutor knew that the blood on Robert's jeans, the blood she had told the jury belonged to Jiminez, in fact belonged to somebody else. And she said nothing to set the record straight.

It is the regular practice of the New York City medical examiner's office to conduct DNA tests of blood or other bodily fluids in cases involving allegations of sexual assault and murder. In all other cases, a written request for DNA testing must be submitted by a prosecutor, outlining the need for the evidence. It is possible for defense attorneys to request a sample of the forensic evidence for testing by an independent lab or to push for testing by the medical examiner. But in all the years I have been practicing, I have never seen that happen, probably because if DNA evidence exonerates a client, he will have no need for my services. In the cases I handle, inevitably it is the prosecution that obtains the DNA test results.

Jiminez had survived the attack, so this case had not involved murder allegations. The prosecutor, Yasmin Krane, waited until a month before the trial began to ask the medical examiner's office to test the blood evidence, which included the blood recovered from Robert's pants and Martin Gray's underwear. Because of the lateness of the request and the demands of the ME's office, the results were not available until a month after the jury's verdict. Turns out the blood splashed on Robert Angelo's pants did not belong to Ramon Jiminez after all. It came from two other unknown sources. Only the blood on Martin Gray's underwear was conclusively matched to Jiminez.

The medical examiner's office immediately faxed the DNA test results to Yasmin Krane. In addition to faxing the results of the DNA evidence extracted from Robert's pants to the prosecutor, the medical examiner's office also entered the DNA profiles into its own database, sort of like filing anonymous fingerprints.

Months later, when Corrie Angelo and Juan Peres were sent upstate to their individual prisons, they were forced to surrender samples of their own DNA pursuant to the standard practice of the Department of Corrections. Every person who serves time in a New York State prison has his DNA recorded in a statewide database. Eventually, both Corrie's and Juan Peres's DNA profiles were compared with the ones recovered from Robert's pants. Contrary to the prosecutor's summation arguments at trial, Robert did not have the victim's blood splashed all over his jeans; rather, it was Corrie's blood, and some from Juan Peres as well.

The medical examiner's office then notified Krane of the match. And the prosecutor again did not disclose this information to anybody.

The blood evidence was important for several reasons. It supported the defense position that Robert, and by implication Corrie, never came into close contact with Ramon Jiminez. That the victim's blood had been recovered from Martin Gray's underwear further underscored its absence from Corrie's clothing. If Corrie had actually stabbed Jiminez, it seemed logical that he would have been more likely than Martin to be splattered with the victim's blood. But the police claimed there had been no blood whatsoever on Corrie's clothing.

"This is big," I told Jennifer on hearing the news. "It would have been better if it were Mario's blood somewhere—then we could prove he was lying about never going near the scene of the attack—but it really backs up Robert's and Corrie's accounts that they never went near Jiminez."

"Yeah, it also means there was a hell of a lot of blood running through the streets," Jennifer observed, as sweet and perky as ever. "Your client's blood is splashed all over. Juan Peres's blood is there. The victim's blood is on Gray's underwear. The only people who seemed to have escaped unscathed were Sergeant Malone and his crew of merry men."

"Yeah, just lucky, I guess."

Even though I should have been feeling hopeful, I knew that while the blood evidence was good, standing alone, it probably was not good enough.

......................................

Discovering the true nature of the blood evidence made me crave more of the hard stuff—objective evidence, not based on live witnesses vulnerable to accusations of lying or bias. I had hoped that the blood on Robert's jeans would belong to Mario Gonzalez. There would have been no denying his lying if his blood had been splashed all over the scene.

Now I needed a different way to reveal Mario's dishonesty. I started to focus on Janet Avery, the mother of Mario's son. She had told the police that Mario had been with her on the night of the incident. Then she had admitted to the defense that she had lied to protect Mario. Her account of Mario's activities was hopelessly conflicted, but the defense attorneys had mentioned during the trial that Avery had been staying at a women's shelter during the relevant time.

When Rich and I discussed whether it was worth trying to obtain a statement from Janet Avery, under oath, setting forth that she had not been with Mario on the night of the stabbing, Rich suggested that I try to determine whether Janet's presence at the shelter had been documented in some way.

"Maybe they kept a logbook of her comings and goings," Rich offered.

"So now I need to find a logbook from three years ago from some shelter whose name I don't even know. Excellent!" I laughed.

I had Roy Swain track down Janet. Roy is the father of several grown daughters, and I knew he would be able to persuade Janet to cooperate one way or another. Over the years, I have learned not to ask too many questions about how exactly Roy persuades everyone to speak with him. But Janet, like most everyone else, agreed to talk, although not to provide any information that could harm Mario. He might be a womanizing, no-good drug dealer, but he was still the father of her son, and that counted for something. When we finally met, I explained to Janet that I understood her position, which, strangely enough, I did. If Mario went back to jail, even the sporadic help he offered was sure to vanish.

Janet's son was three, around the same age as Lila was at the time. It is an age when any mother will take any help she can get from any source. Toddlers can tempt you to rely on the kindness of strangers. Three-year-olds are toddlers in spirit, but with stronger, more sturdy bodies, which allow them to kick harder and cry louder in the grocery store aisles when you refuse to buy them the six-pack of watermelon Bubble Yum.

At three, Lila was not subject to frequent tantrums, but she did seem to suffer bouts of hearing loss when she did not want to go to bed or turn off the television. Her ability to ignore my pleas convinced me she had developed a hearing problem, so I took her to have her hearing tested. The examiner asked me to wait out in the hall but kept the door open. From the hallway, I heard the examiner instruct Lila to raise her hand at the sound of the tones being piped through the headphones into her ears. Ten feet away, I could hear the beeps as the examiner kept turning up the volume. But when I peered into the room, Lila was still as a stone, refusing to raise her hand, despite the blasting beeps ringing in her ears. Within minutes, the examiner stomped out into the hallway to announce the results.

"It's not a hearing problem, it's a personality issue," she announced with great certainty.

There was something vaguely comforting about the diagnosis, expert confirmation that Lila was a ballbuster. So I sympathized with Janet Avery's plight and assured her that she did not need to tell me anything other than the name of the shelter where she'd been staying on the night of Jiminez's stabbing. After we had chatted a bit about the particular challenges presented by our three-year-olds, Janet gave me the name of the shelter and the telephone number of the woman who ran it, Sister Mary Winifred Daniels.

Sometimes in the course of my job, I come across very good people who not only want to make the world a better place but actually are willing to do the dirty work such lofty aspirations demand—to raise the money, find decent space in decrepit neighborhoods, negotiate the leases, sweep the floors, compile a collection of children's books and lightly worn clothing—in the hope that maybe, at the end of the day, a small group of poor women and their children will have a clean, safe place to stay. Sister Daniels is one of those people.

I was apprehensive about calling her because I guessed, using my superior powers of reasoning, that Sister Daniels was a nun. Coming from a place where I did not know anybody who was Christian until middle school, I tend to be nervous around nuns. While I had not hesitated to visit Mario Gonzalez to accuse him directly of being Ramon Jiminez's true assailant, dialing Sister Daniels's number made my palms sweat. I was afraid she might reach out over the phone and smack my hands with a ruler or something.

As it turned out, Sister Daniels was stern. Before she agreed to a meeting, she demanded that I explain over the phone not only who I was but the entire story of Corrie Angelo's trial and what I was hoping to accomplish. As I spoke through the phone, I was surprised to hear the passion in my pleas for her help. My voice was so filled with emotion that at times I had to stop talking, take a breath, and compose my thoughts. When I was done telling her about the incident, about Mario, the police witnesses, the victim, and the blood evidence, Sister Daniels did not hesitate for a second.

"I'll do whatever I can to help you," she promised.

The next afternoon, I had Janet Avery accompany me to the shelter, both so that I would not get lost in yet another unfamiliar Bronx neighborhood and also to assure Sister Daniels that Janet was consenting to the disclosure of records reflecting her whereabouts. Sister Daniels was waiting to meet us. She was a nun right out of central casting—starched habit, upright bearing, a large cross hanging from her neck, neatly combed straight dark hair streaked with gray. Her face was plain, with a prominent chin.

I was not surprised to find that the records she handed me were meticulously kept journals recording the comings and goings of each of the shelter's occupants down to the minute during May 1999. Whenever a woman left the shelter, she had to sign the logbook. The precise time would be noted. When she returned, she signed the book again. The entire process was overseen by the nuns.

The logbook reflected that on May 15, 1999, Janet Avery left the women's shelter at 1:55 p.m. with her infant son and returned at 9:45 p.m. that same evening. She had not left again until 12:05 p.m. the following day, May 16, 1999. Ramon Jiminez had been stabbed at approximately 2:00 a.m. on May 16, 1999, and Mario had testified that Janet had been with him at that time, as she had been the entire evening of the party. But the party location was miles from the shelter.

The prosecutor had argued that Mario had been with his girlfriend and their baby at Ronnie's party, not fighting with the victim. But the logbook showed that Mario's girlfriend and baby had been miles away, asleep at a women's shelter. Unlike Janet, Sister Daniels's records could not be persuaded to lie to provide Mario with a false alibi.

A few days after my visit to the shelter, Sister Daniels sent me copies of the relevant logbook entries and a sworn, signed statement explaining their relevance. The statement was notarized by another nun, Mother Mary Murphy.

I showed Rich the statement and the logbook entries with great satisfaction.

"Two nuns. I have a written statement from a nun notarized by a nun. That has to carry some weight. Even more than a priest," I joked.

"It doesn't get much better than nuns," Rich agreed.

# PRIDE AND ENVY

As my investigation dragged on through the summer and deep into the autumn of 2002, Rich worked on writing the brief to the appellate court. The brief challenged Judge Albert's various evidentiary rulings. Rich and I did not agree about the timing for filing the direct appeal in Corrie Angelo's case. The case had been on the appellate court's dismissal calendar, meaning that if we did not submit a valid explanation for delaying filing our brief, we risked the case's never being heard. But the appellate court is pretty understanding when we provide a valid explanation for a delay. In Corrie Angelo's case, we were trying to prove that our client had not done the stabbing. To me that was a most valid reason not to rush forward with the appeal.

But Rich wanted to file the brief, seeing no real advantage in delaying further. Technically, he was right. We could pursue an appeal and then lodge a motion to vacate in the trial court afterward. But strategically, I always prefer going into trial court first, because once a case has been affirmed on appeal, any subsequent motion to vacate seems more desperate. I also knew that in Corrie Angelo's case, if we lost on the direct appeal, the appellate court would make sure to comment on the overwhelming evidence of our client's guilt.

Where proof of guilt is deemed overwhelming, it is easier for an appellate court to reject a defendant's claims as "harmless error." Appellate courts adore harmless error analysis. Just as in some ancient Greek dramas, where a seemingly insoluble crisis would be solved by the intervention of a god, usually dropped onto the stage through some elaborate mechanical device, harmless error analysis is the deus ex machina for appellate judges, an analytical device capable of forgiving a multitude of sins. But before such analysis can be employed, there must be a determination that proof of a defendant's guilt is overwhelming. If ten eyewitnesses claim that they saw the accused commit the crime, fingerprints found at the scene are matched to him, and the defendant ultimately confesses, the fact that the prosecutor was allowed to pose a few leading questions is hardly likely to have changed the outcome. Appellate courts tend to deem most convictions supported by overwhelming evidence of guilt. The evidence does seem stronger once that guilty verdict has been returned. In Corrie Angelo's case, a higher court's finding of overwhelming evidence would not exactly help my efforts to vacate the judgment before a lower trial court judge.

But I did not fight Rich very hard over the timing issue. My role in the case was limited. Corrie was not even on my client roster, the list maintained by my office to record which cases each attorney is responsible for handling. I stated my position and then I let Rich decide what to do.

I also spoke to Jennifer Stein about when she intended to file a brief on Robert's behalf. She wanted to file sooner rather than later, too.

"I think we have a really good shot of getting the conviction reversed based on the court's throwing Robert out of the courtroom before the verdict was recorded," Jennifer explained, brimming with her usual enthusiasm.

Although I remembered that the judge had ordered the court officers to forcibly remove both Corrie and Robert when the verdict was initially announced, I did not have much hope for a challenge to the judge's conduct prevailing on appeal. For some reason, I found Jennifer's optimism vaguely annoying.

"It's tough to win on appeal in a violent case on a technical issue like a defendant's right to be present," I explained, suddenly feeling the need to school Jennifer in the ways of the world.

"Still, I really think we're going to win on this one," Jennifer replied, not letting my cynicism dampen her mood.

"I hope you're right. It would make my life a lot easier."

When I relayed my conversation with Jennifer to Rich, he agreed with me that Jennifer's enthusiasm for the issue about Robert's being thrown out of the courtroom was unfounded.

"That's not going to fly on appeal," Rich predicted with the same confidence I had voiced to Jennifer.

By the winter of 2002, briefs had been filed in both brothers' cases. Rich did not ask me to supervise Corrie Angelo's brief. He later explained that he felt I was too close to the case to review the brief objectively. Maybe he thought I would insist that the introductory paragraph declare in bold type: **Corrie Angelo is an innocent man, wrongly convicted. The whole system sucks.**

My pride was hurt by Rich's choice to forgo my insights. I knew the case better than anyone but Rich, but once again, I did not confront him about his decision. I accepted it and moved on. I did not even review the appellate brief until after it was filed. It was well written, well researched, and well argued, effectively challenging, for example, the prosecution's failure to disclose Sergeant Malone's history of substantiated complaints against him. But it did not raise the issue about our client's ejection from the courtroom before the verdict was recorded. Robert had one outburst before the court warned him to shut up or face expulsion. Corrie kept complaining. Rich considered the issue so weak that the brief did not even mention that Corrie had not been present for the verdict, and I entirely agreed with his assessment of the issue's lack of merit.

In April 2003, wearing maternity clothes, I accompanied Rich to the oral argument. I was at this time four months pregnant with my third daughter, Maya, and I had already gained twenty-two pounds. There was something vaguely embarrassing about being so large so early in a pregnancy. People would approach me in elevators, nod knowingly, and predict "any day now . . . ." I stopped mentioning that I had five months to go.

The entire Angelo family had come to listen to the arguments: Carlos, Renee, Corrie and Robert's sister Kayla, and some cousins. Corrie's case was scheduled to be heard first, followed immediately by Robert's. Although the brothers' fates had been determined by one jury at a single trial, on appeal each case would be argued and ultimately decided separately several weeks later in two distinct written decisions. While the court does not officially rule until the written decision is issued, it's rarely difficult to predict the outcome. We lose the vast majority of our cases, and the appellate judges are not shy about voicing their respective opinions of our claims.

Rich argued his points effectively. When one judge asked him about his client's being evicted from the courtroom, Rich responded that only Robert was raising that claim. It was one of those rare appellate arguments where I could not predict the outcome with any certainty, even after Rich had sat down.

By the time Jennifer Stein sat down, she had won Robert Angelo's case. To my utter amazement, each judge agreed that Robert Angelo should not have been evicted from the courtroom before the verdict was recorded. The judges accepted that Robert had acted inappropriately when he initially spoke out, but after he had been warned to be quiet, Robert, unlike Corrie, did not say a word. He did not deserve to be excluded from a critical stage of the trial, the judges' comments reflected over and over again.

The appellate prosecutor looked shaken when she left the courtroom, knowing that she would have to return to her office with news of her impending defeat. Even a casual observer could have predicted that Robert's conviction was going to be reversed and his case sent back for a new trial. But Corrie's fate was far from certain.

Outside the courtroom, I waited to congratulate Jennifer and hoped she had forgotten my earlier insistence that the court would never reverse on such a technical issue in an attempted-murder case. Jennifer could not stop smiling. There is no win like your first win.

Watching Jennifer beam as she spoke with the Angelos, a complex series of emotions overcame me. I was happy for Robert, that he would get a new trial, at which the defense would be much better prepared. I was also happy for Jennifer, whom I liked. But mixed in with that happiness was real concern for Corrie. I hoped that the court would just reverse both convictions. If there was going to be a retrial anyway, why not let both Robert and Corrie benefit? The costs to the state would be the same. It seemed cruel to grant one brother a new trial and allow the other to languish in prison.

I knew the appellate court did not share my sensibilities. To the judges, Robert and Corrie Angelo were just two criminal defendants whose cases presented different legal claims. I looked over at Renee Angelo and saw my own feelings reflected in her face, which was not streaked to its usual degree with mascara. There were some tears for Corrie, but there was also jubilation over Robert's good fortune.

In the weeks following the oral argument, Corrie Angelo slipped into my dreams. With my belly growing ever larger, I would dream that the court had reversed his conviction. A great feeling of relief would come over me. I would wake up still tired each morning to face another day of waiting for the court's decision.

The wait ended at the beginning of June 2003. The court reversed Robert's conviction and ordered a new trial, finding that his unjustified ejection from the courtroom deprived him of his fundamental right to be present for the verdict.

Corrie was not so lucky. His conviction was affirmed. In rejecting all of our claims challenging Justice Albert's rulings as being without merit or harmless error, the appellate court made sure to observe that there was overwhelming evidence of Corrie Angelo's guilt.

It was hard to find a silver lining in the clouds that descended following that decision. Rich and I both took the loss a lot harder than most. You cannot be an appellate defense attorney if you fall apart after every loss, because then you will spend most of your professional existence in pieces. But undeniably some losses hurt more than others: the ones where you grow to know and like a client and his family; where you feel the issues were strong and the court's reasoning forces you to second-guess your approach; or worst of all, when you think your client might actually be innocent. The loss in Corrie Angelo's case was a perfect storm of misery. Adding to the gloom, there was little to entice the court of appeals to review the case, because the legal evidentiary issues were not particularly novel.

There was much to envy in Robert's victory. Following the reversal, he was almost certain to serve less than the fifteen-year prison term to which he had originally been sentenced. Often when an appellate court reverses a defendant's conviction, he winds up pleading guilty to a much-reduced sentence simply because the prosecution does not want to go through the effort of a new trial and the defendant just wants to get out of prison sooner rather than later. Jennifer Stein could close out the file knowing that she had truly helped a client, secured him a brighter future in which he would not be deprived of an entire decade and a half of his life.

I was left with two file drawers filled with interview notes, court file papers, witness affidavits, and transcripts, not to mention the latest addition to those files, a decision declaring my client overwhelmingly guilty. I pushed a copy of the decision into the drawer and sat down with my back against the cabinet, my hands folded across my enormous belly. With a little less than four months of pregnancy to go, I had gained forty-two pounds. I found myself envying even overweight women I saw on the street, simply because they could button their pants, a task that was destined to be beyond my capabilities for months, if not years.

Sitting on my office floor, perfectly still, after spending an hour in Rich's office conducting a postmortem of the case up to that point, I found the silver lining. The reversal of Robert's conviction meant that the proceedings would start all over again. Robert Angelo would be entitled to request information from the prosecution, including any information about Mario's involvement in the Bryant Avenue organization. Robert's attorney could ask the court to sign a subpoena compelling the police department to disclose the reports I had unsuccessfully tried to obtain. Perhaps this time, with the benefits of court-ordered disclosure, the true nature of Mario's relationship with the police would finally come to light.

I hoisted myself off the floor with the aid of the cabinet's handles, which threatened to snap off under the strain of my weight, and dialed Jennifer Stein's number. I wanted to get the name of the trial attorney who would be handling Robert's case. In the months before my maternity leave, I would help Robert's new attorney draft a motion compelling the production of the police reports relating to Mario and the Bryant Avenue organization. Then I would wait to see what turned up.

## OVERWHELMING EVIDENCE OF GUILT

Any doubts I had about my sanity and judgment were reconfirmed when I found myself standing at the entrance to the American Girl Place café in February 2004 silently praying that the hostess would find a table at which to seat Lila and me for the 2:00 lunch. When I had called earlier in the week in a futile attempt to make reservations, I was told that the café had been booked for months, but that I could put my name on a waiting list a half hour before the seating I wished to attend. I knew that if we did not get a seat, all that Lila would remember of our afternoon together in the years to come was being shut out of the promised land.

We had come to the American Girl Place at Lila's insistence after Jessie had attended a birthday party there. Months after Maya's birth, four-year-old Lila was not adjusting well to her newly acquired middle-child status. The breeziness that had always surrounded her was stilled. She was quieter now, more prone to crying for no discernible reason, and subject to bouts of fear so fierce that when I picked her up to comfort her, I could feel her heart racing in her chest through my own clothes.

Before Maya came along, I had grown used to thinking of Lila as my "easy" daughter, the one who would never cling when I left her at preschool, who had slept through the night dependably since early infancy, and who potty-trained herself long before her second birthday. With a new infant to care for, I needed Lila to be her usual easy self. But the immutable laws of motherhood dictate that what you have learned to expect from your children often must be unlearned with great rapidity.

Convinced that all Lila needed was a little more mommy time, I agreed to take her anywhere she desired. An afternoon with me would cure Lila's growing doubts, her mourning her lost place as the baby of our family. A little "quality time" was all she needed, I assured myself.

But I cringed when Lila mentioned the American Girl Place. I had never been there myself. From the little I knew, it was no place I wanted to go.

My worst fears were confirmed when we entered the store. It was mobbed in a way that only a store in Manhattan near Rockefeller Center can be during Presidents' Week vacation. Apparently every school-age girl in the country had convinced her mother to visit. Still carrying at least thirty pounds of extra weight, I immediately noticed that most of the other mothers were slim and well dressed. Several looked as if they had had some serious body "work" done. One woman's breasts were so filled with silicone that the skin revealed by her low-cut white cashmere sweater was stretched parchment thin.

In addition to the hordes of well-coiffed mothers and daughters, there were mounds of merchandise flying off the shelves. Dolls, clothes, accessories—from hairbrushes and curlers to antique furniture—were all dangling price tags of mind-boggling proportion. Lila's grandparents had already bought her an American Girl doll, and I had not paid much attention to the prices in the catalogs that regularly arrived in our mail after that. Jessie snatched them up and pored over them. But she rarely asked me to buy her anything in particular. She just liked to look.

The girls in the store were barely looking before asking their parents to buy. I had allotted fifty dollars for Lila to spend. She picked out a cookbook and a lip gloss for well under the limit. It hardly seemed worth joining the massive lines for such a meager purchase. But I figured we could read the book and play with the lip gloss while we waited to get into the café.

As I stood in line for the cashier, I noticed a gorgeous young woman standing behind a cash register with no line in front of it. Something told me that the woman worked for the store. But she was too glossy to be relegated to standing behind a counter—straight, waist-length black hair, eyebrows threaded into perfect arches, skin that seemed to have no pores whatsoever, and a frame so narrow she looked as if she could slip into some of the doll clothing on display. I approached to ask if she could ring up my order.

She looked at me with utter disdain and explained that she was not a cashier but "a personal shopper." Apparently some children are now too busy to spend their valuable time shopping for their own playthings. For a price, the store provides personal shoppers to outfit these elite clients' dolls for them. At that moment, the American Girl Place symbolized for me everything wrong with modern-day parenting in all its overindulgent glory—a store that pushes a treacly sweet celebration of girlhood at prices beyond the reach of most families with products bearing "Made in China" stickers.

After Lila and I were lucky enough to win a table in the café, I sat examining the menu, trying to remember if my own mother had ever subjected herself to anything like this ordeal on my behalf. I couldn't think of one. When I was Lila's age, I did everything with my mother, the grocery shopping, waiting for hours to buy gas during the energy crisis of the 1970s, driving my brothers to their guitar lessons and basketball practices.

The concepts of "quality time" and "floor time" had not been invented. There was only time, lots and lots of time. And in that time, there were so many great spontaneous moments, playing Go Fish in the gas lines, tearing into fresh hot bread we had just bought at the bakery, dropping in on a whim to the café at Lord & Taylor for a cup of hot chocolate.

There was no need for my mom and me to "celebrate" our time together with

American Girl mousse cups while my dolls sat in booster seats secured around the table. *Overwhelming evidence of guilt,* I thought to myself as I picked up an untouched heart-shaped, pink, sugar–coated cookie. It was guilt that had brought me into Manhattan that day. The guilt of knowing that soon I would be returning to work and would have even less time to spend with Lila. That smaller quantity of time would now have to be spread thinner over three girls. I dropped the cookie, paid the check, and led Lila back into the gray February air.

The highlight of the day came at Penn Station when we found a juice stand and the woman working there let Lila select each piece of fruit to drop into the juicer. Lila watched in awe as the oranges, apples, and grapefruit sections were magically transformed into a cloudy liquid concoction. Her smile at the first sip radiated pure joy.

She could not wait to get home to show her book and lip gloss to Jessie, partially to gloat but mostly because for Lila nothing is good until her older sister declares it to be so. But when we arrived home, before going to find Jessie, Lila kissed Maya and hugged her, a little too tightly for my liking but with such love that tears clouded my eyes as I gently pried the baby away.

As I sat feeding Maya, I felt more relaxed. It was true that Lila would have less of my undivided attention in the future. But she had gained something that I had always wanted during my own childhood, a little sister. There would be lots and lots of moments, mundane to spectacular, for them to celebrate together.

........................................

By March 2004, when I returned to work following Maya's birth, Robert Angelo had pleaded guilty to attempting to murder Ramon Jiminez. Was he actually guilty? Under the law he certainly was. A conviction entered as the result of a guilty plea is legally equivalent to a jury's verdict pronouncing a defendant's guilt. But do I believe that innocent people plead guilty at times to avoid the risks inherent in going to trial, namely the possibility of the court's imposing a much harsher sentence afterward? The answer to that question is also unequivocally yes.

The prosecution had offered Robert a six-year sentence in exchange for his guilty plea. With the time he'd already served—over four years—plus time off for good behavior, the offer meant that Robert would walk out of prison a free man within months of admitting participating in the stabbing. There was very little reason for Robert to risk a retrial with that offer on the table. Robert agreed to the deal on the condition that he did not have to admit that his brother had been involved in the incident in any way.

The deal had been offered only after the trial judge in Robert's case had ordered the prosecution to disclose whether Mario Gonzalez had been acting as an informant for the police department. "The status of Gonzalez as an informant provides an obvious motive for the police officers to tailor their testimony," the trial judge ruled in ordering the disclosure. Despite this direct ruling, the prosecutor refused to disclose the information and avoided a confrontation with the judge by making Robert an offer too good to refuse. Once Robert pleaded guilty, the prosecution was under no further obligation to disclose the discovery ordered by the court.

As far as Corrie Angelo's case was concerned, I was essentially in the same position with the investigation as I had been before Robert's conviction had been reversed. I could have given up at that point, closed the file, and moved on. Rich would not have faulted me for doing so. But he wouldn't order me to stop either. After working with me for over a decade, Rich knew enough to give me time and space to make my own decision about how to proceed. "Decision" is sort of a misnomer. A lot of times, I don't consciously decide to keep fighting a case. It's more that the thought of closing the file makes me feel vaguely ill, and so it lies fallow until that feeling passes and I accept the defeat or I figure out another avenue to pursue.

In Corrie Angelo's case, after reinvestigating the crime for two years, I was convinced that my client was innocent. The prosecution's staunch refusal to disclose whether Mario Gonzalez, who I believed was the actual culprit, had been a police informant, even after being ordered to do so by the court, made me even more certain that I was right. Mario must have been an important cooperator in the Bryant Avenue organization investigation.

I decided to file a motion to vacate Corrie's conviction back in the trial court based on the information that I had uncovered, the evidence that the blood on Robert's jeans had not belonged to the victim as the prosecutor had claimed at the trial and the logbook entry from Sister Daniels's shelter proving that Mario had lied about being with Janet and his son on the night of Jiminez's stabbing. I also compiled all the evidence suggesting that Mario was a police informant: the reported decisions from the Bryant Avenue organization federal prosecutions; the NYPD's response to my Freedom of Information Act request, suggesting they had reports documenting Mario's cooperation; the motion practice and decisions surrounding the issue preceding Robert's guilty plea.

In July 2004, I filed a fifty-five–page motion to vacate the Corrie Angelo conviction, with sixteen exhibits setting forth the investigation I had pursued. It took the prosecution's office five months to file its reply, which included sworn statements from every prosecutor who had been involved in the original trial and Robert Angelo's retrial. Each swore that he or she did not know whether Mario Gonzalez had been an informant for the police department. None of them had ever bothered to find out.

There was also an affirmation from a police lieutenant explaining that in response to my Freedom of Information Act demand, no police department official had ever searched for records responsive to my request. They had simply filed a form response that supplying the requested records would endanger witnesses, apparently without being too concerned about its accuracy.

Only in response to my motion to vacate the conviction did anyone involved with the prosecution or the police actually try to ascertain whether Mario was a police informant. A commanding officer in the department's legal bureau claimed to have directed personnel under him to search their records. That search revealed that Mario was not on any NYPD informant list, past or present. Reading the People's response, I knew that it would be sufficient to defeat my claim. I didn't know whether the police department had merely gone through the motions of conducting a valid search or whether I had actually been wrong and Mario had never been a police informant. But I knew that the prosecution's papers would convince the motion court of the latter.

As to my other points, the prosecution dismissed them as trivial. The evidence that the blood on Robert's pants did not belong to the complainant was not likely to have changed the outcome of the trial, the prosecution argued. There were five eyewitnesses who had testified that my client had stabbed Ramon Jiminez, after all. That Mario Gonzalez had lied about being with his girlfriend and son on the night of the stabbing was also unimportant.

It took the judge responsible for reviewing my motion less than a month to conclude that the issues it raised were frivolous. "This motion is: DENIED," the court declared. In a single paragraph, the judge reminded me that there were five eyewitnesses. "While counsel's motion is premised on the assumption that Mario Gonzalez was an informant, her assumption cannot create facts where none exist," the court observed. The blood evidence did nothing to "alter the crime scenario as involves Corrie Angelo's participation." The judge did not even bother to address the logbook evidence.

Reading the decision, its summary dismissal of all my work, actually frightened me for a moment. I could feel my confidence cracking, my heart beating harder, my face flush. There it was in black and white, confirmation that I had lost all perspective. It felt sort of like reading your own name typed on a commitment order to the insane asylum.

To me, it seemed so clear that Corrie Angelo had not stabbed Ramon Jiminez. To the justice system, it was equally clear that my client was overwhelmingly guilty. Nothing I had done had convinced anyone otherwise. Corrie Angelo was in the exact same position he would have been in if Rich had never mentioned the case to me years earlier, if I had never cracked open the file.

In the months that followed the loss, I had to decide whether to pursue my claims in the federal courts. By the time my motion had been denied, Corrie Angelo had already served six years of his fifteen-year prison sentence. It would take months for me to draft a federal habeas petition, followed by additional years for it to be decided. Without habeas relief, my client would most likely serve approximately twelve years in prison on his fifteen-year sentence.

I made my decision based on the numbers. Six years left in which to pursue habeas relief that could in any real way benefit my client. Given the complexity of the case, most likely a habeas petition would not be finally decided, with all the appellate avenues exhausted, for at least four years. The numbers made it easy for me to justify quitting.

But it was not just the numbers. Losing the case, the cavalier manner in which all my claims had been dismissed, temporarily embittered me. It felt as if a big chunk of my self-confidence had been removed and replaced by doubt. Not just doubt in my own judgment, but in my ability to continue being part of a system that seemed so flawed and indifferent. Never had I put myself in harm's way so many times, taxed my office's limited resources to such an extent, and simply worked so damned hard to accomplish absolutely nothing. It was time for me to stop.

When Carlos Angelo called me to ask if I would pursue his son's case in federal court, I explained only the numbers to him, the cost-benefit analysis I had coldly run in my head. Carlos did not judge or scold me. He thanked me for all I had done for his son. I could not have felt more guilty if he had cursed me.

Sometimes numbers do not tell a clear story. In retrospect, it would have been easier to have filed the habeas on Corrie Angelo's behalf. I might not have won, but I would have earned myself peace of mind, known that I had done everything within my power to fight a gross injustice. That knowledge would have been worth the effort. Sometimes the stones left unturned weigh heaviest on your soul.

......................................

In the months that followed my spectacular defeat in Corrie Angelo's case, Lila grew more troubled. As her fifth birthday approached, despite our trip to the American Girl Place and my regular attempts to carve out time for just the two of us, my middle child refused to wear the "easy" label I had affixed to her soon after her birth. She clung to me as I left for work; on the days I stayed home, she cried and begged not to have to go to school. At night, I would awaken to find her standing silently by my bed. Although I would accompany her back to her room and stay until she fell back to sleep, many mornings I would still find her curled up at the foot of our bed when I awoke. Even the mildest forms of entertainment, a magic show or movie, seemed to provide endless fodder for her nightmares. An exhibit at a children's museum about the hidden world of bacteria frightened her for weeks.

I sought help and insights from every source, Lila's teachers, school administrators, social workers, psychologists, my own parents. My mother told me that all

Lila needed was some time to grow into herself, that the best thing I could offer was patience.

Nobody else seemed to have better advice, and so for once I listened to my mother. I let Lila cling and cry without admonition. I slept in her room when she seemed to need me there. Slowly she seemed to regain her footing; some semblance of her former cheerfulness returned. There was nothing in particular that I or anybody else did that made her better. It was just a rough time that we had to endure. I learned the power of stillness and waiting.

That lesson is one I now carry with me into the office. Sometimes when you don't know which way to go, the best way is no way at all. I have learned to stay still and wait to see what happens.

I have never been able to bring myself to close out Corrie Angelo's file. It has remained in the same spot, taking up two entire file drawers. And so it was there when a reporter from the *Daily News* recently called me inquiring about the case. The Angelo family had forwarded a copy of my motion to vacate the conviction to the paper, and the reporter was interested in writing a story about the two brothers' cases to illustrate the arbitrary nature of the criminal justice system. When the reporter said that it seemed clear to him that Corrie Angelo was innocent, that Mario Gonzalez had done the stabbing, I felt a flicker of hope. At least I had convinced one other person of my client's innocence.

There are five people, four police officers and Mario Gonzalez himself, who also know the truth about what happened that early spring morning in May 1999 on Hunts Point Avenue. Some part of me is waiting, patiently, for them to answer the pangs of conscience they must feel about their respective contributions to Corrie Angelo's fate. If and when they listen to their consciences, I will be waiting to hear their confessions—hoping that by doing so I will earn the chance to assuage my own guilt.

# part 6

# Where's Your Outrage?

Every New Year's Eve, my resolutions are pretty much the same: to give up junk food, exercise more, yell at my girls less, and leave the job at the office when I walk out the door on Thursday evenings. But usually by February I'm hitting the doughnuts. Early March sees the end of my exercise routine. Inevitably by April I am raising my voice a bit too frequently, and by the time the flowers begin to bloom in May, I am calling in to work for messages on Fridays, sometimes several times a day.

True to form, on a Friday afternoon in May 2006, I called in to find a message from a reporter wanting to speak to me about Benny Rinaldo's case. Of course I knew it was a bad idea to return the call with all three of my daughters racing around my backyard shrieking with glee as they took turns dousing each other with the garden hose. But the last time I had failed to speak with a reporter, his article concluded by announcing to the world that "the defendant was represented by Claudia Trupp, who could not be reached for comment." *Because she had been driving her daughter to her piano lesson at 4:00 that day,* I'd thought to myself when I later read the article. Anybody reading about my unavailability might have concluded that I had been in court covering another case. More likely, the casual reader would not have paused over her morning coffee at all or even bothered to turn the page to find the article's final paragraph. Only I knew that I had skipped out of the office early that day and thus sensed some thinly veiled indictment of my professionalism.

I wanted to say *something* about my most recent victory. Benny Rinaldo had been convicted of attempting to murder a man in a jealous rage after finding the guy with his pants down in the company of Benny's wife. I had convinced a court to vacate the attempted murder conviction based on the incompetence of Benny's trial attorney. Such wins are unusual. The justice system goes easy on criminal defense attorneys when their actions are being challenged as a basis for vacating a conviction. There are reported cases where defense attorneys actually slept through portions of their clients' trials and reviewing courts upheld the convictions because the defendants could not show that they had been harmed by their attorneys' napping. At least if you're asleep, you can't make things worse.

The judge who vacated Benny Rinaldo's conviction had written a scathing decision lambasting the trial attorney's conduct. Benny's trial attorney had disclosed client confidences and didn't bother to move for a hearing to suppress identification evidence or to discover that Benny was actually mentally retarded. It was a pretty pathetic performance from beginning to end. But the court's decision had not named the attorney involved, referring to him only as "counsel."

When I dialed the reporter's number, the first thing he asked was my opinion of the trial attorney whose identity he had uncovered from the court file. I had no desire to bash another defense attorney. I remarked that while the trial attorney's efforts had been ineffective, I was sure he'd done the best he could given the complicated nature of the case and Benny's complex mental health state, which included not only mental retardation but mental illness as well.

"That's very diplomatic of you," the reporter remarked, obviously disappointed by my refusal to give him any colorful language to quote.

"I just wouldn't want to be judged from my worst mistakes. We all make them," I offered.

"But where's your outrage on behalf of your client?" the reporter asked earnestly.

His reaction startled me. I felt as if he had pointed out that my wedding band had slipped unnoticed from my finger, as if I had lost something important that I took for granted would always be there. Nobody had ever before accused me of not being angry enough.

"Believe me, I have plenty of outrage," I assured him. "I just don't need to splash it across the front page of the paper."

Through the window panes above my kitchen sink, I could tell that the girls' frolicking was devolving into squabbling. Lila snatched a toy from Maya, who reacted by stomping around like Rumpelstiltskin after the maiden has guessed his name. Jessie was unsuccessfully trying to broker a peace accord between the two. She crouched down to speak to her baby sister face-to-face. Maya slapped Jessie, picked up another toy, and threw it with all her two-year-old fury at Lila's head.

It was time to give the reporter a quote he could use and end the interview. "I'm just grateful that Mr. Rinaldo will have an opportunity for the system to treat him with greater fairness. That's about all I'm going to say."

The reporter thanked me for not dodging his calls. I dropped the phone on the kitchen counter, opened the back door, and raced outside before Maya hurt someone. She had definitely not lost any of her outrage in her two short years on the planet.

......................................

I spent most of my twenties angry. There was almost no issue over which I could not work up a head of steam: the state of public education, welfare reform, animal rights, a woman's right to govern her own reproductive decisions, police brutality, violence against women. Any cause, anywhere, anytime. I was ready to march, organize, letter-write, and most often to voice my opinions a little too stridently over dinner tables with those who did not share my views.

The first time I met the fiancé of my oldest friend, Anne, we got into a bruising debate over whether courts should be allowed to compel implantation of birth control into women who had given birth to crack-addicted infants. He thought that was just a nifty idea. I expressed my disagreement in less than civil terms. Charlie and Anne cringed and ordered additional drinks as they watched the battle unfold. The friendship is still recovering almost fifteen years later.

Immediately afterward, Charlie asked why I had gotten so angry about the whole thing.

"He just pissed me off," I explained.

"What *doesn't* piss you off?" Charlie wondered. "I don't agree with his position either, but he seemed okay. Why do you have to be so angry all the time?"

He had a point. Objectively speaking, I had nothing to be angry about. Lots of people disagree over policy issues without almost coming to blows. But I couldn't help it. The argument had made my blood boil.

Until recently, I never could trace the source of my anger. I came from a background of privilege with a family that was always ready and able to encourage me to follow whatever path my heart desired. Sheltered, bright enough, attractive enough, I always realized I was fortunate. But that realization hadn't prevented me from being angry at the state of the world.

A heightened sense of outrage is common in criminal defense attorneys, particularly public defenders. The anger does not come from the lousy pay or poor treatment from judges or clients. It is anger that draws you to the field in the first place.

Maybe anger is too simple a term. It is a sense of otherness, of resentment from being out of the mainstream. Whether it results from being raised by an authoritarian father; growing up gay in Mayberry, USA; being an awkward adolescent shunned by the popular crowd; or being the day-student at an elite boarding school; a deep distrust of authority and an identification with the underdog is a prerequisite to being a good criminal defense attorney.

The job gives you so many chances to give voice to your anger on behalf of your clients, upon whom the criminal justice system regularly doles out indignities large and small. Once I read a transcript in which the defense attorney was objecting because his client had been brought to court naked with just a blanket wrapped around his shoulders. The lawyer's outrage was palpable.

"There's no excuse for the Department of Corrections to produce my client without any clothes!" he sputtered. The court and prosecutor could not disagree.

Clothes were eventually found for the client, and the court session proceeded. The client calmed down a lot sooner than his attorney, who was still seething at the end of the day as he demanded a further investigation into the incident. The following morning, the client was clothed when he came to court. That particular storm having passed, the defense attorney steeled himself for the next battle.

I noticed a change in the intensity of my personal storm systems around the time that I first became pregnant with Jessie. Although I had been a vegetarian pretty much since my college days, once pregnant I developed intense cravings for meat almost immediately. The lack of resistance I put up before abandoning years of vegetarianism should have shocked me. But I was too busy scarfing down medium-rare steak to think much about it. I could no longer see beyond my own yearnings for flesh to consider the cruelty being inflicted on the animals I was eating as I piled my grocery cart high with shrink-wrapped animal parts.

The years of pregnancies and child rearing continued to take their toll on my political activism, if not my ideals. I cannot remember the last time I attended a march or demonstration. And there have been so many things over the past decade, particularly the last five years, to be outraged about. The political climate during the Bush administration made me nostalgic for the Cold War missile proliferation I was protesting in college.

But if my political activism waned, at least I maintained my outrage on behalf of my clients. When reading a transcript, I could always be sure that my indignation would flare at the first hint of injustice inflicted or due process denied. At least that was my experience until Benny Rinaldo's case landed on my desk.

# LOVE CAN MAKE YOU MAD

In 2005 my New Year's resolutions were exceptionally short-lived. I did not make it beyond January before returning to junk food and backsliding into my natural sedentary state. Shortly after New Year's Day, Marie, my nanny of over seven years, told me that she wanted to move down to Georgia to avoid the harsh northern winters. I needed to find a replacement caregiver, a prospect I dreaded.

I am particularly inept at making hiring decisions. Marie came to me magically, like Mary Poppins. A close friend of mine knew Marie's previous employer, who'd decided to quit her job and stay home just as I was getting ready to return to work. By that time, I had interviewed around fifty perfectly nice prospective nannies and rejected them all. They wore too much perfume or lipstick or laughed too loudly. These seemingly innocuous flaws were warning signs of alcohol abuse, sexual promiscuity, and violent tendencies, I explained to Charlie. When Marie arrived on our doorstep, Charlie escorted her to meet Jessie, who miraculously chose that moment to smile, a rare occurrence during her infancy. I watched silently and offered Marie the job on the spot.

Over the years, I had come to respect Marie's instincts and judgment as much as (and often more than) my own. I had never needed to interview another nanny. I had interviewed a few attorneys seeking jobs with my office, but Rich had stopped asking me to participate in personnel decisions after he figured out that I would spend hours talking with people about their personal lives without ever getting around to discussing work. When Rich would ask me for my views on a particular applicant, I would comment that her current relationship was heading for trouble because her boyfriend did not seem ready to commit. So, when Marie told me that she was leaving, I wept at the prospect of losing her and having to find a replacement. Then I reached for the Oreos.

The same month that Marie announced her decision to leave, my father came down with a strange illness. By February he had lost thirty pounds and was hospitalized. When a seventy-one–year-old man starts to lose weight rapidly, the most obvious answer is cancer, and that February the doctors were scanning and probing every inch of him looking for its source.

Then Charlie needed foot surgery and he remained on crutches for weeks. His inability to walk left me in sole charge of our dog and cat, not to mention fetching every glass of water for the kids, hauling every bag of groceries from the car, and taking out the garbage. With three children to care for, a new nanny to find, a father to visit in the hospital, and a dog with serious digestion issues requiring 6:00 a.m. walks, I could feel my sanity snapping, like the cables of a suspension bridge being ravaged by the winds of a fierce hurricane.

At the time, work was not providing any solace. Benny Rinaldo's case had been sitting in my file drawer for months. I had read the record several times, taken prodigious notes outlining the proceedings, researched some potential issues. But the evidence of my client's guilt seemed overwhelming even to me. The recent loss in Corrie Angelo's case still stung. I felt depleted and hesitant to veer from the beaten path.

I could have written the brief in Benny's case in a week, raising one or two evidentiary issues, and moved on from there. Every lawyer with whom I had discussed the case advised me to do just that. Write it, file it, and move on. The police had obtained a full written confession from my client in which Benny admitted stabbing the victim in a jealous rage after finding the man in the stairwell of a building trying to have sex with Benny's wife.

*Write it and move on,* I told myself over and over again. But I couldn't bring myself to do it. I would sit looking at my blank computer screen, unable to start writing the appellate brief.

It was because of the weeping. There was evidence in the record that before confessing, my client had been sobbing in a holding cell for six hours straight, really sobbing hard. Even at my weepiest, I had never been able to sustain a sobbing session for that amount of time. Even Jessie during her worst infant bouts with colic had never approached the six-hour mark. None of my other kids had come close either.

The image of a grown man sitting alone in a cell crying for hours on end haunted me. I opened the file drawer for what seemed like the fiftieth time, pulled out the file, and started reading the case again from the beginning, determined not to let my shattered confidence or the chaos of my personal life force me onto the path of least resistance.

The story began on July 4, 2002, when Benny Rinaldo's common-law wife, Felice Diaz, wandered into the Fortieth Precinct, determined to declare some independence from my client. To Felice—a former prostitute who had realized that it was easier to steal my client's Social Security disability checks than to turn tricks—getting Benny arrested seemed as good a way as any to get him out of her life and keep collecting those checks.

At the precinct, Felice complained that Benny had been hitting her again and asked what had happened to the previous assault complaints she had filed against him months earlier. She had a habit of filing assault complaints when she and Benny fought and then failing to cooperate with the police when the time came to follow up. It's a pattern that is seen often in domestic violence situations.

But this time Felice was determined to make the police listen. So she also mentioned that, in addition to slapping her around, Benny had stabbed somebody weeks earlier. Felice claimed that she had been present for the stabbing, but she could not recall the victim's name or the date when it had occurred.

As Felice was imparting this information to the police, Benny, who apparently had been following her, walked into the precinct and took the opportunity to tell the police that he was having problems with Felice. The officer on duty, Larry Cortes, told Benny to stay in the lunch room. By noon Benny was under arrest for assaulting Felice and was placed in a holding cell. That's when he started to cry.

Meanwhile, Cortes drove Felice around the neighborhood where she said the stabbing had taken place. Felice pointed out a specific building, and people in the area directed Cortes to the apartment of a man whose cousin had been stabbed weeks earlier. The victim, Dario Guzman, was still at Lincoln Hospital in the intensive care unit, under heavy sedation and unable to speak. Upon visiting the hospital's ICU, Felice told Cortes that Guzman was the man Benny had stabbed.

Cortes drove Felice around some more until she showed him where Benny had discarded the knife. After searching an abandoned lot for a couple of hours, the police turned up a small silver folding knife. Cortes then went back to the precinct, where he obtained a formal written statement from Felice recounting the stabbing.

It was not until after 6:00 p.m. that Cortes and his partner, Manuel Joseph, began interrogating Benny. During the interview, Benny was "really crying," according to Detective Joseph. They read him *Miranda* warnings, advising him of his right to remain silent, to have an attorney present, and that anything he said could be used against him in a court of law. Benny was told to write "yes" after each warning to indicate that he understood each right. He signed on the dotted line. The police told Benny that they had a witness to the stabbing, that they had recovered the knife, and that Benny should give his side of the story.

Almost immediately, Benny confessed to the stabbing. When the police told him to write out a statement, he agreed to do that, too. Although the written statement was filled with grammatical errors, strange patterns of capitalization, and misspelled words, Benny admitted that he had followed Felice and this "DuDe" into a building. Benny recalled seeing Felice "grabin is pines and he was on top of her to having sex." According to Benny, he then stabbed the guy for having sex with Felice before running from the building and throwing the knife over a fence. "I mean to Do this By stabing the guy," Benny's statement concluded.

Looking at Benny's written statement, his shaky handwriting, his sloppy spelling, I found it hard to believe that he had not struggled to write it. But according to the police, Benny dashed it off in a matter of minutes.

The first time I read Benny Rinaldo's confession, Jessie was in second grade. At age seven, she was spelling better, writing more neatly, and using more complex words than my twenty-three–year-old client. Benny would later testify at the suppression hearing held to determine whether his statement was admissible that the police had basically told him what to write and that he had written down the story they told him. He did not remember receiving any warnings until after he had written out the statement. Then the police told him to sign the *Miranda* form. Benny explained that he could not read very well.

The hearing judge determined that Benny's confession would be admissible. Not surprisingly, the judge chose to believe the two police officers' accounts of the interrogation over the one provided by Benny. In doing so, the judge observed that Benny's account appeared to be "tailored" to support suppression.

Once the statement was deemed admissible, Benny's chances of being convicted increased dramatically. As the United States Supreme Court has recognized, a confession is like no other evidence. There was a time when I would open a file, read a client confession, and immediately begin looking for errors that could result in automatic reversal without any consideration of the evidence. A confession was considered the gold standard of criminal proof, too compelling to be challenged.

The most startling revelation relating to cases where defendants have been exonerated based on DNA evidence has been the discovery that innocent people, especially the young and the mentally retarded, are prone to falsely implicate themselves in crimes. People have confessed to raping and murdering victims and then been proven innocent when the real culprit has come forward and his admissions of guilt have been corroborated by previously untested DNA evidence. The most notorious such case in recent New York history involved the young men wrongly convicted of sexually assaulting a Central Park jogger. Years after they had confessed, a serial rapist came forward and admitted sole responsibility for the attack. After DNA tests corroborated that admission, all the youths' convictions were overturned.

But despite the well-documented phenomenon of false confessions, few people can believe that anybody would confess to a crime he had not committed. At Benny's trial, once the confession and the knife were introduced, the prosecutor had to do little else. She called the victim, Dario Guzman, who recalled that on his eighteenth birthday he had gone out to celebrate when a woman approached him offering to sell him a CD player, an offer that did not particularly interest him. But when she offered to have sex with him for twenty dollars, Guzman's ears pricked up. The only problem was that he was living with his large family in a tiny apartment that had little room to entertain prostitutes. Felice was not the type of prostitute who demanded a room. She told Guzman they could go to his building and take care of business in the stairwell. When they got to his building, they went all the way up to the sixth floor.

Felice leaned against the door leading to the roof and began taking off her pants. While Guzman watched the show, he was struck on the back of his head. He turned to see a stranger's face and then instantly became nauseated and dizzy. Guzman grabbed for the railing and was stabbed in the elbow. He heard a man and a woman screaming . . . and then nothing.

He woke up in the hospital sometime later with a breathing tube down his throat. He had been stabbed several times, including in the back of his head, a wound that had pierced the occipital bone, the quarter-inch-thick base portion of the skull. As a result, Guzman would suffer bouts of nausea and double vision. He remained in the hospital for three months. That he survived at all was a minor miracle, anecdotal evidence that teenage boys are superhuman.

While in the hospital, Guzman never viewed a lineup to identify his assailant. At trial, he said at first that Benny just looked like the guy. Guzman then became increasingly insistent that Benny was his attacker. But Guzman admitted that before his testimony, the prosecutor had taken him into the courtroom and pointed out where Benny would be sitting. Sort of a dumb thing for a prosecutor to do, because it suggested to the jury that without the help, Guzman would have been at a loss to recognize anybody.

In addition to this less-than-compelling identification evidence, there was nothing at the crime scene that tied Benny to the attack. No fingerprints were recovered. Although the attack had taken place on the sixth floor, where condoms had been strewn, Guzman had been found on the fifth floor in a pool of blood. He did not have any recollection of how he had ended up there. The prosecutor admitted it was a mystery, because the medical evidence suggested that Guzman would have lost consciousness right away. This evidence suggested to me that perhaps somebody had moved the victim after the attack, a scenario supported by pictures from the crime scene depicting smudged blood on the stairs leading down to the fifth floor, as if Guzman's body had been dragged.

The sole witness called in Benny's defense was none other than Felice Diaz herself—a strange choice, given that she was the person who had fingered Benny in the first place. Nevertheless, Felice took the stand and explained that, on the night of the stabbing, she had offered to have sex with Guzman but had intended to take the money and run without going through with her part of the bargain. Once in the stairwell, Guzman got rough with her and tore the buttons off her shirt. Felice told him that the deal was off.

She then saw two men she did not know, a "black" and a Puerto Rican, walking up the stairs toward her and Guzman. The men asked her what was going on, and although she was being manhandled by Guzman, Felice told them that it was none of their business. One of the men told her to leave before she got hurt, and Felice took his advice. On her way down the stairs, she heard Guzman screaming. She then coincidentally ran into Benny. She told him that something was going on upstairs, and they ran out of the building together. As they ran, the Puerto Rican man and the black man ran past them, and she saw them discard a knife.

Felice testified that she later falsely told the police that Benny had stabbed the victim because she was mad at him for calling her names. That's when her trial account really started falling apart (although it hadn't been too convincing even up to that point).

On cross-examination, the prosecutor asked Felice about every detail of the prior statement she had given to the police on Independence Day the previous year. Felice was forced to admit that she had told the police that Benny had "snapped" upon seeing her "hanging out" with a "friend" in a building and had stabbed her friend a number of times before throwing Felice down the stairs. Benny then chased her from the building, threatening her with the knife, which he eventually threw over a fence. Over the objection of trial counsel, the prosecution was allowed to introduce a copy of Felice's prior statement.

In the end, Felice was a disastrous defense witness. She was a prostitute and crack addict who had given a formal written statement contradicting her trial account. Under the rules of evidence, her prior inconsistent statement was technically admitted only to allow the jury to assess her credibility, not as evidence of what had transpired. In reality, such legal niceties most likely were lost on Benny's jury. Felice's statement, because it was consistent with Benny's confession, strengthened the reliability of the confession rather than undermining it.

Even if Felice's trial account had not been contradicted by her previous statement to the police, it was inherently unbelievable. What woman who was being assaulted by a stranger would tell two men interrupting the assault to mind their own business? And Benny's arrival in the building was a little too convenient to be believed.

Benny never took the stand in his own defense to explain the conditions under which he had confessed, which was another strange development. In order for the defense to have any chance of prevailing, Benny's confession had to be rigorously attacked. At the pretrial suppression hearing, Benny had explained that he had not been given the proper warnings until after he confessed, and that the police had essentially told him what to write down. But at trial Benny explained none of these things.

When Benny's trial attorney, Daniel Gordon, announced that his client would not be testifying, the prosecutor sought to put on the record that if Benny had testified, she would have asked him about a prior statement he had made. *What prior statement?* I wondered. The record could not answer my question, because the trial judge cut off the discussion, observing that the prosecutor could not ask Benny anything if he wasn't going to testify.

On summation, Gordon urged the jury to credit Felice's account of the incident despite her "speckled past." As far as the confession went, Gordon argued that the police had held Benny for six hours, that Benny was "probably sleepy" and definitely not well educated when he confessed.

The prosecutor, Mandy Mason, responded that the case was about a jealous boyfriend who followed his girlfriend and stabbed a total stranger, leaving him for dead. Mason characterized Felice's trial account as laughable. "You got an in-court identification, Felice Diaz's statement, and a confession," the prosecutor reminded the jury.

Concerning the defense argument that Benny's statement had been coerced, the prosecutor observed that six hours of detention was unlikely to compel a person to confess to attempted murder involuntarily. After all, Mason asserted, Benny was an adult, who could have asserted his right to remain silent at any time.

During their deliberations, the jurors asked to see both Benny's and Felice's statements together, to view the knife, and to hear again Guzman's description of his attacker. The following day, the jury convicted Benny of attempting to murder Guzman.

Less than a month later, the parties appeared before the trial judge, the Honorable William Fields. The prosecutor asked the court to impose the maximum sentence, twenty-five years' imprisonment, because of the brutal nature of the attack.

Benny's trial attorney, Daniel Gordon, asked the court to impose ten years, setting forth that Benny had a long history of mental illness, had always been in special-education classes, and had never been able to work due to his limitations. Counsel explained that Benny did "not have the full understanding of things as they occur" and continued to maintain his innocence.

Judge Fields found the only sympathetic factor to be Benny's history of mental illness. Declaring the attack vicious and senseless, he sentenced Benny to eighteen years in prison.

Immediately after I had been assigned to Benny's case, I called Daniel Gordon to ask him about some of the decisions he had made. He was willing to discuss his representation without a hint of defensiveness. He had nothing to be defensive about, he explained, because he had made no mistakes in Benny's case, only strategic decisions that had not turned out as well as he had hoped. It was not a case for an ineffective assistance of counsel argument, Gordon explained, because he had carefully considered his options and then acceded to his client's wishes.

I asked why Gordon had not pursued some form of diminished capacity defense. The evidence that Benny had "snapped," that he was a person of limited intelligence who had been overcome by a jealous rage, suggested to me that Benny could not have formed the intent to kill required to support an attempted murder conviction. He was obviously acting under the influence of extreme emotional disturbance, a recognized defense to attempted murder in New York. If Benny had been convicted of acting under the influence of extreme emotional disturbance, the highest sentence he could have received would have been fifteen years.

Gordon explained that Benny had not wanted to raise a partial defense that would have resulted in prison time. They wanted a defense that could result in Benny's walking out of the courtroom. Gordon wanted to raise a justification defense, and Benny had originally told Gordon that he had stabbed the complainant in response to the complainant's attacking him. But then Felice came forward insisting that two other men had done the stabbing, and they decided to go with her testimony instead. Gordon didn't know who or what to believe. He didn't make those "judgments," he explained. They went with Felice's account at the insistence of Benny and his family.

"But what do you actually think happened?" I asked, wanting his assessment of the truth.

"I think love can make you do crazy things," Gordon responded.

I didn't see any point in arguing with that truth. I asked Gordon to send me his defense file and told him I would be calling him again after I had reviewed the case more thoroughly.

## FINDING A VILLAIN

Every story needs a villain. Every case is a story. Ergo, every case needs a villain. It's simple logic. For the prosecution, the villain is always the same at the trial and on appeal—the defendant, my client.

For my purposes, there are several characters to choose from to play the wrongdoer whose actions have denied my client a fair trial. The wrongs could have been inflicted by an overzealous prosecutor, who suppressed favorable evidence or made arguments that improperly appealed to the jurors' emotions and fears. The culprit could have been the judge, whose slanted evidentiary rulings or instructions favored the prosecution and skewed the scales of justice in the State's favor. It could have been a lying victim who, for his own base purposes, duped the system into falsely convicting my client.

But the human mind craves simplicity. Children do not play cops and robbers and Indians. Or cowboys and cops and Indians. No, the forces of good and evil must be squarely matched, the lines clearly drawn. The best stories have one strong villain.

It is the same with appeals. In Stephen DeLuca's case, the villain was Justice Lake, who failed to supervise the jury selection, thwarted the defense efforts to create an adequate record to reveal his errors, and then refused to instruct the jury about a legitimate defense justification theory. In Janet Flores's case, it was the prosecutor, who argued that the court and jury should credit Derrick Fabio's custodial confession because it was given under oath, without revealing that it had been recanted under oath weeks before Janet's trial. In Eric Eastman's case, it was mainly David Johnson, who claimed to have been sexually assaulted, at first merely to earn a transfer off the cell block and then to recover millions of dollars from the city. All clear stories, with clear villains who committed real wrongs against my clients.

Alleging too many villains, too many wrongs, mucks up the narrative, creating the real danger that the audience will dismiss my claims as the creations of a paranoid conspiracy theorist. That was the problem with Corrie Angelo's case—too many villains, not enough clarity. Mario was the stabber. Malone and his team of officers were liars. Justice Albert was biased. Too much for any harried (and/or lazy) trial court judge to wrap his mind around.

When I am reading a transcript, looking to cast the villain's role, my least favorite prospect is the trial defense attorney. There are several reasons for this bias. Having represented a small number of clients at the trial level—before their guilt had been determined—I understand that it is very easy to second-guess strategy decisions after the case has ended badly. The pace of appeals is exponentially slower than trial work. Appellate attorneys have endless hours to mull over issues and research the law. At trial, there is no such luxury. Often objections must be formulated and registered in a matter of seconds.

Also, a claim that a client has been denied a fair trial due to the ineffective assistance of counsel almost always requires filing a motion in the trial court to afford the attorney an opportunity to explain his actions. I find such hearings uncomfortable and unpleasant to litigate. There is something unseemly about a defense attorney testifying about the inner workings of his relationship with his client. Defense trial strategies are like sausages; I'd rather see them fully formed without being privy to the grinding process.

My instincts are to deem reasonable almost any defense strategy, even the most disastrous ones. But I have to fight those instincts, because with a properly developed record, the federal courts are still most likely to reverse a state court's criminal conviction due to a defendant's failure to receive the effective assistance of counsel. While such reversals are rare, if the courts have to choose a villain, their favorite candidate is the defense attorney. Another reason I hate raising ineffective-assistance-of-counsel claims: Criminal defense attorneys are held in low enough regard without their fellow criminal defense attorneys casting aspersions.

But by the time I had gone through Benny Rinaldo's record and Daniel Gordon's trial file, it was clear to me that Gordon would have to be my villain. There were just too many mistakes that had been made.

The first one that struck me was that Gordon had filed a highly unusual motion, asking the court to suppress physical evidence, although no physical evidence had been recovered as a result of Benny's arrest. While motions seeking to bar the prosecution from introducing evidence obtained in violation of a defendant's rights are routinely filed in criminal cases, there has to be evidence to suppress before it makes any sense to file such a motion.

In Benny's case, the sole piece of physical evidence, the knife, had been recovered from an abandoned lot weeks after the crime. A defendant can only challenge the search of an area if he has a "reasonable expectation of privacy" in the place searched. The Fourth Amendment recognizes that you can't dump your dirty laundry out onto the street and then complain if people see your underwear.

Still, Gordon moved to suppress physical evidence, and in doing so, he admitted that Benny had stabbed the victim. His motion, filed within ten days of his taking over the case, set forth that Benny had discovered the victim preparing to have sex with Felice and confronted them. The victim had then pulled out a knife and slashed Benny on the wrist, after which they struggled for the knife. Benny momentarily gained control of the knife and stabbed the victim in self-defense. Thus, Gordon's motion conceded that Benny had actually stabbed the victim—just as the prosecution claimed—before the admissibility of Benny's confession had been determined.

*Thou shalt not reveal your defense theory to the prosecution in filed court papers* is among the major commandments of criminal defense practice. There are times when the discovery statutes compel disclosure, such as when the defense intends to call an alibi witness. Even then, a lot of defense attorneys are slow to comply. Telegraphing the defense to be asserted at trial is never a good idea—inevitably such a revelation gives the prosecution a better opportunity to disprove the defense claims. For example, based on Gordon's disclosure, the prosecution would be prepared to offer evidence that the nature of the victim's wounds (to the back of the head) was more consistent with a surprise attack from behind than the type of damage likely to be inflicted if Benny had merely been defending himself.

In all the years I had been practicing, I had never seen a defense attorney reveal his defense in a motion to suppress. When I read the papers to Beth Fried, a friend of mine with years of criminal trial experience, she actually gasped in horror. Beth is magical in a courtroom. She can charm the birds from the trees and make a jury not merely want to acquit her client but take him home to fix him a hot meal.

"He revealed the defense in his suppression papers? What was he thinking?!" Beth exclaimed.

"What makes it even worse is that there was no physical evidence to suppress," I said.

"Ugh. Was justification the defense at trial?"

"No, they claimed my client hadn't done it. Justification was never really a viable defense. The wounds were all to the back of the head and abdomen."

"That's bad. Really, really bad," Beth said.

I asked her if she could think of any explanation for Gordon's actions.

"Not any good ones."

There was nothing equivocal in Beth's response. Gordon's revealing a subsequently abandoned self-defense claim to suppress nonexistent physical evidence was an enormous blunder. And that blunder came back to haunt the defense during the trial. It was this statement—the self-defense scenario set forth in the motion papers—that the prosecutor referred to when the defense announced Benny's decision not to testify. Benny could not take the stand because if he did, the jury would have learned that he had admitted to his own attorney that he had stabbed the complainant, contrary to Felice's trial account that Benny had not done the stabbing. In other words, Gordon had begun the case insisting that Benny had stabbed the victim in self-defense and ended up claiming that Benny had never gone near the victim at all. The raising of such dramatically inconsistent defenses always makes me nervous; it is often the first sign that an attorney has failed to plot his course carefully. And then I have to go back to square one to figure out where it all went wrong.

After hanging up with Beth, I sat on my office floor leafing through hundreds of pages of the victim's medical records. In several spots, there were notations by the medical staff suggesting that while he was hospitalized, Guzman was incoherent and having difficulty recognizing his own brother. There were also police reports reflecting that during that same time period, the police had shown Guzman a group of photographs to see if he could identify his assailant. According to the police reports, Guzman had been able to identify Benny as his stabber from that photo array.

The victim's alleged ability to identify Benny, a stranger whose face he momentarily glimpsed in dim lighting, at a time when he was having difficulty recognizing his own brother, strongly suggested that the police had singled Benny out in some way. But Gordon had inexplicably failed to exercise Benny's right to request a hearing to explore the circumstances surrounding the identification procedure. Nor did Benny's jury ever learn of the notations in Guzman's chart. Gordon never questioned the treating physician about the victim's inability in the days following the attack to recognize his own family members.

And still there was more. Within Gordon's trial file, there was a page of Benny's school records. That single page reflected that when Benny was sixteen years old, he had a reading comprehension level of a child in the second grade. His verbal IQ fell within the mentally deficient range.

I did not know exactly what all the terminology meant, but it was clear to me that a second grader with difficulty understanding verbal concepts would have a hard time understanding the *Miranda* warnings—the right to remain silent, to have an attorney present during questioning, to be assigned an attorney if he could not afford one, and that anything he said could be used against him in a court of law. I pictured my own second grader, Jessie, sitting in a holding cell, hysterically crying, while police officers placed a form in front of her face. Jessie would sign because someone in authority told her to, not because she had any idea what she was signing.

I knew that there had to be additional records maintained by Benny's school about his mental impairments. From the moment we are born, we are assessed. It begins with the Apgar score that measures a newborn's well-being and continues throughout our lives. We are measured, judged, and graded, our physical growth charted on curves, our intellectual development mapped on charts. A child like Benny, who had attended special-education classes in New York City's public schools for years, would have built up quite a record of assessments, I imagined. Yet no objective evidence of Benny's mental impairments had ever been placed before the suppression court determining the admissibility of his confession, or the trial jury, which also needed to determine the confession's voluntariness and reliability. I could not imagine why Daniel Gordon had failed to explore the extent of Benny's mental limitations.

Also within Gordon's trial file was a videotape, unmentioned on the record. The label on the outside was handwritten in blocked print. "TO THE JUDGE," somebody had penned in black ink.

I was instantly intrigued. I carried the tape down the hall into the conference room and pushed it into the video player. A woman's image appeared on the screen. She had greasy-looking hair, gaunt cheeks, terrible teeth, and flat, dark eyes that darted back and forth. Off camera, there was whispering. Then the woman started talking in a thick Bronx Hispanic accent.

"My name is Felice Diaz. I want to say that Benny Rinaldo is innocent. I lied when I said he hurt anybody 'cause I was mad at him. It was really two black guys who did it. Benny just saw me running out of the building. He's innocent. So you should just let him go. Okay. Thanks."

The screen went blank. Then Felice came back. Again off camera, somebody whispered something.

"I'm saying this because it's true. Nobody forced me to do it. Benny's innocent." The screen went blank again. I continued to watch to see if Felice would come back. But she didn't. After a few more minutes, the screen turned to snow. I popped the tape out of the player, put it back in its case, and returned to my office.

Anybody viewing the tape should have foreseen that Felice would make a terrible witness. She hadn't seemed believable even without an experienced prosecutor confronting her with her prior statement accusing Benny of the stabbing. It also appeared that Felice was being told what to say by the person off camera. Her story about two black men doing the stabbing contradicted her trial account that a black and a Hispanic man were responsible. While I understood why Gordon had not wanted to disclose the tape to the prosecution, as he was bound to under New York's discovery laws, I could not understand how he could have decided to call Felice as a trial witness if he had viewed the tape himself. Felice's story was patently incredible.

After reviewing the file completely, I knew that I would have to bring a motion to vacate Benny's conviction based on Daniel Gordon's ineffectiveness. That meant going up to speak with him so that I could set forth in my motion his purported reasons for the disastrous decisions he had made during Benny's case.

I dreaded the prospect. It is never a pleasant task to confront another person with the news that, in your opinion, he fucked up royally. I wanted Daniel Gordon to admit that he had made serious mistakes, to prove that there were no reasonable strategic explanations for his actions. But the chances of his agreeing to do so were slim. Generally, trial attorneys, especially private practitioners, are reluctant to admit that they have committed malpractice. Such an admission can result in a client's suing his attorney to recover money damages, thus increasing malpractice premiums. At the very least, an ineffectiveness finding tarnishes an attorney's professional reputation.

I walked into Rich's office and flopped into a chair.

"What are the chances of my getting Gordon to admit that he fucked up Benny Rinaldo's case from here to Honolulu?" I asked, knowing in my own mind that they were near zero.

"You never know. Maybe he'll fall on his sword," Rich remarked, smiling slightly. He didn't personally know Gordon, but he knew as well as I did that any trial attorney was unlikely to admit his own ineffectiveness.

"I doubt it. He's been practicing criminal law since I was two years old. He's going to want to lecture me about how to try a case. I don't know that I have the patience for that right now," I said, my mind slipping toward my father, who was still in the hospital, his condition undiagnosed. I could feel tears stinging my eyes and I looked down so Rich wouldn't notice them.

"Just charm him," Rich responded.

"I'm not feeling very charming lately," I said, my voice catching. I faked a cough.

"What's wrong?" Rich asked, undoubtedly sensing the darkness of my mood, the tightness in my voice.

"Nothing, just tired as usual."

I pushed myself out of the chair and forced a smile onto my face. I did not want to share my morass of personal problems. Rich didn't want to hear about them anyway. I could not begin to explain that I was losing my nanny, perhaps my father—and still hadn't mastered even the dog walking. Starting to get into any one of these personal catastrophes would have made my cheerful facade crumble.

I returned to my office and called Daniel Gordon to arrange a sit-down. He explained that he had a packed schedule but that he could squeeze in a meeting with me around lunch the following day.

I left my own office the following morning an hour before our scheduled meeting for the forty-five–minute trip on the Number 4 train up to the Bronx courthouses. But the subway broke down around 146th Street, leaving me many blocks away from my destination. I walked onto the street and hailed a livery cab. After I closed the car door, I realized that I did not even know if I was actually in a cab or whether my driver had just decided to give me a lift because he thought I was hitchhiking. *This is how people disappear,* I thought to myself. But a few minutes later, the driver dropped me near the courthouse and demanded five dollars.

There was nothing stately or even particularly lawyerly about Daniel Gordon's office suite. But for the sign in the front window announcing the firm's name and the availability of legal services, the office could have housed a car rental or tax preparation franchise. Gordon was still in a meeting somewhere else when I arrived, but his secretary told me that he was expecting me. I walked around the office casually snooping.

Nailed to the inside of the door frame of Gordon's office was a mezuzah, one of the small encased prayer scrolls Jewish people affix to the doorposts of their houses. *You shall love the Lord your God with all your mind, with all your strength, with all your being. Set these words which I command you this day, upon your heart. Teach them faithfully to your children; speak of them in your home and on your way, when you lie down and when you rise up. Bind them as a sign upon your hand; let them be a symbol before your eyes; inscribe them on the doorposts of your house, and on your gates.* I knew the prayer by heart both in English and in Hebrew. Seeing the mezuzah made me feel a small twinge of remorse. In addition to being a fellow defense attorney, Gordon was a Member of the Tribe.

My guilty musings were interrupted by the sound of a door opening, followed by a rush of cold air that penetrated my stockings and sent a chill up my spine. A large, heavyset man in his sixties, wearing a tan trench coat and brown hat, was standing at the receptionist's desk, looking over his messages. Daniel Gordon rushed to greet me, apologizing for his lateness. I sensed he was actually happy he had made me wait; it conveyed that he was a very important man, rushing from one urgent appointment to the next.

When we sat down next to each other in his office to review the papers from his trial file, Gordon removed a cloth handkerchief to mop his brow. Another pang of sympathy for him came over me. I was making him sweat even before I had asked a single question.

I explained that I had concerns about his motion papers. Why had he moved to suppress physical evidence when none existed? Why had he disclosed his privileged communications and strategy in filed court papers? Why had he failed to move for a hearing into the circumstances surrounding the hospital identification procedure? Why had he not offered any evidence of Benny's mental impairments? And why had he called Felice Diaz as a witness even though she had previously told the police that Benny had stabbed the victim in a jealous rage?

Gordon answered every question without a moment's hesitation or defensiveness. He explained that it was his standard practice to move to suppress physical evidence. He unfailingly did it in every case. He revealed what Benny had told him about stabbing the victim in self-defense because Gordon believed this explanation demonstrated that the police had wrongly arrested his client. Gordon could not remember exactly why he had failed to move for a hearing into the identification procedure, but he surmised that he must have had a reason.

Concerning the school records, Gordon explained that anybody looking at the confession could tell that Benny was "slow" and that no other evidence was needed to make that point. Anyway, Benny had told him that the police had not given him the *Miranda* warnings until after he had confessed, a fact scenario that supported suppressing the confession at the pretrial hearing.

As far as Felice Diaz was concerned, Gordon had not wanted to call her at all. Benny and his family had brought him the tape and insisted that he present her testimony. While it is not uncommon for an attorney to agree to call a witness at a client's insistence, ultimately it is the attorney's decision to determine which witnesses will testify. With a witness like Felice, a disaster waiting to happen, deferring to the wishes of Benny and his family made no sense whatsoever.

I didn't press Gordon too much on his explanations. None of them appeared reasonable to me. Moving to suppress nonexistent physical evidence and revealing client confidences in the process should not be part of any attorney's standard operating procedure. Moreover, Gordon's suggestion that the police should not have arrested Benny, because he had stabbed the victim in self-defense, bordered on the ridiculous. The victim had almost died from numerous wounds to the back of his head and abdomen.

Gordon's explanations suited my purposes just fine. I had to show that his actions did not comport with those of a reasonably competent defense attorney. Then I had to prove that his errors had undermined the fairness of Benny's trial.

I asked Gordon if he would be willing to sign a sworn affirmation setting forth his explanations. I told him apologetically that I was going to file a motion to vacate Benny's judgment claiming that he had been ineffective. Gordon smiled and appeared amused. He refused to provide me with a sworn affirmation, explaining that he would rather not sign anything that could come back to haunt him. Still, he was far from hostile.

"It's fine. I've raised those claims before. Sometimes it can't be helped," Gordon remarked amiably. He said good-bye and wished me luck with my efforts to help Benny.

His good cheer only made me feel worse as I trudged into the freezing-cold air, hoping that the subways going back to Manhattan would be running.

# HEAD BANGING

After meeting Daniel Gordon, I knew that the prosecution would seize on his attempts to blame Benny and his family for the disastrous decisions that had been made. To me that seemed like blaming the victim. The law recognizes that a defendant represented by counsel retains the right to make a few critical decisions, such as whether to testify in his own behalf, whether to plead guilty to the charges, or whether to take an appeal following a conviction. But most strategic decisions, such as which questions to ask on cross-examination or which witnesses to call, remain with the defense attorney. For the sake of smooth client relations, some attorneys simply accede to their clients' wishes, hewing to that path of least resistance even when they know it could lead to disaster.

Generally, a reviewing court will not be sympathetic if a defendant specifically asks his attorney to do something and then complains after the conviction because his attorney complied with his demands. A defendant cannot come to the table with unclean hands and expect a court to serve up any relief.

But Benny was so obviously of limited intelligence. Gordon himself had told me that Benny seemed "slow." *What exactly does that mean?* I wondered. Nobody had bothered to find out. Now I needed to answer that question to argue that it was unreasonable for Gordon to have charted a course based on Benny's suggestions.

I contacted Benny's family and spoke with his brother—the only one who seemed to speak English—to set up a meeting for the following day. I knew from the pre-sentencing report contained within the file that Benny had been raised by his father, Michael. I asked his brother to tell Michael to bring every piece of paper he had relating to Benny's mental condition—school records, medical records, anything.

The next morning, Benny's father arrived at my office right on time. Michael Rinaldo was a small, wiry man, with dark hair graying slightly at the temples. I led him to the conference room and asked our receptionist, Inez, if she could translate our conversation.

I love Inez. She always helps me with a smile and never fails to ask regularly about each of my girls. She keeps her hair long, jogs most every day, and is a strict vegetarian. Although she looks around forty-five, Inez has grandchildren, so I doubt she is younger than sixty.

Once we were seated around the conference table, I asked Michael to tell me everything he could about Benny's childhood and mental development. Michael Rinaldo nodded to indicate that he understood the question, took a deep breath, and momentarily looked away from my gaze. It was the same technique I had used with Rich days earlier so that he would not see the tears spring to my eyes. I looked down for a moment to allow Michael to regain his composure. A minute passed. Then Michael started to tell me the story of Benny Rinaldo's childhood.

Benny had been born in Puerto Rico, the youngest of several children. As a baby, Benny used to regularly bang his head against the side of the crib. As he grew, he developed a habit of hitting himself in the head whenever he felt frustrated. These symptoms worried his father, because by the time Benny entered school, his mother had suffered a mental breakdown of some sort. The precise diagnosis was unclear.

Michael moved with his children to the Bronx, while Benny's mother remained in Puerto Rico. The loss of his mother devastated Benny and would inevitably lead to his infatuation with Felice, a woman old enough to be his mother, years later. Benny became a quiet, withdrawn child, with no friends.

While his siblings learned to read and write without much trouble, Benny had severe learning difficulties. Despite Michael's efforts, all the assessments, and individual educational planning meetings, Benny never learned to read very well. By the age of sixteen, Benny was still reading on the second-grade level. The Board of Education referred him to the Social Security Administration for further evaluation to determine Benny's eligibility for disability benefits based on his low intelligence.

Also during his teenage years, Benny became more and more depressed. He attempted suicide on several occasions and was treated in various mental health clinics. While he was on Rikers Island awaiting trial for stabbing Guzman, a little over two years earlier, Benny had tried to hang himself with a bed sheet and had been taken to Bellevue Hospital for treatment.

I held up my hand, signaling that Michael should stop.

"You mean that during this case, in 2002, Benny tried to kill himself?" I asked. There had been vague references in the pre-sentencing report to past suicide attempts, but I did not realize that one of those attempts had been so recent.

"Yeah, during this case," Michael responded, pressing his finger onto the table for emphasis.

"Do you know if Daniel Gordon tried to get any of Benny's mental health records?"

"No. I told him that there were all these records. I gave him a page of the school records to show him what I was talking about, but he didn't care. He did nothing to help Benny," Michael answered, anger seeping into his voice.

There was no reason I could think of, other than laziness, for the defense not to have obtained the records relating to Benny's mental disabilities. Learning about his mental history would not have meant that the defense had to use any of the information contained within the records. But there was no harm in gathering them up to see if there was anything in them that could help. I sighed and shook my head in disbelief.

Michael Rinaldo asked me what happened next, how I intended to proceed with his son's case. I explained that I was going to file a motion arguing that Benny had been denied his right to an effective lawyer during his trial. If we won that motion, Benny would be entitled to a new trial at which he could be represented by a better lawyer.

Michael Rinaldo looked at me intensely and asked the question that I dread, but have to answer, in almost every case.

"What are the chances that we'll win?"

Inez looked at me, waiting to translate my response. She knew as well as I did that the chances of winning in a case involving a violent attack were always slim. I answered slowly, choosing my words with care.

"It's always difficult to obtain relief after a jury has convicted someone of a violent crime. Courts generally don't want to upset a conviction, especially when they think the person who has been convicted is guilty. But I promise that I'll fight as hard as I can for your son."

Michael Rinaldo nodded as Inez translated my response, then he addressed a question directly to Inez. She answered in Spanish without translating for me. They both started laughing.

"What did you say?" I asked.

"He said you look too pretty to fight. I told him not to worry, that even though you might not look like it, you're as tough as any street fighter."

Well, at least Inez believed in me. I collected the records Michael Rinaldo had brought from Benny's various school assessments and walked him to the door. I promised to keep him informed of my progress and said good-bye.

• • • • • • • • • • • • • • • • • • • • • • • • • • •

I needed to visit my father, who had been in the hospital for nearly a week. Before he was admitted, he had assured me that he would be discharged in two days, that he just needed a course of intravenous antibiotics to battle an infection he had been unable to shake. Five days later, there had been no discussion of his discharge. During our daily telephone conversations, he told me everything was fine, that the doctors were just being overly careful. But fear had started to plague me.

A weeklong stay in the hospital did not suggest to me that all was well. More likely he was shielding me from something.

The day after meeting Michael Rinaldo, I dragged Lila into the office with me and set her up in the conference room with seven different shades of high-lighters and markers, file folders, tape, Post-its, and scissors, while down the hall I returned phone calls and wrote a few letters. Rich discovered Lila thirty minutes later and came to find me in my office.

"I assume the child with the pigtails in the conference room is yours," he remarked.

"Could be," I responded. "What'd she do?"

I walked down the hall and opened the conference room door. Lila was deep in concentration. Several folders had been cut into various shapes and taped together into a sculpture of some sort. She did not look up when Rich and I opened the door.

"Lila, this is my boss, Rich, the one who's always yelling at me."

I knew my words would be lost on Lila until we captured her full attention. Rich looked mortified.

"Don't tell her that," he said seriously. "She'll be scared of me." He bent down to meet Lila face-to-face. "It's nice to meet you," he said in his most respectful tone.

Lila looked up from her art project and was suddenly overtaken by shyness. She bolted up from the table and hid behind me. I pried her off my hip and reminded her to say hello.

"We're going to visit my father in the hospital," I explained to Rich, mentioning my father's illness for the first time.

"What's wrong with him?" Rich asked.

"We don't know yet."

Rich grimaced. "Well, I hope he's okay." He bent down again to address Lila. "It was nice seeing you," he said. He stood up and wished me luck, leaving Lila and me alone in the conference room to discuss our lunch options.

A short time later, we were outside eating hot dogs with sauerkraut and mustard bought from a street vendor. Lila wolfed hers down in minutes. She was excited at the prospect of riding the subway to the hospital.

Once at New York Presbyterian, she was thrilled with the bustle. She begged to stop in the gift shop to buy my father a present and selected a basket full of candies decorated with a balloon announcing "It's a Boy!"

We found the geriatric ward to which my father had been assigned. I knew he would be insulted by his placement there. In his mind he was barely middle-aged, never mind that few live to see 142.

Upon arriving at my father's room, I stood in the doorway, unable to reconcile the image of the drawn, pallid figure sitting in the hospital bed with my vibrant, bigger-than-life father. There were intravenous tubes and monitors everywhere. I could not will my feet to move and remained paralyzed at the threshold.

Lila's hand immediately slipped free from my own as she bounded into the room and leapt onto the bed to hug my father.

"There's my girl!" he announced, his face lighting up instantly as if a switch had been flipped inside him. Lila found a place among the tubes and begged him to demonstrate how the hospital bed's controls worked. Within moments, they were raising and lowering their heads, their feet, the entire bed, laughing all the while.

Their game was interrupted by teams of doctors and medical residents asking my father to sign legal waivers so that he could undergo additional tests, scopes, and scans. I glanced at the forms over my father's shoulder as he signed them without reading a word. "Risk of complications, bleeding, infection, death" seemed to appear on each one. I knew the forms were simply outlining the most dire and unlikely dangers, that they had been drafted by lawyers to make sure each patient's consent could be deemed informed. But my father looked so sick and fragile. The prospect of his being subjected to such a battery of tests worried me.

After the last form had been signed, I followed the chief resident into the hallway. The resident seemed harried, carrying a bunch of charts in his arms as he strode toward the nurses' station. He looked ten years younger than I. I introduced myself and asked whether all the tests that had been ordered were really necessary.

"That's why we ordered them," he replied curtly, without looking at me. Wrong answer.

"Look," I said, my voice instantly too loud, "I'm not some alternative medicine guru, but it seems to me that when you have a seventy-one-year-old man whose immune system is being taxed, subjecting him to every invasive procedure you can think up just doesn't make sense. I don't want you to cure the disease and kill my father!" I shouted.

"Mommy?"

Before the resident could respond to my tirade, I heard a familiar voice from behind me and turned to see Lila standing in the hallway. She looked frightened, unused to hearing me yell at total strangers. I lifted her into my arms and returned to my father's room to continue the visit. By the time we left, I had not spoken with anyone who had a definitive answer about what was wrong. My father had a rampant blood infection, but nobody knew what was causing it, where or why he had contracted it. I pressed my mother to get a second opinion by reaching out to infectious disease experts from another hospital. But she and my father were not inclined to do so, and I felt I had to defer to their wishes. The visit only made me feel more uneasy.

I was grateful to be back at work the following morning, sitting on my office floor, a defined task before me that I could conquer and control. I carefully reviewed Benny Rinaldo's school records. All of them reflected the same thing. Benny had particular problems with tasks tapping his ability to understand verbal concepts. His ability to articulate his ideas was also impaired, and he frequently used "incomplete sentences and mispronounced words" when he spoke.

Those limitations would be a serious handicap during a police interrogation. Benny would have a hard time understanding the *Miranda* warnings and telling a coherent story, making it likely, I surmised, for him to just go along with whatever information the officers suggested to him. At the time of his interrogation, the police already had Felice's account of the attack. They could have easily worked off Felice's story to come up with a matching one for Benny.

I called up Bellevue Hospital and asked the administrative office to fax me a release form allowing me to obtain Benny's mental hospitalization records from his most recent suicide attempt. I went online to the Social Security Administration's Web site and downloaded a release to obtain Benny's disability records. I sent both off to Benny, who quickly signed his name next to the X that I had marked on each form and returned them to me. Then I waited and prodded each bloated bureaucracy until it coughed up the records I had requested.

The records from Bellevue revealed that Benny had a long history of depression with psychotic traits. He had complained of hearing voices that urged him to kill himself, although at the time of the Bellevue assessment in August 2002, Benny reported that the voices had quieted some. The doctors at Bellevue prescribed Prozac and advised that Benny needed to be closely monitored at Rikers to prevent any further suicide attempts.

I called my father and read the Bellevue records to him over the phone, the various psychiatric phrases and scaled ratings along the diagnostic axis mental health professionals use to chart a patient's condition. My father had been discharged from the hospital, having received a diagnosis of septicemia, a bacterial infection of the blood that has settled in his heart. Still on intravenous antibiotics, he had not returned to work. But his mind was as sharp as ever.

"It sounds to me like your client is functioning on a very low level of intelligence," my father confirmed.

The Social Security records, which I received weeks later, revealed just how low. As I had expected, Benny had been evaluated many times throughout his life, his intelligence and disabilities documented and measured. It was the same old story. Nobody had bothered to learn the true nature of Benny's disabilities when years of his life were at stake, but when money was on the table—in the form of monthly disability allotments—nobody was writing a check until some serious evaluations had been done.

Only 1 percent to 3 percent of the population has an IQ score that measures lower than seventy-five. Benny's scores consistently measured in the low fifties. He was not merely "slow," as Gordon had claimed. Benny was mentally retarded.

Mentally retarded people are generally more suggestible, more easily manipulated, and more eager to comply with authority than people of even average intelligence. It has been demonstrated that people with mental retardation typically have difficulty understanding the *Miranda* rights and warnings. The same year that Benny had been interrogated by the police, the United States Supreme Court held that mentally retarded people could not be executed, in part because of the risk of their falsely confessing to crimes they had not committed. But long before that landmark ruling, courts had recognized that a person's limited mental abilities needed to be considered when evaluating the voluntariness of his response to interrogation.

I called Charlie at work to tell him what I had discovered. Charlie has never practiced criminal law, but he has a way of seeing to the heart of any problem I pass by him. He is the "reasonable man" against whom I measure all of my legal arguments. If Charlie doesn't buy it, I pretty much know that no judge will.

"You know my slow client? The one whose lawyer blamed him for all the mistakes made during the trial? Turns out he's actually mentally retarded," I explained.

"The lawyer or the client?" Charlie asked absentmindedly. I could hear him typing at his office computer as we spoke.

"Not the lawyer, my client. C'mon, focus here. What do you think?"

"Let me get this straight, the lawyer was letting his mentally retarded client call the shots in his own defense? It sounds like there should be a punch line in there somewhere, like what do you call a lawyer who listens to his mentally retarded client?"

"I'm hoping the punch line's 'ineffective.'"

"Seems it should be. But is there any chance your guy doesn't seem mentally retarded when you meet him? Is that even possible?" Charlie wondered.

As usual he had asked exactly the right question. While Gordon had admitted that Benny had appeared "slow," maybe Benny seemed more normal than his IQ scores reflected. The prosecution would undoubtedly argue that it was reasonable for Gordon not to have investigated the true nature of Benny's mental disabilities. The only way to answer that argument was to sit down with Benny himself.

Fortunately, Benny was being housed at Sing Sing Correctional Facility, only an hour from my office. I arranged to visit him the following week.

........................................

Sing Sing Correctional Facility is the ultimate maximum-security prison in New York State. It actually birthed several common phrases for imprisonment. Being "sent up the river" and "going to the big house" both refer to being sent to Sing

Sing, as the plaque at the prison gate proudly proclaims. Sing Sing sits along the banks of the Hudson, in Ossining, New York, about twenty-five miles up the river from the island of Manhattan and its outer boroughs, which provide the prison with a steady supply of inmates.

It is an institution with a notorious history, built by one hundred prisoners from Auburn prison, who in 1825 were sailed down the Hudson to the suburbs of Manhattan to quarry marble from the hillsides and build a model facility. They quarried so much marble that the extra was sent down the river to Manhattan, where it was used to build portions of New York University, as well as up the river, where it was incorporated into the state capitol building in Albany. In its early years, Sing Sing's warden insisted on absolute silence from the prisoners. The silence was enforced with regular lashings and beatings. That warden eventually impregnated a female prisoner and was fired in disgrace. Whipping and torturing prisoners was fine, but never sex outside the sanctity of marriage.

The only word to describe Sing Sing is hulking. My heart always starts to beat a little faster when I approach it. Inevitably my distraction results in my missing the public entrance and finding myself trapped in the staff parking lot. Once there, the only access to the visitor's reception center is over a ramshackle wooden bridge beneath the stone turret of the guard tower encircled with razor wire. It is a bridge right out of "Three Billy Goats Gruff." "Clip, clop, clip, clop," my high heels thump as I wobble across, half expecting each time to fall right through. But oddly there is not a single sign stating that the bridge is off-limits to the public. Maybe the warden believes no such sign is necessary. *Res ipsa loquitur*: The thing speaks for itself.

On the day I went to visit Benny Rinaldo for the first time, I actually found Sing Sing's public parking lot, maybe because I was so focused on the task before me that I failed to take in the prison's aura upon my approach. When Benny walked into the counsel room, I immediately sensed a gentle softness about him. He was big and doughy, with pale skin, chubby cheeks, and slightly slanted eyes that appeared a bit too wide set. He blinked his eyes twice as often as a normal person, probably as a result of his psychotropic medications.

I tried to explain to Benny who I was and the approach I would be taking to his case. With a client of average intelligence, such a meeting would have taken twenty minutes. With Benny, I spent an hour. He would nod and smile as I explained basic concepts to him. Then when I would ask him to explain to me what we had just discussed, he couldn't find the words. Fortunately, Jessie was in second grade at the time, about the same level on which Benny was functioning. So I was used to explaining complex thoughts in simple terms.

Before I left, I wanted to test Benny's understanding of the *Miranda* warnings.

"If I were to tell you that you have the right to remain silent, what would that mean to you?" I asked.

"That I didn't have to talk," Benny responded, smiling, obviously pleased to know the answer.

The right to remain silent is probably the simplest warning. I needed to try a harder one.

"If I told you that anything you said could be used against you in a court of law, what would that mean?" I continued.

Benny looked up at me blankly, searching for the answer in my face. Not finding it there, he asked me to repeat the question. I repeated the *Miranda* warning again, slowly. Benny shook his head.

"I don't know," he said softly, hanging his head for a moment, before looking up again with his blinking eyes.

"That's okay," I assured him. "That's a hard one. I'm not even sure I know what that one means." I smiled at Benny, not wanting him to feel as if he'd failed some pop quiz. There had been enough failures in his life, I intuited. I promised that I would be in touch and made him promise to call me if he was having any problems at Sing Sing.

I left the meeting convinced that there was no way Gordon could have reasonably concluded that Benny's mental disabilities did not warrant additional exploration. Any reasonably competent defense attorney would have known that Benny's cognitive impairments, his complex array of mental retardation and mental illness, would be critical to challenging the voluntariness of his confession. Gordon's failure to obtain this information from the long list of institutions that had documented Benny's mental difficulties throughout his life—the schools, the mental hospitals, the Social Security Administration—simply defied reason.

# DON'T PISS OFF THE JUDGE

Roy Cohn, who achieved infamy as Senator Joseph McCarthy's right-hand man during the communist scare of the 1950s, is a great study in paradoxical outrage. By most accounts, Cohn was a rabid anti-Semite, even though he was Jewish, and a gay basher, although he himself was homosexual. Before he became a national figure, Cohn practiced criminal law in New York. He prosecuted Julius and Ethel Rosenberg, who were both executed in the electric chair at Sing Sing, another proud moment in the prison's history. In his later years, Cohn became a criminal defense attorney. Before being disbarred for stealing client funds, he represented several high-profile organized-crime figures. "I don't want to know what the law is, I want to know who the judge is," Cohn used to say.

On this point, I happen to agree with Roy Cohn. Often when I am discussing an issue with a colleague, the first question I will ask is, "Who was the judge?" Almost always the question meets with blank stares from newer attorneys, who have yet to realize that judges are not robots in black robes. They are individuals with prejudices and life experiences that make them receptive to certain arguments and unreceptive to others. Nobody is a blank slate.

Knowing the identity of the judge is only the first step, a means to an end. Once you know who will be hearing your motion or your argument, it is important that you don't piss him off. You can know every rule of criminal procedure, every substantive case supporting your arguments, every fact in your favor. But if you piss off the judge, most likely none of your brilliance is going to matter. I actually had a professor in law school who was honest enough to incorporate the "don't piss off the judge rule" into her lectures. Hers was the most useful course I took.

While it is always important to know the judge so that you can pitch your arguments in the most persuasive manner, in Benny Rinaldo's case I knew that which judge would hear the motion would be critical to the outcome. A lazy or nonintellectual judge would simply look at the evidence of guilt, the confession, the eyewitness testimony, the recovered knife, and Felice Diaz's pathetic testimony and conclude that no lawyer could have done any better than Gordon.

There are also judges who harbor a deep distrust of any claims relating to mental incapacity, who believe in their heart of hearts that mental illness really does not excuse criminal conduct and that psychology is mumbo jumbo trotted out by criminal defense attorneys in an attempt to excuse the inexcusable. If Benny's trial judge harbored either of those predispositions, the motion would have to be skeletal. I would simply lose quickly in the state court and proceed to federal court.

I didn't know anything about Justice William Fields, the judge who had presided over Benny's trial. None of the Bronx trial attorneys with whom I spoke seemed to know much either. Benny's was apparently Justice Fields's first case as a supreme court judge. He was not even from the Bronx, but rather from Brooklyn criminal court. I needed to change my focus.

I started with one of my best friends, Celine Bond, whom I have known since my earliest Legal Aid days. Celine is the real deal, brilliant and beautiful, who spent her adolescence as a scholarship student at St. Paul's, an elite New England prep school, and has never lost her outsider's passion for battling on behalf of the underdog. If I were ever accused of a crime, Celine would be the first person I would call. Charlie would not know how to bail me out of the pens. Celine would.

"Bond!" I barked into the phone. Ever since Celine started trying a lot of felony cases, we have been addressing each other by our last names in a pseudo-macho fashion.

"Trupp, how are you?"

"I need to know what type of buzz saw I'm about to walk into on behalf of my mentally retarded client. Tell me everything you know about Judge Fields."

"Smartest boy in the room. Harvard law. Filthy rich. His wife is a famous fashion designer."

Celine mentioned some designer brand name. No slave to fashion myself, I had never heard of it. I stopped buying new clothes when it became clear that

I was unlikely to get out the door without being drooled upon or used as a tissue by at least one of my daughters.

"Is he going to think my client's faking being mentally retarded and psychotic?" I asked.

"Actually, I think I heard that one of his kids had some problem, serious learning disabilities or something. Rumor has it anyway. He should be pretty up on that stuff," Celine assured me.

"What else? I need someone smart who doesn't think IQ tests are like voodoo."

"He's a former prosecutor. Don't think he's going to welcome you with open arms," Celine warned.

"Aren't they all former prosecutors? Except for the ones who are presently prosecutors, of course." I laughed at my own joke.

Celine didn't; she seemed distracted, obviously in a rush to get to some courtroom somewhere.

"True enough. Let me know how it goes with Fields," she said brusquely.

After I thanked Celine for the report and hung up, I felt strangely optimistic about Benny's case. All I needed was a smart judge who was open to the radical notion that a mentally retarded man should not be running his own defense. Justice Fields seemed perfect.

I drafted the motion without worrying that too much detail or analysis would overwhelm the judge or that my reliance on Benny's mental disabilities would be ignored. Once finished, the motion was over sixty pages long. On top of that, I attached every school record, mental health record, and Social Security Administration record that I had uncovered.

Thankfully, by the time I filed the motion in July 2005, my house was more or less back in order. Charlie's foot had healed, and I no longer needed to wake before dawn to walk the dog. My father had been successfully treated. And Marie had decided to move back north, at least temporarily.

For the five months Marie had been gone, I had learned just how hard life could be. I had selected Edie, Marie's replacement, simply because she reminded me of Marie, with a similar Haitian accent, proper bearing, and warm smile. But like most rebound relationships, this one was destined to fail. Turns out, Edie was nothing like Marie. Marie had never missed a day of work in over seven years, but within weeks of her hiring, Edie was regularly coming late or calling in sick. Often on the days she actually came to work, she would call me at my office at noon to announce unexpectedly that she had scheduled a doctor's appointment for 3:00 that day. More and more, work began to feel like a luxury I could no longer afford.

Eventually, I called Marie in tears one afternoon after Edie had failed to pick up Jessie from school. Jessie had apparently wandered around the neighborhood crying until a stay-at-home mom had taken pity on her and brought her home. In addition to the terror of knowing that my eight-year-old daughter had been wandering the streets alone, I felt the shame of having to be bailed out by a stay-at-home mom, who did not even have the decency to be judgmental about the whole thing so that I could get properly defensive.

"I'm sure you'd do the same," she told me with total sincerity.

Of course I would help out a crying child, I assured myself. If she happened to wander into my field of vision on my regularly scheduled day off, I would be the first one to help. Still, I felt horrible that I had not chosen Marie's replacement wisely and that Jessie had suffered the frightening consequences of my poor decision. When I relayed the story of the missed pickup and Jessie's wanderings to Marie, she announced without a moment's hesitation that she would be back the following week to stay for a while.

By the time Marie had been back for a few days, all the previous months' disasters seemed a distant memory. Wrestling with child-care issues is like banging your head against a wall. It feels great when you stop.

I filed Benny's motion and waited for the prosecution's response. The prosecutor handling the case, Gina Nielson, called several times to ask for extensions. She was getting married that summer and planned on taking a few weeks off. I agreed to every adjournment. Far be it from me to get in the way of a new bride and her honeymoon.

Meanwhile, the appellate court was threatening to dismiss Benny's case unless I explained the delay. There was no way I was going to file an appellate brief so that the higher court could declare Benny's guilt overwhelming before my motion in the trial court had been determined. I had learned my lesson from Corrie Angelo's case and resolved to delay filing the appellate brief until I got a decision on my motion to vacate from the trial judge.

I called Gina to ask if she would agree to adjourn the case, which would allow me to refrain from filing an appellate brief for several months. Although she ultimately agreed to do so, Gina had to ask a supervisor before consenting. Her voice actually seemed to tremble slightly when she spoke with me. *Was I ever that green?* I wondered every time I hung up the phone after speaking with Gina. If the prosecutor's office had deemed my motion strong, I surmised, such an inexperienced assistant district attorney would not have been handling Benny's case.

That impression was confirmed when I received the prosecution's response. It was short and sweet. According to the prosecution, Daniel Gordon was a brilliant tactician who represented Benny with skill and care throughout the proceedings. Gordon's disclosure that Benny had admitted stabbing the complainant in self-defense? Obviously an attempt to impress the prosecution with the strength of the defense case to stimulate beneficial plea bargaining. The failure to move for a hearing into the circumstances surrounding the photo array identification procedure? It was obviously the result of a strategic determination that identification would not be an issue because the defense was going to be that Benny stabbed the victim in self-defense. The failure to uncover the mental health records? A legitimate tactic in light of Benny's insistence that he had never been given *Miranda* warnings in the first place. Calling Felice Diaz despite her previous sworn statement that Benny had stabbed the victim? A valid choice because Felice was the only eyewitness other than the victim and she admitted she had lied when she told the police Benny had done the stabbing.

I quickly wrote a reply pointing out that the prosecution's attempts to justify Gordon's actions, several of which were not based on Gordon's own explanations, defied all reason. Gordon could have participated in plea negotiations without disclosing the defense in filed court documents. The decision that identification would not be an issue in the case had been made before Gordon had interviewed a single witness other than Benny himself, which was not exactly conduct comporting with a defense attorney's obligation to investigate the facts. Similarly,

Gordon's decision to rely on Benny's account of the interrogation, which Gordon knew would be contradicted by at least two police witnesses, could not be excused. Calling Felice could not be deemed reasonable, because Gordon failed to anticipate that her prior inconsistent statement would be introduced into evidence.

Soon after I had served the reply, I received a call from Justice Fields's chambers advising me that he intended to hear oral argument on my motion a few days before Thanksgiving: a good sign, because it suggested he was taking my claims seriously. I had been intending to take that day off to cook, but I heard myself agreeing to the proposed date without any protest.

The day of the oral argument, I was up before the sun in order to have time to get into my office, review the briefs, and still make it to the Bronx by 10:00 a.m. Half-expecting the subway to break down again, I gave myself additional time and arrived at the courthouse before anyone else. Justice Fields's courtroom was beautiful—high ceilings, dark wood railings, antique light fixtures, leather seats in the jury box. It was a courtroom right out of the movies of the 1950s, a courtroom meant to reflect the majesty of the law itself.

I sat down and looked over my notes. A short time later, Gina Nielson walked in. As I had expected, she was just-out-of-law-school young. I smiled and introduced myself, feeling a strange warmth toward Gina. It's hard being a young attorney. Law school teaches you very little of any use when it comes to actually practicing. She was so young, she did not even know what she didn't know. As I was chatting with Gina about her wedding and gently probing to discover how she came to be assigned to Benny's case, a man approached us. He was wearing a blue oxford shirt, had curly hair, and looked around thirty-five.

"Are you Claudia Trupp?" the man asked.

"Yes," I answered, trying to place the face, wondering if he was a former colleague from somewhere whose name I had forgotten.

"I'm Justice Fields. I just wanted to tell you that your motion papers were exceptional, probably the best I have ever received."

There was an intensity about Justice Fields, a bluntness I found startling. A random urge to laugh overcame me. I wanted to tell Gina not to worry, that the judge's compliment was the kiss of death for Benny's case, a consolation prize for my impending defeat. But I suppressed the urge to be flip. I had been teaching my daughters the importance of accepting a compliment with grace. For once I decided to practice what I had been preaching.

"Thank you, Your Honor," I said seriously.

"It's true. The best." Justice Fields seemed to notice Gina for the first time. "Your papers were very good too, Miss Nielson. I don't mean to belittle your efforts."

From that moment on, I was playing not to lose. I figured that I had said everything I had to say, the best way I could have said it, in my papers. I didn't want to say anything to undermine my position during the argument. Still I argued Benny's case for a full half hour, with the judge probing my position on several points. It was one of those arguments where the ball stood still and I could hit every question out of the park.

Unbelievably, by the time the prosecutor sat down, it seemed clear that Justice Fields was prepared to grant the motion to vacate and order a new trial. The judge asked us whether either side believed a hearing was necessary to explore Gordon's explanations for his challenged conduct. Both of us said no hearing would be necessary, because Gordon had pretty much given us consistent explanations for his decisions. Judge Fields announced that he would issue a decision within the month.

I turned to walk out of the courtroom and noticed Beth Fried, the talented criminal defense attorney with whom, months earlier, I had discussed Gordon's mistakes. Beth had been sitting on the front row bench reserved for lawyers throughout the argument.

"What did you think?" I asked, not quite believing that I was going to win.

"I think you kicked ass," Beth said laughing. "You're gonna win."

I should have known it would not be that simple.

. . . . . . . . . . . . . . . . . . . . . . . . . . . . . . . . .

Few people believe that the criminal justice system provides its participants with a level playing field. It's not just the prosecutors, defense attorneys, victims, and defendants who believe that the system is stacked against them. The men and women on the street pretty much believe it, too. Each year I read the responses of hundreds of prospective jurors, regular men and women from all walks of life, discussing their feelings about criminal justice. Some are obviously just trying to avoid jury duty. They'll say they cannot be fair because their car radio was stolen twenty years earlier or that a distant cousin was convicted of disorderly conduct and got a bum rap. But the vast majority of people will voice genuine concerns about the system's bias. Some will say that the cops lie, poor people are punished to a greater degree than the wealthy, sentences for nonviolent offenses are too harsh. Others will insist that the system bends over backward to protect criminals, that nobody is really concerned for the victims or the truth, that defendants too often get off on technicalities. Very few people who are called to serve exclaim that our justice system is the greatest in the world, something to be emulated and admired. Deep down, despite all too many bitter experiences, I have never been able to shake that belief.

As a criminal defense attorney, in my more rational moments, of course, I believe the system favors the State. That bias grows exponentially once a defendant has been convicted of a crime. So many of the procedural safeguards accorded to the accused vanish the moment the jury announces a guilty verdict. The defendant is no longer presumed innocent. The prosecution has no further burden of proving his guilt. There is no right to demand additional information from the State through discovery motions.

Sometimes being an appellate attorney feels like being a coroner. You can dissect each portion of the case, determine what caused the harm, but at the end of the day your client is no better off than a cadaver after the autopsy.

Appellate prosecutors are so used to winning, to having every one of their arguments endorsed by the court, that they have very little compunction about asking for the moon. So I should not have been surprised when the day after the oral argument in Benny Rinaldo's case, after Gina Nielson had specifically stated on the record that she did not believe the court should conduct a hearing at which Gordon would testify in order to explain his actions, she called me to say that she had decided to request a hearing after all.

"I don't get it. Your position all along has been that we don't need a hearing," I sputtered.

"Well, we've reconsidered. When I spoke to Daniel Gordon, he said that there were certain aspects of his representation that he believed were covered by the attorney-client privilege," Gina explained.

"You know the privilege is waived by our filing the motion," I said, wondering if Gina had failed to grasp the basic rule that once a client accuses his attorney of being ineffective, the attorney is free to reveal client confidences in order to defend his decisions.

"I guess you're opposing the hearing?" Gina asked.

A hearing would cost me several trips to the Bronx so Gordon could testify. It would also give him time and an opportunity to come up with better explanations for his conduct. I found neither prospect particularly appealing.

"Yeah. I'm opposing," I responded, trying not to sound too snippy.

I couldn't really get angry with Gina. She obviously had gone back to her office, told them what had happened during the argument, and was ordered to request a hearing. But I was shocked at the prosecution's brazenness. I never would have had the guts to ask for a hearing a day after announcing in open court that none was required. If I did, there would be little chance a court would seriously consider my request. Plus, I'd probably get a good reaming from the judge in the process.

To his credit, Justice Fields was not about to grant a hearing simply because the prosecution asked for one. He made Gina file supplemental papers formally setting forth the prosecution's position. But a few days later, he ordered a hearing over my objection. Even worse, it was scheduled for the first week in January, a time I was expecting to be home on vacation and had no child-care coverage. Marie, who has arthritis, had scheduled a vacation down south to get a break from the cold northeast winter. But once again, I heard myself agreeing to a totally inconvenient date. This time without even knowing who would be available to care for my children.

I called Charlie as soon as I could and told him he would have to block off the hearing dates for child-care duty—a radical request I rarely make. Charlie has a real job. One that actually pays the bills.

I approached the pending hearing with trepidation for so many reasons. I hated the idea of forcing Daniel Gordon to testify against Benny. I was worried that information would be revealed that I had not previously learned about. No matter how hard I have worked on a case, dread of the unknown always descends upon me right before a hearing.

Added to this trepidation was my uncertainty about whether to disclose to the court and the prosecution a copy of the videotape containing Felice Diaz's account of the stabbing. The tape still sat in the trial file on my office floor. I had considered including a reference to the videotape in my motion papers, but I didn't know exactly what to say about it. I could have used it merely to depict Gordon as an unethical and sleazy lawyer, but I had no desire to besmirch Gordon unless it affirmatively aided some argument. Now that a hearing had been ordered, I knew that I probably had to disclose the videotape, but I still didn't want to do it.

Later, when I broached the topic with Rich, his position was clear.

"You've got to turn over the tape to the prosecution first thing," Rich advised me.

"Why? What does it get me?" I asked.

"It's gonna come up, and if you're not the one who brings it up, it looks like you're hiding something," Rich explained.

"I just don't want to get Gordon in trouble," I admitted sheepishly.

I knew I should have felt more hard-core, eager for a chance to destroy Gordon's credibility to make him appear an incompetent fool. I just wasn't feeling it. I kept picturing him in his office, mopping sweat from his forehead, slightly winded, before I had even asked him a question. The image of the mezuzah flashed across my mind.

"It's not about getting anybody in trouble. It's about not looking sleazy yourself," Rich said, forcing me to focus on my hearing strategy instead of Gordon's office decor.

"I don't mind looking sleazy. I think it sort of suits me," I joked.

"Just turn over the tape. That's an order. And I think you're going to need someone to second-seat you. I don't think you should go in there alone."

"Thanks for the vote of confidence."

"You think Gina's gonna be by herself? I'd bet the prosecution's going to have someone there to help her on this one," Rich predicted.

"Gina has been practicing for, like, two minutes. I've been at it slightly longer," I said peevishly.

"And Gordon's been practicing for close to forty years. Experience doesn't necessarily prevent you from messing up. Ask Vanessa to help you. She won't step on your toes."

Vanessa Paige had been a supervisor when I met her working at the Legal Aid Society years earlier. She is a no-nonsense, savvy lawyer and deeply legally analytical—a quality that I am often too harried to achieve. I was grateful when she agreed to help me.

I spent New Year's Day 2006 preparing for the hearing. It seemed as if my entire holiday season was going to be eaten up by Benny's case. Something about working in an empty office on a national holiday felt strangely exhilarating. I get so little time to be alone. There is almost always a child, a colleague, or a fellow commuter standing nearby. Being alone, listening to the quiet, was a rare treat. No phones ringing; no photocopiers flashing; no voices raised in intellectual debate. Just me, the files, and my thoughts. It felt more luxurious than a day spa—not that I have actually ever been to one. By the time I shut off my office light and left, I felt ready, actually prepared—another luxury.

When Vanessa and I arrived in Justice Fields's court for the hearing, there were two prosecutors waiting for us, a team, just as Rich had predicted. Gina looked strangely relaxed. I guessed that the blond-haired, long-legged, short-skirted woman sitting next to her was Mandy Monroe, the prosecutor who'd originally handled Benny's trial. I asked to speak with the judge in chambers with the prosecutors so that I could turn over the videotape and get it off my mind.

When we were seated around the judge's desk, I explained that there had been a videotape in the file recording a statement by Felice Diaz that I believed had never been disclosed. I handed over the tape to Mandy Monroe and outlined Felice's statement. Justice Fields merely nodded. Mandy was immediately on the offensive.

"Can I ask why you did not disclose the tape's existence in your motion papers?" she asked pointedly.

"I didn't think it was relevant to my claims. Daniel Gordon explained his actions consistently to me and Ms. Nielson. I didn't believe there was any issue about Gordon's credibility. Now you have requested a hearing, which has been granted over my objection, and I thought you might consider the tape relevant to assess Gordon's credibility and I'm disclosing it to you," I explained.

"Sounds right to me," Justice Fields said.

Things between Mandy and me went downhill from there. She kept mispronouncing my name in really weird ways. Finally Judge Fields had heard enough.

"It's pronounced TROOP, not TRIP or TROMP or TRUPT," he snapped. "That's right, isn't it, Miss Trupp?" he asked.

"Yes, Your Honor," I said, in a monotone I seemed unable to break out of in his courtroom. Despite my serious tone, I was liking him more and more.

There was only one witness, Daniel Gordon himself. His testimony stretched out painfully over several hours. He described every job he had ever held, dropped every name of every judge he had ever worked for, and recounted most every case he had ever won. There were quite a few over his thirty-eight–year career. Practicing primarily in the Bronx, he had accrued an impressive eighty-five percent acquittal rate.

Gordon was totally unrepentant about the manner in which he had represented Benny. If he had the opportunity to try the case over again, he would conduct the defense in the exact same manner, he explained.

Gordon even went so far as to accuse me of sandbagging him when we met to discuss Benny's case, insisting that I had never told him I would be lodging a motion to vacate Benny's conviction.

"So when I left your office and I told you that I would be raising a claim of ineffective assistance of counsel against you, what didn't you understand?" I asked on cross-examination.

"I thought you were going to be raising it just in your brief on the appeal. I didn't think I'd be called to testify about our conversations," Gordon insisted.

I didn't press the point or contradict his response. Any experienced attorney should have known that a claim of ineffective assistance would first need to be raised in a motion at the trial court level. If I had intended to raise the claim based only on the existing trial record, I would not have needed to speak to Gordon at all. I couldn't have used anything he said off the record on the direct appeal.

Gordon's attempts to excuse his ineptitude when representing Benny only created a deeper hole for the prosecution. He testified that he had never made the decision to abandon the justification defense and to rely on Felice Diaz's testimony. That decision, Gordon emphatically insisted, was made by Benny Rinaldo himself. I couldn't believe that Gordon was actually admitting under oath that he had let his mentally retarded client chart the course of his own defense. But apparently Gordon believed that this explanation excused his own failures.

When we broke for the day and Gordon had left the courtroom, Vanessa turned to me with a perplexed look on her face.

"I don't understand something," she said seriously.

"What?" I asked, hoping that she had not spotted some weakness in my arguments, some problem I had missed.

"Why do you feel bad for Gordon? The guy's a total asshole," she remarked, her voice dripping disdain.

"I don't know. I guess because he's a defense attorney and he's old and he tried his best and I think he usually does a good enough job and I wouldn't want to be him right now," I explained, omitting the Jewish thing. Vanessa is not Jewish.

"None of that changes that the guy is a total asshole," she insisted.

# TWENTY-THREE POUNDS OF FURY

I walked home from the train station to my house in the frigid January darkness, having spent the hours after the hearing preparing to further cross-examine Gordon the following day. It was too late to be walking alone, almost 10:00 p.m.

I should have arranged for someone to pick me up, but I hadn't thought of it. Charlie had been at home alone with the girls all day. They would be in bed asleep by now. Another full day of me not seeing them at all. Tomorrow would be better, I assured myself. There was no way Gordon's testimony could last another entire day.

When I arrived home, the upstairs bedrooms were all dark. There was only a light on in the kitchen. I opened the door expecting to be greeted by the dog. Instead, there was Maya sitting on the kitchen floor, her mouth ringed with cookie crumbs, a half-eaten cookie in one hand, a whole one in her lap.

"Mama home!" she shouted, dropping the cookies onto the floor and crushing them with her feet, the bottoms of her pink footie pajamas now covered in dirty black crumbs.

"What are you still doing up?" I asked, lifting her into my arms, knowing full well the answer. Her father had not had the strength to fight with her over going to bed. Holding Maya close to me, I could actually feel the tension of the day subsiding, a slight change in my own blood chemistry, a dose of pure joy.

"Mama, mama, mama," Maya continued to hum, a gleeful mantra. She threw her arms around me, tangling her hands in my hair, leaving a residue on the nape of my neck, cookies and cream, sticky and sweet-smelling. Maya struggled in my embrace. I returned her to the floor.

"It's time for you to go to bed, young lady," I announced.

"No! No! No bed!" Maya shouted, the sweetness of the previous moment gone in an instant. I braced myself for the pending storm.

"NO! NO! NO!" Maya continued to holler, as Charlie entered the kitchen.

"Welcome to my world. She's been waiting for you," he announced. "How'd it go today?"

"Long and painful," I said. I could have been describing Maya's nightly bedtime routine.

By this time, Maya had hurled herself onto the kitchen's hard tile floor and worked herself up into a picture-perfect tantrum, arms pounding, legs kicking, screams rising into a crescendo.

I bent down to scoop her up, and her body stiffened in my arms. Maya has always been tiny. Back then, at just over two years of age, she weighed twenty-three pounds, the size of an average one-year-old. People were always remarking on her incredible vocabulary, thinking that she was actually much younger than two.

I trudged up the stairs with Maya still screaming, her arms pounding on my back, her legs kicking my stomach with surprising power—from all that sugar coursing through her veins, I imagined. In her room I took a wet washcloth and wiped her face and teeth. Then I shut off the lights and climbed into bed with her next to me. She was starting to quiet down now. I began singing "Twinkle, Twinkle, Little Star" as I did every night.

"NO TWINKLE! NO TWINKLE!" Maya yelled.

"Okay, okay, what do you want to hear?"

"NOTHING! NO SINGING!" she ordered.

"Okay then, hush, hush. No singing, I get it."

Within minutes I could feel Maya's body relaxing, her breathing becoming calmer, until there was almost silence, just the feel of her warm breath on my neck. I counted backward from one hundred and slowly slipped off the bed and out of the room.

I walked down the hall to our bedroom, where Charlie was reading the paper in bed.

"God, she's tough," I sighed. "What does she have against 'Twinkle, Twinkle, Little Star'? I could have sworn that was her favorite yesterday."

"That song always pissed me off too," Charlie answered, not looking up from the paper. "She's two."

"It's more than that. Jessie was two. Lila was two. They weren't like Maya. It seems like she's always on the brink of exploding," I mused.

"How else is she going to get anyone's attention when she only weighs twenty pounds?" Charlie said, putting down the paper and smiling at me.

"She's always the center of attention. The other two are lucky if they get a minute of uninterrupted time. Jessie told me the other day that I'm not doing a very good job of disciplining Maya, and she's right. Maya's a tyrant," I complained, suddenly feeling overcome with fatigue.

"She'll grow out of it," Charlie promised.

I slipped out of my work clothes into pajamas, brushed my teeth, and got into bed. But even after I had turned off the light, I couldn't sleep.

*What does she possibly have to be so angry about?* I wondered. It was the same question Charlie had directed at me years before, following my brawl over court-mandated contraception for the mothers of crack babies.

Maya and I had more than our anger in common. We were both third children. The age differences between me and my older brothers were exactly the same as the ones separating Maya from her sisters. Like me, Maya was always in a hurry to grow up. She had walked at nine months, begun speaking in full sentences at a year, was out of diapers by eighteen months. But all her efforts could never change the fact that her older sisters would always be just that, older. When she tried to join their games of Frisbee or catch or their tea parties, she would inevitably wind up flat on her back wailing in frustration. Jessie and Lila adored her and catered to her whims, but even their kindness could not quell Maya's temper. She didn't want to be accommodated. Maya wanted to be their equal, and that goal was unattainable; it was simply not possible for a two-year-old to catch or throw like an eight-year-old, or even pour pretend tea like a six-year-old. Maya remained on the outside, fuming.

My own brothers had been far less sensitive. In addition to being older, they had shared the bonds of brotherhood, complete with its own language in which they discussed their boyhood secrets, plans, and schemes. I was perpetually left out while they inhabited a shared world apart from my parents and me. Contemplating Maya's anger, I understood for the first time my own identity as an outsider. It had been forged to a large degree by my brothers, by a childhood of exclusion in my own home.

It is probably not a coincidence that I have spent most of my professional life representing men who had no choice but to share their secrets with me. When a client complained that he wanted a man to represent him, I would essentially respond, "Too bad, you're stuck with me." Then I would double my efforts to win his trust. Almost always, I would succeed. I proved to myself over and over again that I am a worthy confidant and as tough an advocate as anyone—that I never deserved to be excluded. It was having Maya, watching her struggles, that finally helped me pinpoint the source of my own angry outsider identity.

Children do shrink your world in some ways. It is virtually impossible to find the time to read all the books on the best-seller list or even to get through the newspaper on some days. Catching a movie or a play in the theater is rare. My memories of traveling the world grow more distant every day.

But there is a depth of understanding of human nature, of myself, that I have gained only through becoming a mother. Buddha said that to understand everything is to forgive everything. Perhaps that is why I no longer find myself so quick to anger, to let my outrage overtake me. Or maybe I am simply too tired.

# HAPPY ENDINGS

In May 2006, Justice Fields granted my motion to vacate Benny Rinaldo's conviction, finding that Daniel Gordon had failed to provide Benny with the effective assistance of counsel. The judge agreed with every single one of my claims and acknowledged that the evidence of Benny's guilt appeared overwhelming only because Gordon's blunders had pervaded every aspect of the proceedings. Justice Fields went so far as to compare Gordon's representation of Benny to the toxic ministrations of a parent suffering Munchausen syndrome by proxy, which sicken the child. In other words, the judge recognized that Gordon's efforts had harmed Benny's chances of mounting a successful defense.

We reached out to the prosecution's office to see if they intended to appeal. To their credit, they recognized the strength of Justice Fields's reasoning. There would be no appeal.

Soon after receiving the winning decision, I was back at Sing Sing, traipsing over the rickety wooden bridge to visit Benny. I slowly and carefully explained the details of the court's opinion in simple terms. When I was finished, Benny regarded me silently with his blinking eyes.

"Do you have any questions?" I asked.

"This is good news, right?" Benny wanted to know. In my effort to explain the case to him, I had forgotten to smile and appear happy. Benny was used to taking his cues from people's expressions, not the contents of their words. My somber tone had thrown him off entirely.

I smiled at him, although an incredible sadness overcame me. There really was no good news for Benny Rinaldo. Win or lose, his prospects for the future were not bright. Even if he won at a new trial, his life would resume with subsidized housing and disability benefits. It would be a life better than the one he was spending in Sing Sing, but far from anybody's ideal of happily ever after.

"Yes, Benny," I said softly, "this is really good news." I forced an even broader smile onto my face, shook his hand, and said good-bye.

· · · · · · · · · · · · · · · · · · · · · · · · · · · · · ·

I arranged to have Beth Fried represent Benny Rinaldo for the retrial, and after a lot of maneuvering, she and a colleague wrangled from the prosecutor's office one of those offers too good to refuse. Ultimately, Benny pleaded guilty to attempted murder in exchange for a seven-year sentence—eleven years less than the one he had been serving when his file landed on my desk. He was released in July 2008.

Daniel Gordon, when interviewed by the same reporter with whom I had spoken, continued to insist that he had done nothing wrong, that he had been placed in an impossible situation by Benny's demands. He continues to practice today.

Maya remains a stormy force in our house—a tiny, adorable, stormy force.

The chagrin that engulfed me after Benny failed to understand that I was delivering good news to him proved only temporary. There are never perfect happy endings in my work. That truth does not fill me with either anger or despair. I accept that my job—as both a lawyer and as a mother—is not to make things perfect. It is only to make them better.

# Afterword

## THE CALL

On an unseasonably warm November morning in 2006, I arrived at my office early to find the phone ringing and raced to grab the receiver. Although I had not spoken to Carlos Angelo for several months, I recognized his voice immediately. When I learned the reason for his call, the irrational part of me that had been waiting stirred, eager for action.

The next Friday, I found myself with Roy Swain, my private investigator, sitting in the cafeteria of Coxsackie Correctional Facility. An inmate serving time on a robbery bid strode casually up to our table and silently sat down across from us.

The years had not been kind to Mario Gonzalez. Gone was the cocky young man who had answered the door wearing only a low-slung towel and attempted to dazzle me with his radiant smile. Mario was heavier now. His skin, his hair, even his teeth appeared to have dulled. Dark circles ringed his eyes.

"Do you remember me?" I asked.

"Yeah," Mario said after looking at me for a long moment, "I do."

"I understand you have something to tell me," I said stonily.

"Yeah," Mario practically whispered. But he did not look away.

For the next fifteen minutes, Mario Gonzalez spoke to me of that warm May night in 1999 when Ramon Jiminez had come back to Hunts Point from visiting friends in Manhattan and was attacked while walking home to his parents' house. Mario explained how he had seen Jiminez and had mistaken him for somebody else, a guy named Jose, with whom Mario had fought days earlier. Set on revenge against Jose, Mario punched and stabbed Jiminez in a drunken haze, while his cohorts joined in the pounding. When the police came to break up the fight, an officer hit Mario over the head and he fell to the ground. Mario pretended to be unconscious while the cops wrestled with the other men on the street, including Corrie Angelo—who Mario confirmed had not been involved in the attack on Jiminez.

As the struggle continued, Mario had been able to sneak away and hide in a nearby alley. There he'd stayed until all the others had been arrested and removed from the scene. Mario had run home, his clothes spattered with Jiminez's blood down to his sneakers. Once home, he'd thrown his bloody clothes in the trash and eventually called Janet Avery, the mother of his son, and persuaded her to tell the police that he had been with her on the night of the stabbing.

"I just didn't want to go back to prison," Mario said.

As I listened to Mario's confession, I did not feel vindication, only bitter sadness.

"So because you didn't want to go back to prison for a crime you committed, Corrie Angelo's daughter has grown up without her father for seven years," I said snidely. "Do you know what you've done?"

Mario did not fight back. Instead he met my gaze.

"I do. I have a son too," he replied. His eyes seemed to plead for understanding.

Hearing the sadness in his voice, I could feel my anger vanish, like the pop of a soap bubble. When I spoke again, my voice was kinder.

"So why tell me this now, after all this time?" I asked.

"I'm just so tired," Mario explained wearily. "I haven't been able to really sleep in years. I dream about Corrie. I just want to be able to close my eyes at night and not see his face."

"What are you willing to do to get some sleep?" I asked, searching his face for signs of duplicity.

Mario had waited to come forward until the statute of limitations had expired—assuring that he would never be prosecuted for the stabbing. If his confession had any chance of helping Corrie, Mario would have to be a steady, flawless witness. The cost of redemption was higher than merely speaking to me.

"If you're going to deny your guilt to the DA, let's just not bother," I explained. "The Angelos have been fucked with enough."

"I'll do anything you say," Mario responded without hesitation. "I just want to make it right."

"Will you sign a sworn, written confession?"

Mario nodded.

"Speak to the DA's investigators if I can convince them to come up here?"

"If you tell me to," Mario said.

"Testify in court?"

"Yes."

"Submit to a polygraph exam?"

"If you think that'll help."

"And no one's threatened you or forced you to say these things?" I asked.

I knew that Corrie had not threatened Mario. While Mario had remained free to deal drugs and rob others on the outside, Corrie had spent the years working in the prison's hospice program comforting the sick and the dying. He was active in the prison's religious programs. But I also knew that if the district attorney failed to concede on a new motion to vacate the conviction, he would argue that Mario was somehow being coerced.

"Haven't been no threats," Mario assured me.

I sat for a moment silently looking at Mario. He made no attempt to interrupt my contemplation.

"Okay, then," I said. "We'll try to make it right. I'll let you know what I need from you."

I pushed back my chair from the table and stood up.

"Thank you for speaking with me," I said, holding out my hand.

"Thank you," Mario answered and reached up to grasp it.

As Roy and I walked away from the prison, I asked him what he thought of Mario's confession. Roy stopped walking for a moment and turned slightly back toward the gate, as if he expected to see Mario watching us from within.

"I think he genuinely feels bad," Roy answered. "He really did seem sincere."

I had to agree. Roy smiled at me mischievously.

"Soon as I get back to the office, I'm phonin' in for the weather report in hell. Must be *cold* down there today!" he declared, sounding like an old-time gospel preacher.

I laughed, hugged Roy, and walked quickly to my car without looking back.

....................................

When I arrived home, the house was empty: the older girls still at school, Maya somewhere with Marie. I set the dining room table without interruption and started to prepare dinner, listening to the quiet. I realized that such times of peace were becoming more common. My thoughts were interrupted by Maya's noisy return, her immediate demands that I let her help me cook. I set her up at the sink with lettuce to tear for the salad and watched in wonder as she conquered the task with the skill of a sous chef.

A short time later, Jessie and Lila came crashing through the back hall into the kitchen, a blur of discarded backpacks and jackets.

"Are we getting ready for Shabbat?" Jessie asked and raced into the dining room, announcing that she would get the candles.

"I'll get the teacups!" Lila offered, following Jessie.

Instructions instantly rose to my lips. *Don't run! Wash your hands! Be careful!* But I willed myself to remain silent, in the kitchen, even as I heard the china cabinet open and the sound of glasses being removed. Lila handling antique porcelain—the thought would strike terror in the heart of any rational adult.

I dared to look only after I heard Jessie practicing the piano in the living room. The piece she was playing was somber, but the music was not dampening the spirits of her younger sisters. I could hear them giggling and racing around. At any moment I would be summoned to restore order. But before heading to the living room, I paused to soak in the sounds of laughter accompanied by music, the smell of bread just beginning to bake, the beauty of my grandmother's teacups set with obvious care around the table.

# Acknowledgments

I read somewhere that the acknowledgments section of a book is like a speech at the Academy Awards, inevitably too long and self-important. The critic who made that analogy probably never wrote a book. I have been astonished to learn just how many people have to work so very hard to create the finished product.

My husband, in this venture, as in all others over the past twenty years, has provided unwavering support and invaluable advice. He was my first reader and the person whose guidance I have relied on the most.

Usually he would simply tell me to follow the sage advice of our friend and my agent, Tina Bennett, who represented this book with unparalleled passion and energy. It is hard to come up with superlatives to describe Tina that have not already been used by her other clients. I can only agree that she is brilliant, indomitable and kind—and add that she can make me laugh on the worst day.

Fortunately, there were not too many bad days during this project, thanks to the dedication and attention of the team at Rodale. Leigh Haber understood this book immediately and helped me greatly in my efforts to clarify my thoughts and writing. Karen Rinaldi offered additional, critical support. Working with and getting to know Shannon Welch has been a real pleasure. Invariably her advice has been well-reasoned, thoughtful, and always honest. I'd also like to thank Andy

Carpenter, Carol Angstadt, Meredith Quinn, Nancy N. Bailey, Beth Davey, and Blanca Oliviery for their respective contributions.

If you recognize yourself in these pages, despite the name changes, then you deserve acknowledgment. Every colleague, client, friend, and family member mentioned here has enriched my life in some critical way. But the efforts of a few have not been adequately recognized. From the time I was twelve, I have relied on Debbie Epstein Henry's advice, love, and humor to make the hard times easier and the good times better.

Without Marie Edouard, who has cared for my family with unbelievable devotion and skill, I could not have left for work each morning certain that my children were in the best possible hands.

I don't know that I would have wanted to walk out the door if I did not work with such an impressive group of intelligent and talented people. Particularly, I would like to thank my boss for his steady support and innumerable insights over the years.

I cannot adequately express my gratitude to my parents for their devotion, wisdom, and generosity. It is their example, in both the personal and professional realms, that I strive to emulate every single day.

Last, but certainly not least, I must thank my daughters. The three of you have brought me more joy than I could have ever imagined possible.